DISCOVERING THE AMAZON

READER'S DIGEST

Travels & Adventures

DISCOVERING THE AMAZON

Published by The Reader's Digest Association Limited
LONDON • NEW YORK • SYDNEY • CAPE TOWN • MONTREAL

◆ COVER:

Main picture: **The Rio Negro, the Amazon's largest tributary, in flood.**

Smaller pictures, from top to bottom: **Benedict Allen beside his canoe in the Amazon basin. Jaguars fighting. Kayapo men from Brazil's Xingu region perform a war dance. Hummingbird sipping nectar. Gold-and-turquoise mask from the Andes.**

Spine: **Kamayura Indian from the Mato Grosso, Brazil, decorated for a fertility ritual.**

◆ FRONTISPIECE:

A family of Chacobo Indians in northern Bolivia navigate their canoe through floodwaters.

◆ TITLE PAGE:

A barred leaf frog from the Amazon rain forest.

◆ OPPOSITE:

A bat-pollinated bloom of the rain forest.

◆ CONTENTS PAGES:

Left: **The jungle basks in the warm glow of late afternoon sunlight.**

Right: **Benedict Allen beside his canoe in the Amazon basin.**

◆ PAGES 8–9:

The muddy, brown waters of the River Amazon and the black waters of the Rio Negro swirl together a few miles downstream of Manaus.

◆ PAGES 42–43:

Vines densely covered with mosses and epiphytes hang above the thick undergrowth of high-altitude rain forest.

DISCOVERING THE AMAZON was edited and designed
by The Reader's Digest Association Limited, London

The Reader's Digest Association Limited
Berkeley Square House, Berkeley Square, London W1X 6AB.

Mad White Giant: Original full-length version published by Macmillan
London, 1985 and Flamingo, an imprint of HarperCollins, 1992. © 1985 by
Benedict Allen. The Author asserts the moral right to be identified
as the author of this work. British condensed version © The Reader's Digest
Association Limited, 1994, published by arrangement with HarperCollins
Publishers Ltd.

Contributors

Consultant Editor: Donald Payne

Editor: David Scott-Macnab

Associate Editors: Mary Gibson, David Compton

Copy Editor: Jenny Baines

Designer: Louise Dick

Assistant Designer: Rick Lecoat

Picture Researcher: Cathy Stastny

Additional material by: Benedict Allen, John Hemming, Tim Locke

Watercolour illustrations: Mark Entwisle

Cartography: Malcolm Porter

Index: Jean Gay

◆ The publishers and project team would like to thank the many other people who have contributed to the preparation of this volume. In particular, they are grateful to John Hemming, Director of the Royal Geographical Society, Nigel Winser, Deputy Director of the Royal Geographical Society, and Jayne Dunlop, Librarian at the Royal Geographical Society, for their ongoing help and advice.

Contents

A JOURNEY INTO THE AMAZON JUNGLE

Condensed from MAD WHITE GIANT by Benedict Allen

— page 42 —

♦ *with special features:*

Index and Acknowledgments

— page 186 —

PART 1   AN EVOCATION

THE MIGHTY AMAZON

CAYENNE

ENCH
IANA

Cabo Norte

Macapa

Equator

Marajo
Island

Belem

Tocantins

The Amazon Basin

**The mighty Amazon River flows
for an astonishing 4,000 miles
through the Amazon basin—**

SOUTH
AMERICA

an area of over
two-and-a-half
million square
miles and home
to the greatest
rain forest on
our planet.

BRASILIA

| 0 | 100 | 200 | 300 | 400 miles |
| 0 | 100 | 200 | 300 | 400 kilometres |

The Mighty Amazon

THE AMAZON IS A PRIMORDIAL GIANT of a river: a great dark snake, its head in the sea, its body coiling through thousands of miles of rain forest, its tail lost in distant mountains wreathed in cloud. It is unbelievably old—scientists say it existed 60 million years ago—and unbelievably large—its average outflow of 45 million gallons of water per second is greater than that of the world's eight next-largest rivers combined; it has over a thousand tributaries longer than the Thames; it drains an area the size of Europe; and locked up in its enormous basin is a third of the world's rain forest and two-thirds of its fresh water. Early explorers, astounded by the magnitude and complexity of the Amazon's waterways, called it *O Rio Mar*, 'The River Sea'.

How, you may wonder, did such a mighty river-system come into being.

Genesis of a River

Geologists tell us that in the youth of the world, about 150 million years ago, a great river flowed through what we now call the Amazon basin. This was not the Amazon as we know it; for one thing, it flowed in the opposite direction to today's river—from ancient mountains in the east into the Pacific Ocean in the west.

Then, about 120 million years ago, when the dinosaurs were in their heyday, the great range of the Andes started to appear, levered up as a result of friction between two of the huge plates which make up the surface of the Earth. As the Andes grew, they blocked the path of the primeval river so it was no longer able to flow into the Pacific, and at the same time they enclosed its vast sea estuaries, cutting them off from the ocean. The river, however, continued to pour westwards, with the result that a huge inland sea, part saltwater and part freshwater and almost the size of the Mediterranean, built up in what today is the Amazon basin.

Marvels of the Amazon

FOR TENS OF MILLIONS of years, South
America drifted in the oceans as an island-
continent, its plants and animals evolving in
isolation, and developing into some of the
most distinctive and varied life-forms on
our planet.

Nowhere is this diversity more apparent
than in the extraordinary Amazon basin,
which originally developed as a huge inland
sea and which is now home to one of the
world's richest ecosystems. Here a single acre
of forest may contain so many types of trees
that only two or three examples of the same
species recur; and here there are more species
of birds, bats, rodents and insects than on
any other continent in the world. In fact,
there are so many different creatures, and
with such remarkable characteristics, that
scientists are often at a loss as to how to
classify them.

▲ The giant anaconda is
the world's largest snake. It
can grow to over 35 feet in
length and weigh over 500
pounds. This enormous
specimen has been caught
by a group of Suya Indians.

◄ The basilisk lizard
escapes danger by rearing
up on its hind legs and
racing for water, which it
skims across for several
yards before sinking in and
swimming away.

The bird-eating
spider, the largest
of tarantulas, may
measure as much as
10 inches across.
It hunts at night,
and therefore often
catches small
sleeping birds. Its
venom is not as
dangerous to people
as is commonly
supposed. ▶

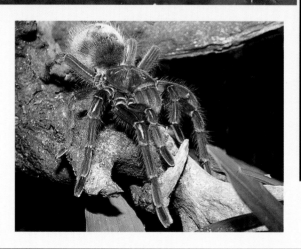

▲ Hummingbirds, known as 'flower-kissers' in Brazil,
can be a minute 2½ inches long. They are the only
birds that can fly backwards and sideways.

Using its sonic radar to detect ripples on the surface of a stream, the fishing bat dives to pluck out a fish with its claws.

During the rainy season vast areas of the rain forest are flooded, making the forest floor a feeding ground for fish.

This inland sea endured until about 80 million years ago, when the entire continent of South America started tilting towards the east. Eventually it tilted so much that the waters of its landlocked sea spilled out through a gap between the highlands of Guyana and Brazil and found their way to the Atlantic. The Amazon was born at last, and was flowing to the east.

A World of Wonders

This curious genesis of the Amazon explains many of its wonders—such as the presence of stingrays (exclusively saltwater dwellers elsewhere on Earth) in fresh water 3,000 miles from the sea. The ancestors of these creatures, scientists believe, did not migrate upriver from the Atlantic; rather, they were swimming in the pre-Amazon's Pacific estuaries and were trapped inland when the Andes rose. They then gradually adapted to fresh water, and are now the only examples of their kind to be found in such conditions.

Much of the area's flora and fauna is similarly unique, giving one the impression of belonging to another era. 'As I came to know the Amazon,' writes naturalist Tom Sterling, 'I had the uncanny feeling that I was wandering the Earth in prehistoric times, before the emergence of man.'

Almost everyone who has visited the Amazon basin admits to this feeling of having been in another, quite different and somehow older world: a world of lizards that walk on water, bats that catch fish and frogs, spiders that hunt hummingbirds, and moths that are bigger than many birds. And these creatures are as diverse as they are exotic. There are, for example, some 2,500 species of fish in the Amazon, compared with 36 in Great Britain, and scientists believe that there are more species of plants and insects in two-and-a-half acres of Amazonian forest than in the whole of the British Isles.

It would be easy to fill page after page with statistics about this amazing world. But perhaps the best way to get to know it is for us to make a journey together, following the Amazon River some 4,000 miles from source to mouth.

The Source

Finding the source of this great river is, however, more easily said than done. No one doubts that the Amazon starts somewhere in the Andes, but authorities have long disagreed about which of the many tiny mountain streams that combine to create the river should be recognised as its official source.

For centuries, Lake Lauricocha at the head of the Rio (River) Marañon was regarded as the source of the Amazon because, of all the Amazon's distant feeders, the Marañon contributes the greatest volume of water. Recently, however, experts have come to agree that the true source of a river lies at the head of its *longest* tributary. And the longest tributary of the Amazon is not the Marañon, but the Ucayali, flowing from the Apurimac, a turbulent mountain river known to the Incas as 'Tears of the Moon'.

But where do we find the source of the Apurimac?

Our search takes us to a labyrinth of minute feeder-streams among snowcapped peaks in the Peruvian Andes, just west of Lake Titicaca. It was here in 1971, at 17,200 feet and less than 120 miles from the Pacific Ocean, that the American photographer and explorer Loren McIntyre pinpointed the most distant source of the Apurimac: a tiny mountain tarn only 100 feet across, named Laguna McIntyre in his honour.

This is bleak, desolate country: a landscape of shale lying well above the tree line. The air is dangerously thin, yet not so thin that it cannot support life. A giant condor floats effortlessly past us on its 10-foot wingspan; and from the valley below comes the wail of an Indian flute as a shepherd drives his llamas to pasture. A thousand feet down are little drifts of golden *ichu* grass, clusters of crimson cacti, and the strange yareta plant that grows only a few feet in a hundred years.

Descendants of the Incas

Following the Apurimac downstream we pass through a terrain of high plateaux, deep valleys, and mountain peaks topped with perpetual snow. At a little under 17,000 feet these parched and dusty highlands are the highest inhabited area on Earth. The Quechua-speaking Indians who live here have larger than average lungs and extra red blood corpuscles to help them cope with the sparse oxygen in the air. These Indians are a mixture of many different peoples from all over the Andes; some are kin of the Incas, while others are descended from people conquered by that nation of warriors and engineers and brought here from distant parts of their empire.

Five hundred years ago the Incas were turning this unpromising terrain into a food-producing Arcadia by means of their roads, terracing, irrigation channels and agricultural expertise. Then came the Spanish Conquistadors and, within the span of a couple of generations, the Indians' well-ordered society had been obliterated. Three out of every five had either been killed by the Spaniards or had succumbed to imported diseases such as smallpox, measles and tuberculosis. Many of those who survived were forced to work in appalling conditions

The bulbous yareta lives for up to 500 years. It is a type of giant moss, yet its wood is so hard that it can blunt an axe blade. ▼

Source of the Mighty River

THE AMAZON BEGINS its 4,000-mile journey east to the Atlantic from just below the icy topmost ridge of the Andes. Water from melted snow trickles into a tiny tarn, known as Laguna McIntyre, from where it spills to form a brook that feeds the Apurimac. An uncounted multitude of minute streams adds to the force of the river, which joins with other mountain torrents to race down the slopes of the Andes into the great Amazon basin. Loren McIntyre, who discovered this furthest source of the Amazon, has remarked, however, that it 'may not always be the most distant water of the River Sea. It could disappear in a single season. The Andes are new mountains; they still buckle and break, and cataclysmic landslides often shatter the stillness of the peaks.'

Loren McIntyre drinks from the most distant source of the Amazon. ▲

◄ **The Apurimac flows through desolate, but spectacular, mountain landscapes on its way to join the Amazon.**

The Andean rivers that feed the Amazon may start from tiny springs, or from icy mountain lakes such as this. ▼

▲ **The Andean condor is the world's largest vulture. Its wingspan of up to 10 feet is exceeded only by that of the biggest albatrosses.**

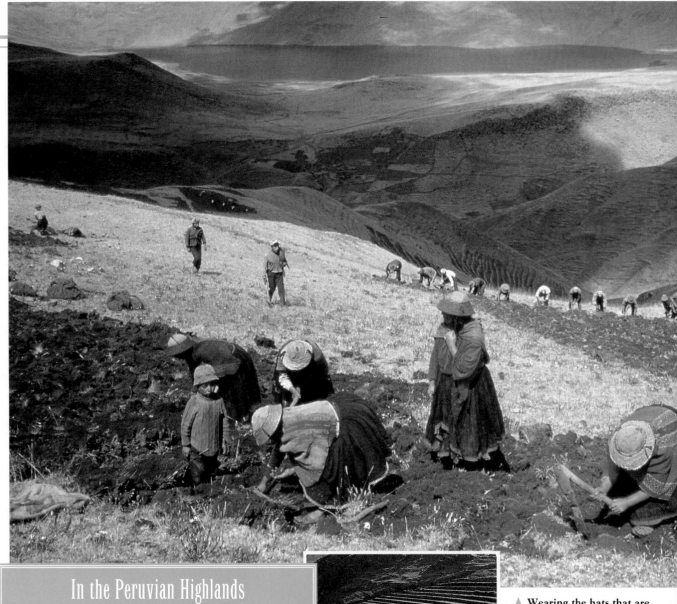

In the Peruvian Highlands

IN THE REMOTE, INHOSPITABLE
highlands of Peru many
Indians follow a way of life that
has changed very little over the
centuries. They live in dispersed
rural communities, building
their thatched stone or adobe
dwellings in places where they
won't encroach on valuable
agricultural land.

Farming has a long history
here, which is all the more
impressive because of the
wildness of the country and
the severity of the climate.
The Andean Indians developed
dozens of varieties of potato
from a wild tuber; cultivated
squash, cotton and maize; and
domesticated animals such as

the llama, the alpaca,
and the guinea pig.
Although the
temperatures here
regularly fluctuate
between intense heat
in the day and bitter
cold at night, the locals have
exploited these extremes to
create special foods: freeze-dried
fish, meats and vegetables that
last indefinitely.

The crop terraces and
irrigation canals built under the
Incas are still in use. And the
coca leaf, a crop dating from
those faraway days, is frequently
chewed as a tonic by the natives
who live and work at these
punishing altitudes.

▲ Wearing the hats that are
typical of this area, these
Indians harvest potatoes in
fields near Cuzco.

◄ The terraced fields built
by the Incas are still used
for farming.

▲ Made of plaited grass, this suspension
bridge spans a chasm cut by a mountain
river. In many places, there is no other
means of crossing from one side to the other.

◄ Llamas have been domesticated for
thousands of years. They are used primarily
as pack animals, but also provide the Indians
with meat, wool, hides, tallow for candles
and dried dung for fuel.

in the silver mines that were to become Spain's principal source
of wealth from her South American empire. It is said that more
than a million Indians died in these mines, often choking to
death in the dust 700 feet beneath the surface. And the mines
are still working today: gaping pits, squat kilns, acrid fumes,
harsh arc lights, and adjoining squalid shantytowns.

The Great Gorge

For its first hundred miles the Apurimac is little more than a
slow-moving trickle confined to a shallow volcanic trench. But
as we approach the old Inca capital of Cuzco, the river is joined
by a plethora of feeders that broaden and quicken it. Then,
suddenly, it begins a spectacular descent. In a gradient five
times steeper than that of the Colorado River as it swirls
through the Grand Canyon, the Apurimac plummets 15,000
feet in altitude down and across the east-facing slopes of the
Andes in a series of gorges that are among the most dramatic on
Earth. One of these, the Apurimac Gorge, is over a mile deep,
and is the second-deepest gorge in the world (the deepest is the
nearby Colca River Gorge, measuring just over two miles from
clifftop to riverbed). Here we can tell how the river got its
name—*Apu* in Quechua meaning 'great' and *rimac* meaning
'speaker'—for the noise from this riot of foaming water can be
heard two miles away. The occasional suspension bridge of
plaited grass makes it possible for villagers to cross from one side
to the other, but none of these modern structures can compare
with the spectacular Inca bridge that once spanned a 150-foot
section of the gorge, hanging 300 feet above the river.

As we continue on our way downriver, the temperature rises
and the countryside becomes increasingly benign. Soon the *ichu*
grass of the highlands gives way to a carpet of moss; and as the
river debouches into the foothills, its banks are transformed
from bare boulders to a mosaic of flowers: white daisies, blood-
red geraniums and wild roses as big as your fist. The river, now
midway between riotous youth and majestic old age, becomes
almost gentle. It is surrounded not by rocks or trees, but by carefully cultivated fields. For although the soil here is poor and the
climate harsh, the Quechua-speaking farmers have a long
history of agricultural expertise and prosperity. Some, it is said,
can trace their ancestry back several centuries.

However, it is not long before the fields grow sparser and the
trees more evident. The atmosphere becomes moister; clouds
and rain are more frequent, and mist collects in hillside
hollows. At first, the landscape is rather unusual. The moss-
covered trees, growing among boulders green with lichen, are

▲ On the raised ground between rivers, known as *terra firme*, the forest is relatively dry and open. Tall trees like this yellow *ipê* reach straight up towards the sunlight.

▲ The appropriately named cloud forest in the uplands is lush from the huge quantities of rain that fall over it. As here, the canopy is shrouded in almost perpetual mist.

◄ The majestic kapok or silk-cotton tree grows near rivers and rises from giant buttressed roots.

▲ There are fewer types of trees in the seasonally flooded forest since few species can tolerate being waterlogged for months at a time.

◄ The dwarf forest of the highlands is typically covered with a thick layer of moss. Epiphytes or 'air plants' such as this bromeliad are abundant here. They grow on trees, but are not parasitic.

The Amazon Rain Forest

THE AMAZON RAIN FOREST, possibly the most varied plant and animal habitat on our planet, covers a vast swathe of South America. Growing everywhere from high mountain slopes to coastal estuaries, the rain forest can be astoundingly diverse in form and appearance.

In the Andes, the first forest vegetation occurs at around 10,000 feet. But it is stunted and sparse—a 'dwarf' forest of twisted trees and shrubs. At 5,000 feet, where there is considerably more rainfall, the moss-covered 'weeping woods' of the cloud forest begin. Epiphytes (or 'air plants') such as orchids and bromeliads grow in profusion here, their gaudy colours rivalled by those of the iridescent hummingbirds and magnificent butterflies which dart from flower to flower.

Below 3,000 feet is the rain forest proper, the oldest and largest in the world. But even this has many forms. Some of the densest forest grows along the banks of rivers and in the permanent swamps of lower-lying regions; taller trees and palms thrive in the areas that are regularly flooded in the wet season; and the tallest hardwoods prosper on higher, drier ground.

twisted and stunted, giving the appearance of belonging to a miniature world. This is often called the 'dwarf' or 'fairy' forest, and is the first manifestation of the great Amazonian rain forest. Lower down, we enter the 'cloud forest', where the trees are taller, the air even more humid. This is the home of startlingly beautiful birds and some of the largest and most colourful butterflies in the world. Lower still, the ground flattens out and becomes so moist that water oozes up from our footprints. Here, at last, we are in the jungle of the Amazon basin.

The Rain Forest

And here the great lake of the age of the dinosaurs has never completely drained. So what we are about to traverse is, in effect, a gargantuan swamp: 50,000 miles of navigable 'trunk' waterways, interspersed with something like 500,000 miles of secondary streams and creeks, all ebbing, flowing and flooding to the rhythm of the rain. And this rain, at times pouring down day after day, combines with the heat of the equatorial sun to turn the Amazon basin into a huge greenhouse in which vegetation goes mad. The result is the rain forest: the most diverse and complex ecosystem on Earth.

No one has described this rain forest better than the 19th-century English naturalist Alfred Wallace:

> I could only marvel at the sombre shades, scarce illuminated by a single direct ray of the sun, the enormous size and height of the trees, most of which rise in huge columns a hundred feet or more without throwing out a single branch; the strange buttresses around the base of some; the furrowed stems of others; the extraordinary creepers which wind around them, hanging in long festoons from branch to branch, sometimes curling and twisting on the ground like great serpents, then sprouting to the very tops of the trees, thence throwing lower roots and fibres which hang waving in the air, or twisting round each other to form ropes and cables of every variety and size.

This forest, so dense that it looks from the distance like a continuous single plant, will line the river for the next 1,500 miles. Only the river itself will change, growing steadily larger, until by the time we have left the Apurimac and entered the Ucayali, it is often more than half a mile wide. The Ucayali is a great intestine of a waterway; looping, twisting, turning, dropping on average less than half an inch in a mile, ever altering course and flooding over its banks to sweep away whole villages. These middle reaches of the river are a navigator's nightmare, but they have a beauty out of this world; especially the side channels, where the foliage, almost meeting overhead, is alive with exotic birds—neon-blue macaws, gold parakeets and red-headed blackbirds; while the waters through which we paddle are alive with the strangest fish—freshwater dolphins, 'water monkeys' which can leap six feet into the air to catch their prey, fruit-eating bream with teeth like a sheep's and red piranha with teeth like razors.

The forest's larger animals, however, can be disappointingly elusive. The growls of a jaguar may sometimes be heard at night, but it could be weeks or even months before we see one of these magnificent creatures. Tapirs, sloths and capybaras are also scarce. But at sunset the sky is often darkened by tens of thousands of bats, setting out on their nightly foraging. And everywhere, all the time, there are insects.

A Plague of Insects

Insects are vital to the rain forest because they help to recycle its detritus and pollinate its plants; but they are often anathema to man. No one knows exactly how many insect species there are in the Amazon rain forest; but scientists have upgraded their estimates over the years, often by millions. Some, like the bird-eating spider, are grotesquely large; others, like the morpho butterfly, are dramatically beautiful; many, like the katydid grasshopper, are cunningly camouflaged; and most of them make life unpleasant for human beings. Joe Kane, who kayaked down the Amazon, complains about the 'bugs':

> spiders, cockroaches, moths, bees, wasps, ants, chiggers, ticks and, of course, mosquitoes. They buzzed and hummed around our eyes and ears, bit our feet and ankles, and embedded their greedy little snouts in our skin, which soon erupted in sores that festered constantly.

Such insects are not merely a nuisance; many of them are lethal. For they may be transmitters of the diseases that, for both indigenous Indians and visitors, are the bane of the Amazon: diseases such as yellow fever, malaria, river blindness and leishmaniasis—an especially nasty ailment that eats away your warm extremities, in particular your mouth and nose.

Jungle Towns

Soon on our journey downriver we are passing fair-sized towns: Pucallpa, Contamana and Orellana. Then, at Nauta, we are joined by the Rio Marañon; and at last we are officially on the Amazon (though Brazilian cartographers prefer to use the name Solimões until Manaus). A few miles downriver we come to a

▲ The magnificent jaguar is the largest predator in South America. Although strong enough to crack a man's skull with a single blow, it rarely attacks people.

This iguana is an agile tree-climber. Like some of the ancient dinosaurs, it has small upright plates along its spine which help control its body temperature. ▼

I N CONTRAST TO THE HUGE VARIETY
of bird and insect life to be found in
the rain forest, Amazonian mammals and
reptiles are comparatively limited in
their diversity. There are very few large
animals, in particular, probably because
they are unsuited to living and escaping
from danger in dense forest.

Most forest animals stay near water,
and have therefore had to adapt in some
way to the area's heavy rainfall and
frequent flooding. The capybara, the
world's largest rodent, has developed
webbed feet, and evades danger by
plunging into a river where it can stay
submerged for ten minutes. Even the
jaguar has overcome its family's hatred of
water to become an excellent swimmer
and a keen fish eater.

Other animals avoid the floods by
taking to the trees. Iguanas, snakes and
anteaters have all learned to live above
the ground; though they must compete
in this habitat with troops of acrobatic
monkeys, many of which have the
benefit of a prehensile or 'grasping' tail.
It is only in the Americas that monkeys
have developed this amazing fifth limb.

**The handsome giant otter can grow to six feet
in length. It is a friendly, inquisitive animal,
but is immensely strong and has been known
to kill caymans and anacondas.** ▼

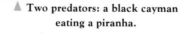
▲ Two predators: a black cayman
eating a piranha.

**Capybara are equally at home on land or
in the water. An adult may stand four
feet high and weigh 160 pounds.** ▶

◀ The endearing emperor tamarin
got its name from the way its long,
droopy moustache resembles that of an
oriental emperor.

major centre: Iquitos, a city surrounded on three sides by the Amazon and its tributaries. During the rubber boom a hundred years ago, Iquitos was the trading centre of the Peruvian jungle: a city where the cost of living was four times higher than in Paris, and where money could buy every pleasure mentioned in the *Arabian Nights*.

We have now come to what might be called the powerhouse of the Amazon: the Peruvian and Brazilian lowlands where the average rainfall is over 100 inches a year. A large part of this huge seasonal deluge finds its way into the river, often by way of other gigantic waterways. One tributary of the Amazon, the Negro, is in its own right the sixth-largest river in the world, discharging into the mainstream four times as much water as the Mississippi discharges into the Gulf of Mexico. No wonder that by the time we come to Manaus, 900 miles from the Atlantic, the river is several miles wide, so deep it is used by ocean-going liners, and so akin to the sea it is the habitat of what are usually thought of as marine creatures—dolphins, flying-fish and sharks.

Manaus is the commercial hub of the middle-Amazon; a city that nowadays has little to commend it to tourists or environ-mentalists. It does, however, still retain a veneer of its former glory. For, a hundred years ago, it was the first city in South America to have electricity, trams and a sewage-system; its streets were paved with cobblestones brought all the way from France, and its ornate opera house, resplendent with marble columns and mosaic tiles, epitomised the flamboyant lifestyle of its inhabitants. Long gone are the days when Manaus's rubber barons lived in palaces rather than villas, kept lions in their gardens, and watered their horses on champagne. Yet the city still exudes a chaotic vitality. It remains one of the world's last great free ports.

Meeting of Many Waters

The river, by this time, is an exotic mélange of waters. The mainstream, up to now fed largely by the Apurimac-Ucayali, the Urubamba and the Marañon, is the colour of creamy coffee, technically known as 'whitewater'. It is muddy and full of sedi-ment, because it has come mostly from the Andes—young, soft mountains that are easily worn away. The 'blackwater' rivers joining it from the north, such as the aptly named Rio Negro, are the colour of Guinness when viewed from above, and the colour of tea when seen through a diving mask. They get their distinctive colour from tannin derived from the enormous quantities of partly decomposed organic matter swirling through

▲ Rubber wealth built the magnificent Teatro Amazonas at Manaus (above and inset), an opera house capable of seating 2,000 people. The legendary tenor Enrico Caruso sang at the opening night in 1896.

These old steamers, moored at Iquitos, date from the rubber boom. They have been painstakingly renovated for modern use. ▼

Boom Towns

FOR ABOUT 30 YEARS—roughly from 1880 until 1910—the Amazon basin enjoyed a spell of extraordinary prosperity. During this period, the rubber tree, *Hevea brasiliensis*, was king of the rain forest, bringing wealth to a few and drudgery to many.

Waterproof clothing developed by Charles Macintosh, and the pneumatic tyre designed by John Dunlop, created a huge demand for rubber in Europe and America. Because the rubber tree in those days grew only in South America, colossal wealth came to the speculators who bought up vast tracts of jungle, to the middlemen who passed the raw rubber downriver, and to the shippers who distributed it worldwide. Most of these rubber barons lived in spectacular style in the riverside towns of Iquitos, Manaus and Belem. They imported building materials—and whole buildings—directly from Europe, and even sent their laundry to Ireland in order to avoid spoiling it with 'dirty' local water.

In contrast, the rubber tappers who were enticed to the Amazon in their thousands by the lure of easy money found themselves virtually enslaved by their masters. They spent their days in squalid, gruelling labour, tapping trees in the wild and then making enormous balls of rubber out of the milky latex. Little wonder that the tappers' lives were usually miserable and short.

The rubber boom collapsed early this century after trees were commercially planted in Southeast Asia. Nevertheless, rubber remains an important crop in the area.

▲ A present-day tapper fixes a pot beneath a deep cut that he has just made in a rubber tree. The tree's latex oozes into the cup and is collected the same day, before it has congealed. The tapper then smears it onto a spindle set over a fire in order to make a ball of rubber weighing up to 80 pounds. ▶

The River Sea

EVERY DAY THE AMAZON RIVER discharges as much fresh water into the Atlantic as the Thames carries past London in one year. Its outflow is five times greater than that of the Congo, 12 times that of the Mississippi. At Manaus, the river is over 300 feet deep, and ocean-going ships can travel as far as Iquitos—2,300 miles inland—on the longest navigable waterway in the world. Small wonder that the early explorers called the Amazon O *Rio Mar*, 'The River Sea'.

Several tributaries of the Amazon are giants in themselves: seven are more than a thousand miles long, and one, the Negro, is in places over ten miles wide. These rivers, together with their tributaries, are the roads of the jungle. But in the rainy season, when they overflow their banks, many forest rivers become difficult to define. They invade enormous floodplains of at least 40,000 square miles; and when they retreat, they often flow through entirely different channels from those of the previous year.

. . . .

When the river is in flood, it can overflow its banks for up to 60 miles on either side. Farmers must then keep their livestock on rafts. ▼

▲ The meeting of the rivers Amazon and Negro at Manaus. The dark waters of the Negro are actually like clear tea, as this photograph of a river dolphin (inset) shows.

▲ After seasonal floods, many rivers change their courses. They leave behind oxbow lakes and former channels which will eventually dry out.

A fisherman hunting for giant pirarucu fish. Amazonian rivers provide a rich harvest of fish for the communities living on or near their banks. ▶

their waters. Finally, from the south flow the 'bluewater' rivers, notably the Tapajos and the Xingu. They are also clear because they come from the Brazilian highlands and flow over ancient, rocky beds that have long since lost any soft silt.

These different types of water are often reluctant to mix. Where the Negro and the mainstream converge—and the river becomes officially known by all as the Amazon—the waters roll side by side for more than five miles before they mingle: a race of great waves and thunderous whirlpools. At the spot where they do finally blend, an enormous cement-plant disfigures the river's north bank. This cement-plant is symbolic, for from now on the Amazon comes increasingly under the influence of man.

Towards the Sea

Below Manaus the river takes on many of the characteristics of the sea. Its waves can be head-high, and many of its birds are seagoing species such as gulls and terns. The craft that ply their trade on it are not only Indian canoes but ocean-going freighters. Lumbering straight towards the sea at a steady four-and-a-half miles per hour, like a runaway colossus, the Amazon is now so huge that it has become featureless and impersonal.

But the greatest change of all is a sad one. It is that much of the primary rain forest which used to line the river's banks is no longer there. There is, it is true, a good deal of secondary and replanted forest. Nonetheless, for the next 750 miles of our journey we will be travelling through a mutilated world. The land on either side of the river has been ravaged and bears the scars of its ordeal: derelict homesteads, deserted lumber-camps and the occasional shantytown; a world of transistor-radios, cheap liquor and cheap Indian labour.

▲ Hundreds of miles from the sea, this huge ocean-going freighter towers over smaller river craft.

Then, about 250 miles from the sea, the Amazon enters its delta. Here, instead of flowing between well-defined banks, it intermingles with a new habitat: swamp-forest, a morass of half-submerged mangroves, palms and vines. There is more vegetation here than we have seen for the last 750 miles and it is good to hear, for the first time since leaving Manaus, the roar of howler monkeys and the screech of parrots. But which of many waterways do we follow to reach the mouth of the Amazon? Some channels lead north past Macapa, while others lead south and east past the island of Marajo. And nothing brings home the scale of the Amazon more clearly than the fact that Marajo is slightly larger than Switzerland.

Whichever route we follow, north to Cabo Norte or east to Belem, we come eventually to open sea at the Amazon's vast mouth, which is more than 200 miles wide. Though even here we may not have reached the ultimate end of our journey.

In January 1500 the Spanish captain Vicente Pinzon was sailing over what he believed to be open sea when he found the water under his keel was changing colour: from blue to bronze, 'like a fire at sunset'. He lowered a bucket and found to his amazement that the water was not salt, but fresh. He called his discovery *La Mar Dulce*, 'The Freshwater Sea'; and it would not be wrong to say that it is here, where the last molecules of fresh water give way to salt, that the great river, over 4,000 miles from its source, comes to an end.

It used to be said that Pinzon (or Amerigo Vespucci, according to some sources) 'discovered' the Amazon. That isn't so. The discoverers of the river were very different people from a very different age.

The First Inhabitants

First to sight the Amazon, and therefore first to discover it, were almost certainly Stone Age hunter-gatherers who came south across the Isthmus of Panama a little over 20,000 years ago.

Man arrived late in South America. In Africa, Indonesia and China human remains have been found that are 200,000 years old; but the oldest human bones ever discovered in South America (in a cave in Peru) have been proved by carbon-dating to be no more than 20,000 years old. In the same cave were found bones of a similar age belonging to giant sloths (*megatherium*). These enormous creatures—15 feet long and 5 tons in weight—had survived in South America long after they had become extinct elsewhere, because the continent had for so long evolved in isolation from the rest of the world. We must therefore picture the first human beings to settle around the Amazon as hunting prehistoric creatures half the size of many dinosaurs, rather than tapir, capybara or llama.

How, one wonders, did Stone Age people settle in such a challenging environment, and what sort of lives did they lead?

It would be simplistic to classify the people of the Amazon merely as 'Indians' and think they are all the same. They are as disparate as the people of Europe. An Indian of the Apurimac is as different from an Indian of Marajo as a blond Norwegian is different from a dark-skinned Sicilian. And at an early stage in their history the Stone Age hunter-gatherers of the Amazon divided into two quite distinct communities: there were the people of the lowlands who lived in the Amazon basin and there were the people of the highlands who lived in the Andes. The dividing line between them was the steep, east-facing wall of the Andes, which neither group attempted seriously to cross.

▲ A group of red-and-blue macaws perch on a liana. These highly social birds spend hours chattering to one another.

Aerial Beauty

THE VISITOR TO THE RAIN FOREST may at first not be aware of any birds at all. Those that live on the forest floor are heavily camouflaged, and those that live higher up are way out of sight. Yet this is home to the world's richest bird population, both in numbers and diversity.

One of the Amazon's strangest birds is the leaf-eating hoatzin, a clumsy and ungainly bird with the added misfortune of having a strong musky smell. Its chicks, however, are even more eccentric because of the claws they have on their wings. Experts are not sure whether these are a special adaptation or a remnant of all birds' reptilian past.

Many colourful birds inhabit the forest undergrowth but, as with flowers, the most spectacular specimens are to be found high in the canopy. Here are gaudy parrots, toucans with bills as large as their bodies, monkey-hunting eagles and countless songbirds. Above them all soar the vultures, the most colourful of which is the king vulture.

▲ Toucans, with their enormous bills, are perhaps the most spectacular inhabitants of the upper canopy.

◄ The vivid cock-of-the-rock has been described as being like 'a fiery comet'.

▲ The enigmatic hoatzin: a type of cuckoo, whose chicks possess hooks on their wings like the prehistoric *Archaeopteryx*. When threatened, the baby birds jump out of the nest, swim downstream, and eventually claw their way back to safety.

◄ A king vulture. This bird soars at great heights, from where it observes the behaviour of other carrion fowl, using them to guide it to a meal.

Harpy eagles are remarkably agile fliers. They are best known for their breathtaking pursuit of monkeys through the trees. ▶

The Tribes of the Amazon Basin

In time, the Indians who settled in the Amazon basin evolved a way of life ideally suited to their surroundings. They survived not by conquering and altering their environment, but by blending into it and becoming as much a part of its lifecycle as the plants and animals. As a result, they managed not only to survive, but to prosper and multiply in the immense rain forest.

About 500 years ago the population of the Amazon basin is believed to have been at least five million—large enough for there to be serious competition for land. The most sought-after land was the fertile floodplains beside the rivers. The people who settled here lived in permanent villages with populations of anything up to three thousand. They cultivated beans and manioc and became the prosperous tribes of the area.

Other tribes settled on higher ground, where they became nomadic, banding together into small, extended-family groups of between 30 and 100 people. They practised contraception and infanticide to ensure that their population never became a strain on their environment, and each group had its own territory, which it vigorously defended. Hence the warlike reputation they soon acquired.

All these people relied heavily on hunting and gathering for their existence. There was no trade, no contact with the outside world, and there were no animals which could be domesticated. Since the lowland people depended for everything on their rain forest, it is hardly surprising that they gradually established an affinity with it, not merely using its plants and creatures, but coming to think of them as spirits, some harmful, some healing. When they wanted to communicate with these spirits they took hallucinogenic drugs, as they do to this day.

These people of the Amazon were not 'noble savages' living in a latter-day Eden. But they did work out a way of life which enabled them to live in harmony with their environment, and they would no more dream of harming this environment than of harming themselves. They have an ancient saying that, 'Each time you cut down a tree you must ask its forgiveness or a star will fall out of the sky'.

The Tribes of the Andes

The Indians who settled in the highlands, in the headwaters of the Amazon, led totally different lives. The Andes are a harsh environment—strong winds and long spells of drought alternate with short bursts of violent rain; the soil is poor; there are few trees and much of the land is too high for conventional agriculture. The Indians here could never have survived simply by

▲ The Indian tribes display an enormous variety of body decorations. This nomadic hunter from the Txukuhamae tribe sports a large, decorative lip-disc and the scars of self-inflicted incisions on his chest and arms.

▲ A pair of Kamayura tribesmen size each other up at a wrestling match that forms part of the festivities to mark the end of a period of mourning.

Jungle Tribes

THE EARLIEST COLONISTS of South America, and the ancestors of today's Indian tribes, are believed to have been people of Asian origin, who crossed from Siberia to Alaska and then gradually migrated down the American continent. They were hunter-gatherers and subsistence farmers, and those who made their home in the jungle settled most densely along the rivers, especially the Amazon.

These tribes adapted to life on the floodplain—the fertile land on either side of a river—by cultivating beans and a root vegetable called manioc during the dry season, and by hunting turtles and their eggs in the rivers. Other tribes adopted a more nomadic way of life. They had to fend for themselves in the jungle, and developed a fearsome reputation for head-hunting and other belligerent behaviour. In general, however, the Indians had a relatively stable way of life—until the arrival of Europeans with their guns and diseases: smallpox, measles, syphilis and the common cold. These had a devastating impact on the peoples of the rain forest, wiping out whole communities and even whole tribes.

▲ A Txikao Indian, whose tribe is famed for its fierceness, adorned with feathers and paint.

▲ A group of Kamayura Indians from the Xingu area assist each other in festive body decoration. Crushed seeds of the urucu plant are kneaded into a red paste (inset), which is used for body paint by many tribes.

▲ As recently as the first half of this century, head-hunting tribes such as the Jivaro believed that the shrunken head of an enemy gave power to its possessor.

◄ Today, this tribe of Kayapo Indians from the Amazonian lowlands perform a traditional war dance to enlist the protection of forest spirits. They are seen here brandishing spears and their lethal wooden war-cudgels.

accepting their environment. They needed to master it, and this is what they did. They domesticated the llama and the guinea pig, and formed themselves into village collectives that improved the land by communal effort. They shored up the hillsides in great flights of fieldstone terracing, and collected and distributed rainfall by canals and irrigation runnels.

Then, with dramatic suddenness, one tribe rose to prominence. The Incas first conquered their neighbours, then built an empire and imposed a short-lived spell of unity and prosperity over almost the whole of the Andes.

The Empire of the Incas

The Incas rose to prominence in the 15th century, largely through the efforts of one man, the Emperor Pachacuti. He reorganised the Inca army and launched a series of campaigns designed to bring the diverse people of the Andes under his control. Within a generation he and his son Topa Yupanqui had carved out for themselves an empire which extended from the volcanic peaks of Colombia to the Vales of Paradise in Chile, and from the Pacific seaboard in the west to the Amazon rain forest in the east: that is to say, it was as large and as populous as the empire of Alexander the Great.

Empires are traditionally more difficult to keep than to acquire, yet the Incas managed surprisingly well. They were expert soldiers, engineers, agriculturalists and administrators. Whenever they conquered new territory, they linked it to their heartland around Cuzco by the most magnificent roads, with storehouses, rest houses and hilltop forts at strategic intervals. They then used their agricultural expertise to make the newly won land more productive.

The Coming of the Conquistadors

How long the Inca empire would have lasted without outside interference will never be known. For in the spring of 1531 Francisco Pizarro and 180 Spanish Conquistadors landed on the coast of present-day Ecuador. Within a couple of years this small group of professional soldiers had done the impossible: they had conquered one of the world's greatest empires, guarded by a quarter of a million first-class troops. But the Conquistadors did

◄ **Machu Picchu. In 1911, the American archaeologist Hiram Bingham discovered the ruins of a fortified Inca city on Machu Picchu (The Old Peak). Why the site was abandoned remains a mystery, since its excellent state of preservation shows that it was never attacked by the plundering Conquistadors.**

more than conquer the Inca empire, they obliterated it. 'What can be burned is burned,' wrote a contemporary chronicler, 'the rest is broken.' To understand why, we need to know their background and their motives.

For almost 800 years the ancestors of the Conquistadors had waged a non-stop crusade against the Moors, the Islamic people who in those days occupied a large part of the Iberian peninsula. In 1492 Granada, the last Moorish stronghold in Spain, was captured and the last Moorish troops ejected to North Africa. And suddenly there was no one left to fight. However, by a strange coincidence, the year Granada fell was also the year Columbus discovered America. So the men who for centuries had fought the Moors set out in the wake of the seamen in search of new infidels to fight and new booty to win. For as Hernando Cortes, the conqueror of Mexico, wryly confessed: 'We have a sickness of the heart for which there is only one cure, gold.' The Conquistadors could never get enough gold. They scoured the Andes and the rain forest remorselessly for it; and, driven by their obsession, lost many lives on fruitless searches for the legendary El Dorado, 'the gilded (or golden) man' and his kingdom.

It was on one such quest in 1541 that Gonzalo Pizarro (a half-brother of Francisco, who had led the invasion of the Inca empire) headed east from Quito into the upper reaches of the Amazon. His expedition is important on two counts: it led to the first recorded journey down the Amazon from headwaters to mouth; and it led to the river getting its name.

Contact with the Amazons

For the Indians of the Amazon basin, their first contact with the heavily armed Conquistadors must have been a terrifying experience. Some fled and let the Spaniards ransack their villages; others greeted them with dignity, and only turned against them when they started to pillage and loot; yet others met them with war drums and poisoned arrows. Describing one of these skirmishes, the Dominican friar Gaspar de Carvajal wrote: 'In a village where the Indians defended themselves with particular fury they were led by women. Ten or twelve of these Amazons were fighting in front of the men as female captains. They were tall, white and naked, with only their private parts covered, and each did as much fighting as ten men.'

This is no more than an imaginative reworking of the Greek legend of a land known as Amazonia, where there was said to be a race of female warriors strongly antagonistic towards men. These Amazons' only contact with men was supposed to be at

The great fortress of Sacsahuaman near the old Inca capital of Cuzco. Some of these stones weigh over 200 tons. ▶

▲ Steep paths, like this one at 11,500 feet, crisscrossed the Inca empire.

Agricultural terraces at an Inca temple in the sacred valley of the Urubamba. Apart from being essential for farming, the terraces were also effective defences. ▼

The Master Builders of the Andes

THE INCAS HAVE BEEN DESCRIBED as the Romans of South America. Their empire, at its height, covered nearly half a million square miles, and they kept control of it by means of an extensive network of magnificent roads that were one of the wonders of the world. Their Royal Road was the longest trunk road in the world prior to the 19th century. It stretched for over 3,000 miles to the north and south of Cuzco, across ravines, swamps, rain forests, deserts, glaciated plateaux and high mountain passes. Regrettably, much of it has now fallen into disrepair.

The Incas were also fine masons. Their fortresses, temples and palaces were built without mortar from blocks of stone that could weigh as much as 200 tons or more. These were cut with such precision that even today a knife blade cannot enter the joins. And, by building vast, loose-stone terraces and irrigation runnels on forbiddingly steep mountain slopes, they turned the Andes into the highest food-producing area in the world. At altitudes of thousands of feet they grew crops of beans, maize and potatoes to feed the people of their realm.

▲ The Incas had no system of writing, but used the knotted *quipu* for keeping records of taxes, crops and populations.

▲ Modern descendants of the Incas in traditional costume enact *Inti-Raymi*, the annual sun festival, at Cuzco.

The Incas' extraordinary skill in dovetailing blocks of stone can be seen in this photograph of two niches set into a wall. ▶

an annual festival, held to ensure the reproduction of their race. They allowed only female children conceived at the festival to live, and cut off one of their breasts so that they could draw their bows more easily. Theirs was supposedly a land rich in gold and emeralds. Like many tall stories, this one became accepted as fact; and the greatest river on Earth has been known from that day to this as the Amazon.

Slave Traders and Missionaries

After the Conquistadors had drawn a blank on their many searches for El Dorado, the Amazon remained in limbo for almost two centuries. The river had an unhealthy climate; there was no particular reason for anyone to go there; and the fact that its lower reaches were controlled by Portugal, and its upper reaches by Spain, discouraged overall development. The only people to take much interest in it were two very different groups: slave traders and missionaries.

Round the periphery of the Amazon cheap labour was in great demand, especially in the mines of the Andes and the sugar plantations of present-day Venezuela and Brazil. It wasn't long before groups of *bandeirantes* (gangs of slavers-cum-gold-prospectors) were rounding up whole communities from the rain forest and forcing them to work in conditions that caused an appalling death-rate. The only people effectively to oppose them were missionaries.

From the 1550s until the 1760s Capuchins, Carmelites, Franciscans and Jesuits penetrated deep into the jungle, intent on converting the Indians to Christianity. We may well question their motives in wishing to 'convert the heathen'; but there can be no denying that many of the 17th-century friars and priests were men of heroic quality. They had intellectual curiosity, surprising practical skills, great powers of endurance and deep piety. They have been described as the first naturalists, the first anthropologists and the first cartographers of the interior. Their work paved the way for that of the 18th- and 19th-century scientists who were soon unveiling the richness and diversity of the Amazon.

Scientists and Explorers

One of the first of these more technical and more modern scientists was Charles-Marie de la Condamine, a French soldier-turned-mathematician. La Condamine was second-in-command of an expedition which arrived in Ecuador in 1736 to measure the exact length of a degree of longitude at the Equator. Once this had been worked out, cartography could become an exact

▲ **A ruined church stands in the jungle, a reminder of the many Catholic missionaries who came to the Amazon.**

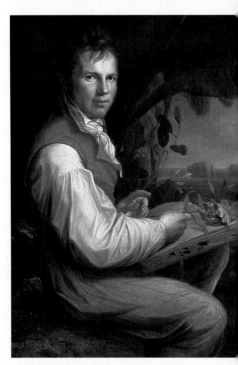

▲ **A portrait of Alexander von Humboldt painted in 1806, showing him pressing flowers in the Amazon.**

The British naturalist Henry Bates prepares to dispatch a cayman caught by Indians while hunting for turtles. ▼

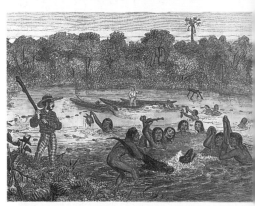

Men with a Mission

THE AMAZON HAS ALWAYS attracted men inspired by a cause. The Conquistadors wanted power and wealth, and the Jesuit missionaries who followed them wanted souls. These priests and monks built huge fortified missions and vast baroque churches, and cultivated the surrounding land for the benefit of the whole community. They were generally men of great dedication and zeal, who succeeded in converting many Indians to at least some observance of Roman Catholicism.

In their footsteps came the explorers and naturalists, eager to open up undiscovered country, or extend the borders of scientific knowledge. The first world-renowned scientist to study the area in depth was the aristocratic Frenchman Charles-Marie de la Condamine, who landed in Ecuador in 1736. At the turn of the century, the German Alexander von Humboldt travelled in the upper reaches of the Amazon, recording his acute observations about the area's people, animals, plants and geology. Then, in the mid-19th century, the English naturalists Alfred Wallace and Henry Bates spent years collecting insect specimens and developing a 'survival of the fittest' theory at precisely the same time as Darwin was writing his famous book on evolution, *On the Origin of Species*.

Today doctors and scientists still come to the Amazon, in particular to learn more about its plants and their potential for curing diseases.

▲ **A Xavante Indian serving at mass in the Mato Grosso. His tribe was among the most warlike in the region, driving away all outsiders until the 1950s.**

Mission schools such as this often provide the only opportunity for Indians to receive a Western education. ▼

▲ Only in the forest canopy are trees covered with a mantle of blossoms.

The Flowering Forest

THE ABUNDANT AND EXUBERANTLY FLOWERING vegetation of the tropical rain forest is produced by heat and rain—conditions that are particularly concentrated in the Amazon basin. And since there is no autumn or winter on the Equator, the forest remains in bloom throughout the year.

There are, however, relatively few flowers to be seen in the deep shade of the forest, and those that do endure the gloom are mostly small and pale. At ground level, bright flowers are generally confined to the occasional clearing that has been penetrated by sunlight. But in the sunlit canopy the situation is quite different. Here are great clusters of brilliant flowers, many of which are enormous in size and pungent in perfume— qualities which have evolved to attract the insects, birds and even bats that tropical plants rely on for pollination.

▲ Epiphytes such as this orchid flourish in the intense humidity of the rain forest. They grow on larger plants, especially trees, but are not parasitic.

The carnivorous sundew secretes sticky droplets, which attract and catch small flies. ▶

▲ The beaked heliconia is a large perennial favoured by collectors.

Many plants rely on specific creatures to pollinate them. This bloom attracts bats.

A cannonball tree in bloom. It gets its name from its fruit, which is as hard as iron and crashes noisily to the ground. ▼

◄ The royal water lily astounded Victorian botanists. Its leaves are large enough to support a small child.

science—but it was only after eight years of painstaking triangulation that success was achieved. La Condamine meanwhile had become an aficionado of all things South American, and he decided to return to France via the Amazon. It was a perilous journey. His raft was sucked into whirlpools. His Indian crew died of smallpox. Nonetheless he kept a detailed record of the river's course, flow and wildlife. And perhaps even more important, when he got back to France he spent the rest of his life promoting a wide range of South American products, among them rubber, curare and quinine.

One of the next major figures to throw light on the Amazon was Alexander von Humboldt, the German scientific traveller. In 1799, Humboldt and his companion Aimé Bonpland headed inland from Caracas to investigate the connection between the Rivers Orinoco and Amazon—contemporary maps suggested that both rivers had their source in an enormous lake. What made their journey particularly remarkable was that they were forever collecting data in so many fields. One day they were studying the symbiosis of ants and fungi, the next day dissecting electric eels, and the next making notes on the rituals of the Orinoco Indians. Their curiosity encompassed every facet of nature. At the end of nine months they returned to the coast, having proved, in Humboldt's words, that 'the great lake does not exist, and must be reduced to an area of swampland only two or three miles in circumference.' They also brought back a cornucopia of specimens, including 16,000 plants.

Wallace and Bates

Even more specimens were collected half a century later by an unlikely pair of apprentices from industrial England: Alfred Russel Wallace and Henry Walter Bates. The two men were brought together by a mutual interest in beetles and in 1848 they pooled their resources to set off on what Bates called their 'rash adventure': a journey to the Amazon to collect insect specimens and ship them back to museums and research establishments at threepence a head.

The museums and research establishments got more than they bargained for! Wallace went up the Rio Negro, which he followed almost to its source. Bates went up the Amazon and over a period of 11 years collected 14,712 different species of insect, of which 8,000 were previously unknown. He also made a detailed study of the mimicry of butterflies. 'On the expanded membrane of their wings,' he wrote, 'Nature reveals the story of the modification of species.' Wallace too was to reach the conclusion that: 'Creatures change in order to improve the species, so the inferior are killed off and the superior remain.' It is not perhaps widely known that at the same time as Darwin was groping towards his theory of evolution, Wallace and Bates were thinking along exactly the same lines in the Amazon.

The Amazon Today

So we come to the 20th century which, until recently, has been a period of pure exploitation.

To start with, it was rubber which was exploited; and for some 30 years the Amazon basin had a monopoly in the production of latex. However, in the early years of this century the boom collapsed after a classic piece of industrial espionage. Seeds from the indigenous rubber plants were smuggled out of the Amazon, germinated at Kew, and then planted in Southeast Asia; soon they were producing rubber three times as cheaply as the trees in the Amazon.

In recent years it is coca that has been exploited. Coca is a bush with laurel-like leaves, about 8 feet tall, which flourishes in the heat and humidity of the east-facing Andes at heights of between about 2,000 and 4,000 feet. It has been called 'the oldest stimulant known to man'—partially chewed quids found in Peruvian middens have been carbon-dated at about 2100 BC, and from that day to this many South Americans have been mildly addicted to it. Then in the 1960s it was discovered that, by a sophisticated process of refining, the coca leaves can be transformed first into a pastelike cocaine-hydrochloride, and then into the 'crack' now selling in the United States and Europe at US $25,000 a pound. The inevitable drug-trafficking has led to an enormous increase in local violence and crime.

Other present-day exploiters of the Amazon are gold prospectors and cattle ranchers.

Garimpeiros (gold prospectors) are today panning for gold along many of the Amazon's tributaries, and are doing considerable harm to the region. They are seducing the Indians out of their rain forest with the promise of wealth, and using them as virtual slave labour. They are also dumping silt and mercury (which is used for extracting gold) into the rivers. Satellite pictures taken in 1980 show the Tapajos River as dark blue, while pictures taken in 1992 show it as pale turquoise, deeply polluted by mercury and silt.

The cattle ranchers are causing an even more serious problem. In the 1960s the Brazilian government moved its capital from Rio de Janeiro to Brasilia, a move that symbolised its determination to open up the untapped wealth of its interior. Politicians hoped in particular to transform the jungle into

▲ Jaguars have been exterminated in many areas by illegal hunting and trapping.

A huge raft of timber being hauled down the Rio Negro. ▶

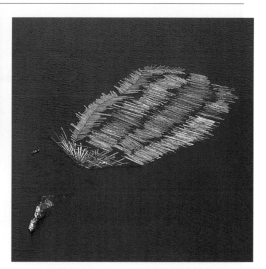

Destruction of the Rain Forest

FOR CENTURIES, THE AMAZON rain forests escaped large-scale destruction by European settlers. Even the great rubber boom had little impact on the landscape since the rubber trees were tapped in the wild and otherwise left undisturbed.

However, since the 1960s the situation has changed dramatically. In the quest for land to breed cattle and raise crops, massive areas of beautiful forest have been felled and burned—according to some estimates, up to four million acres per year between 1977 and 1986, and over five million acres in 1987 alone. Despite the fact that the soil, stripped of trees, remains fertile for a few years at most, ranchers and farmers continue to clear new pastures.

More recently, a new threat has emerged: loggers. Having denuded the tropical hardwood forests of Southeast Asia, they have turned their attention to Amazonia with increasingly devastating effect. Official and clandestine sawmills are springing up all over Brazil, and huge rafts of logs can be seen being towed down Amazonian rivers.

Mines such as this Brazilian open-cast tin mine strip the land of its vegetation, leaving it highly vulnerable to erosion. ▼

▲ Vast areas of forest are cleared every year to make way for farming. The trees are felled, left to dry out, and then wastefully burned.

◀ Forest animals such as this giant anteater are left to starve in a disfigured landscape.

Saving the Forest

THE DESTRUCTION OF NATURAL ecosystems in the Amazon is still very much a cause for concern. However, thanks to changes in government policy, deforestation in Brazil has slowed down significantly. Previously under military rule, Brazil now has an elected government, and the plea of many voters to save the forests is at last being heeded, with scientists and environmentalists from all over the world playing their part.

Work such as the recent Maraca Island Rainforest Project, led by the British Royal Geographical Society, enabled Brazilian field workers to study the devastating effects of rainfall on deforested land, and to learn how trees can be regenerated. Today, mining companies are regularly encouraged to replant land laid bare by their excavations, and hunting restrictions allow threatened animals such as the jaguar and capybara to flourish in forest reserves.

After five centuries of persecution, tribes such as the Yanomami and Kayapo Indians have recently been granted permanent rights to huge reserves of forest. And, perhaps most important of all, there is the growing realisation at home and abroad that the destruction of the Amazon would be a tragedy for future generations.

This Kayapo Indian has been provided with a CB radio in order to monitor and control visitors to his settlement. ▼

▲ Rows of mahogany seedlings, which are being carefully nurtured. Since these trees take only 25 years to reach maturity, many devastated areas could benefit relatively swiftly from replanting.

◄ Many Brazilians are appalled at the destruction of their rain forest. Here two protesters hold symbolic mahogany cuttings to show their opposition to the deforestation caused by a local sawmill.

▲ **The recent Maraca Rainforest Project involved some of the most intensive rain forest research ever undertaken in Brazil. Here, a scientist and her assistant are seen taking instrument readings in a specially prepared forest clearing.**

International research projects enable scientists to study forest wildlife with a view to aiding their survival. This zoologist is examining a boa constrictor. ▼

pastureland for cattle, and to create a beef-producing area like the pampas of Argentina. Vast reaches of the jungle were set on fire and, after the burn-off, planted with grass-seed. What wasn't understood in those days was that once the jungle had been destroyed there was nothing left to enrich the soil, which soon became too poor to support vegetation. Within 18, or at the most 24, months the grass withered and died. So did the cattle. In the past 20 years seven out of eight ranchers in Amazonia have been bankrupted.

Towards a Brighter Future

Today, thanks partly to the protests of environmentalists, the Brazilian government has been obliged to rethink its policy and its attitude to the rain forest, and is now a great deal more enlightened than it was 20 years ago. Some areas are scheduled for conservation and others for sustainable production; there is a commitment to reafforestation, and government helicopters patrol the forest to prevent illegal burning.

People now realise that the Amazon rain forest is unique and too precious to lose; for there is a great deal we can learn from its people, flora and fauna. Scientists and explorers are going there in greater numbers than ever before in search of knowledge. While some people go there for more personal reasons— such as wishing to experience the mystery and wonder of the place. Such a person is Benedict Allen.

Introducing *A Journey into the Amazon Jungle*

In 1983 Benedict Allen, fresh from the University of East Anglia, set out to make a journey through the Amazon jungle. He planned to travel 1,500 miles from the mouth of the Orinoco to the mouth of the Amazon through little-known rain forest in the Guyana foothills. He wasn't a scientist collecting facts. And he wasn't a mystic or a misfit escaping the world. He was simply a young man doing something he had always wanted to do: fulfil a childhood dream.

The remainder of our book is Benedict Allen's account of his adventure: an adventure which ended up as a desperate struggle for survival. His story conveys, more than anything else, what it is like for an ordinary person to venture into such an amazing and often perilous world.

When you have come to the end, you will know a lot more about the Amazon rain forest, its people and its animals; and, most of all, you will know what it is like to be there.

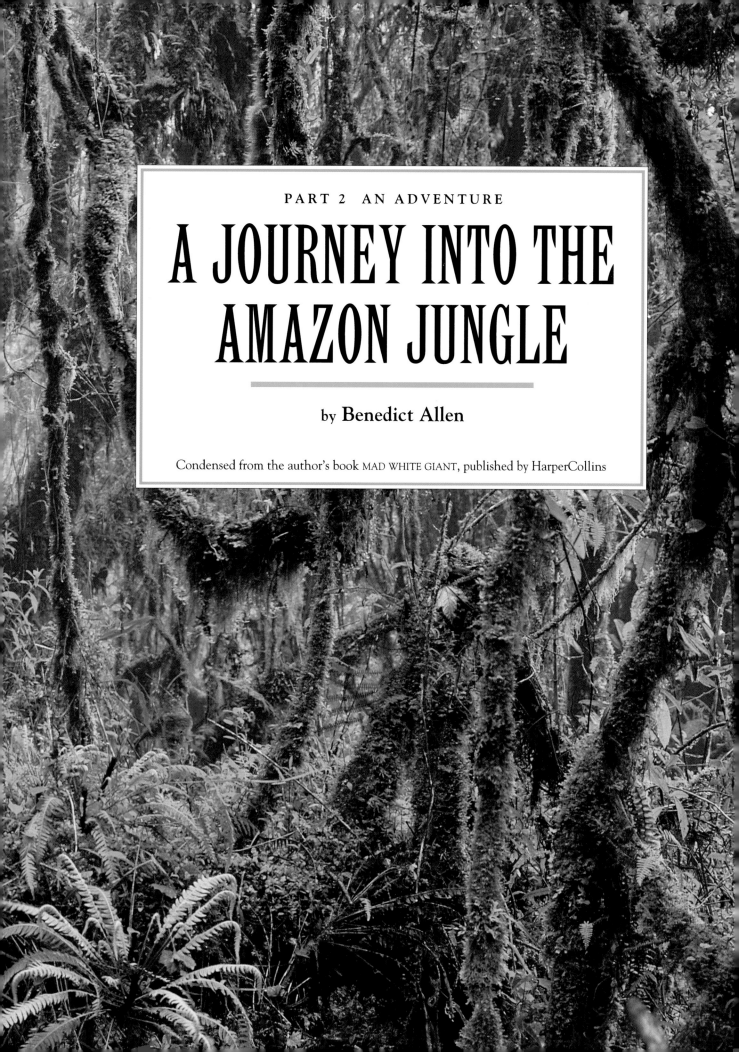

PART 2   AN ADVENTURE

A JOURNEY INTO THE
AMAZON JUNGLE

by Benedict Allen

Condensed from the author's book MAD WHITE GIANT, published by HarperCollins

CHAPTER 1

'No Need to Die'

WHEN I FIRST HEARD ITS NAME, Amazonia was a land of steaming jungle on the equator inhabited by naked savages. All the savages were headhunters and most would eat each other, given half the chance. The fiercest of them were women warriors, who cut off their right breasts to fire their arrows with greater ease. Their targets were mainly explorers, who roamed the forest in search of gold. But amongst these primitives were some Good Indians, and because explorers gave them presents of salt they guided white men through the wilderness. That was how it was to me at school, aged ten.

'The jungle is a mysterious world of darkness and insects,' the class mistress told us one day. 'Enormous snakes hang down from the creepers and wrap themselves around you and squeeze you tight until you suffocate.' The teacher, who was squeamish, had gone ash white. We demanded to know more, but she said nothing. She stood motionless by the blackboard, with her hands gripped tight around her throat.

I imagined thick coils grappling with a moustached white man in a suit. I saw the snake being dispatched with repeated shots of a revolver, the man straightening his tie, then walking away.

Months went by before I met anyone who had actually been to the Amazon. He was the father of Pinkerton-Smithe, a boy at school who had bragged that his father had just recently returned. I met him on Parents' Day.

He was easily recognisable as an explorer. He was tall and had a thick muscular neck. His beard was a black thicket and he had restless, intolerant eyes and looked much like the moustached white man who had executed the snake. I told him of the teacher's jungle and asked him the truth about the savages.

'The truth about the savages?' he said. 'The truth about the savages is that there aren't any.'

This was appalling. 'Aren't any?'

'Nope. Just people who have wars like us and people whose lives aren't cluttered up by possessions, unlike ours. The jungle is their larder. It's their home. What else do they need?' I wasn't sure. But Pinkerton-Smithe's father really seemed to know these people and their jungle. 'No, it's not the *Indians* who are the savages,' he said.

According to him, in the sixteenth century the jungle had been seething with Europeans 'all because a man called Cortez had made his name by conquering the Aztec empire

These fierce Amazonian warriors are shown displaying their traditional hostility to men. This drawing dates from the 16th century. ▼

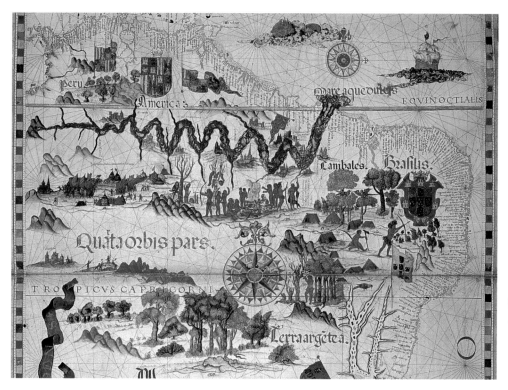

In this 16th-century map the Amazon twists like a snake above a group of cannibals roasting their victims. To their left is a group of heavily armed European invaders.

in Mexico and become exceedingly rich on the spoils, like another man, Pizarro, who had plundered the Incas. And you can appreciate that all the adventurers of the day wanted to obtain the same wealth.' I said I could quite appreciate that. 'Well, straight away it looked as if they were in luck, because many Indians spoke of a lake in the jungle, the lake of El Dorado, the Gilded Man. Here was a tribe of such wealth, they said, that the chief used to anoint his body all over with gold dust and wash it off with great ceremony in the lake water. Many explorers searched the jungle for this chiefdom: Sir Walter Raleigh from the Orinoco River, and the Dutch, Spanish and even Irish from the Amazon.'

'Did anyone find El Dorado?' I asked.

'Nope. But explorers still go out to that jungle in search of it. They go, but some never come back.'

What Mr Pinkerton-Smithe had said, about the lost explorers more than the gold, excited me. Although my teacher had got it wrong—there were no breast-less female savages—this was still a land of mystery. A place for the explorer.

If only I were older, I thought, then I could go there too.

Eight more school years drifted by, during which I developed a passion for fossils. To my parents it was a harmless enough hobby; but tramping mile upon mile of the rich blue lias cliffs of Lyme Regis, I unwittingly fostered the wander-lust that had seeded itself deep inside me. Once I was released from school, I began to work on a plan. It was a simple one: to journey between the mouths of the Orinoco and the Amazon, through the heart of that El Dorado land. I found it was a route no one had attempted before; not even the explorers who had used the lower, slow-water stretches of both during the search for treasure. I bought some maps, inspected them closely, and then saw why.

The mangrove forests of the Orinoco mouth looked straightforward enough. There was even what looked like a dirt track leading south through the jungle, out of the Orinoco system and up through hilly savannah. It was beyond this, at the end of the track, coming down again off the lip of the Amazon basin, that there would be difficulties. I would have to head east for seven hundred miles, across one of the remotest sections of Amazonian jungle, hopping the gaps between half a dozen different tributaries along the way. Only then would I reach the Amazon mouth. For someone who had never set eyes on the rain forest, and whose longest journey had been while backpacking in Greece, it certainly would be hard.

'Impossible' was the word chosen by specialists, when I broached the plan.

'What will happen if one of your expedition party gets a jungle fever? You wouldn't get to a village for months.'

'How do you think you'll get in all your food supplies? By helicopter or something? If so, where are you getting the money from? I can't imagine anyone *sponsoring* a scheme like this. You'll need the army at your disposal and Heaven knows what else.'

'Are you stupid or something?'

I was beginning to admit that I was.

A Lost Explorer

ONE OF THE MOST famous of many explorers to be lost in the Amazon jungle was Colonel Percy Fawcett—a man of remarkable courage and endurance, whose lifelong obsession with the area began when he surveyed the Brazilian frontier in 1906.

After the First World War, in which he was awarded the DSO, Fawcett returned to South America in the hope of finding the Lost City of an ancient civilisation. His only evidence was a dubious 18th-century document unearthed from archives in Rio de Janeiro. Although he had lost several companions on previous expeditions, Fawcett set out in April 1925 with only two guides (who soon turned back), his 22-year-old son and a young friend. His intention was to explore the vast, dense forests of the Mato Grosso in south-central Brazil, but he and his companions never reappeared. In 1928 a rescue mission reported that the party had probably been killed by Indians.

▲ **Colonel Fawcett at his camp in the Mato Grosso at the start of his last journey.**

Nevertheless, sightings of a mysterious, haggard Englishman, believed to be Fawcett, continued to surface for some time afterwards. Some suspected that the colonel had been secretly prospecting for oil; but whatever his mission, no definite trace of the unfortunate explorer has ever been found.

In the next four years I passed through university, clocking up experience on expeditions to the world's last remote scraps along the way. In the virgin jungle of Costa Rica our party scooped up research samples of boiling mud from the cone of a volcano. I joined an expedition of Gurkha soldiers to Brunei, and there netted bird-like moths and bottled jungle wasps for science. Then I led fellow graduates to a distant glacier, where we measured pioneering plants and grew numb in blizzards. It was all very interesting, but it was not enough.

Not knowing what to do with myself, I hung on through one more academic year. Sometimes I dreamt once more of travelling the lands between the Orinoco and Amazon river mouths, but each time I dug out the maps and drew up plans, the experts, through weight of numbers, forced me into agreement. My expedition was just not practicable.

And that would have been that, had I not recalled something Pinkerton-Smithe had said ages ago. The memory came late one summer night and sent me leaping out of bed. He had been talking about the Indians. 'The jungle is their larder. What else do they need?'

The answer was 'nothing', and two thoughts fused together in my mind. The first was that taking an expedition anywhere using alien, Western technology and ignoring indigenous skills has little to do with true exploration. The second was that the Indians, not outsiders, should determine whether or not my journey through the land between the Orinoco and the Amazon was possible. If it was, then I must go alone, place my trust in the Indians, and win their acceptance. I must learn to live much as one of them.

'The jungle is their home,' Pinkerton-Smithe had said. The Indians, if they wished, would guide me through it.

▲ **Only from the edge of a clearing is it possible to appreciate the full beauty of the tall, majestic trees of the rain forest as they stand out against sunlight and mist.**

Jungle Eddie

'Jungle Eddie' McGee, so people said, could survive in the most desolate place anyone could dream up. In any cold or hot desert, he could dine out on the land. The wilderness gave him food, shelter and even medicine. He would treat wounds by binding up the gash with a cobweb. On top of the cobweb he would sprinkle the black spores of puffball toadstools and the penicillin in the fungus would restore him to health. He was that sort of man.

When I first came across him, he was standing on the lawn of the Royal Geographical Society. It was February 1982. There was a bitter wind. Snow was forecast. Eddie McGee was about to talk to a crowd of scientists who were planning modern-style expeditions to the rain forests. The title of the talk was 'No Need to Die'.

'All right. Gather round, please.'

The crowd shuffled forward. Some people were still nattering.

Eddie McGee was a short, compact man with a weathered face and alert eyes. He was sure to know something the Indians wouldn't.

'Now, I'm going to tell you a bit about how to cope if something goes wrong on your expedition. You'll all have your emergency arrangements, naturally—for rescue parties, evacuations and so on—but you can never be too cautious.'

Emergency arrangements. I wasn't going to have any *emergency arrangements* and the words made me flinch.

'What do we mean by a "survivor"? Anyone?'

Silence fell. Someone sneezed.

'Well, I'll tell you. A survivor is a person who fights when others die.' He paused for effect. 'And "survival" is fighting to live on when all hope has gone. Now, if you remember only *one thing* today, let it be this: nothing counts more in a survival situation than our attitude. Our *will to survive*.'

He had said this to set us thinking, but most people were trying to hide a smile. *They* wouldn't be in a survival situation. Not even a panic situation. Those were their thoughts, and their flippancy isolated me. I thought of them in the jungle with their 'emergency arrangements', and then thought of myself alone out there, living like an Indian. The vision in my head was of a gangling white man looking ridiculous in a loincloth. I wanted to forget the whole idea.

Eddie McGee took two paces backwards to a spot on the lawn between two wiry shrubs.

'Come this way, please. Now, the greatest killers in most survival situations are: one, the cold; two, wetness; three, the wind. But in the jungle our main

problem is wetness. So we need to build a shelter, right? This is how we do it.'

He drew a string of fishing line from his clothing and strung some shrivelled leaves on it. Then he made a frame of twigs and covered it with the leaf chains. In a few minutes it was a tent, the leaves like roof tiles over it.

'Remember that in the jungle you've got leaves all around you to choose from.' By now every member of that audience was riveted. Eddie McGee had a habit of conjuring up things from nowhere. This man was a magician.

'One thing in passing. Don't camp near a river. In the tropics they swell and sweep over the banks, even after the shortest of downpours.' He remembered something else. 'Oh yes, and don't camp on a game trail. There was this man who went off to the jungle just last year. It was his own fault. Went by himself, the idiot. Got lost, of course. Lost everything. Followed the survival instructions. Managed to make a lovely tent from leaves, as he'd been taught. At last things began to look up. He even found a nice bare patch of ground to camp on. Trouble was, it didn't belong to him, and at the crack of dawn he was flattened by a hippo. So *think* animal, *be* animal. OK? And that goes for tracking and snaring, which I'll talk about in a minute.

'Next most important thing: making a fire.' He showed how to rub two sticks together. 'You can't use any old sticks, mind you.' When he'd lit up some bark chips with the spark and blown up the flames, he spoke about cooking. 'I assume you all know how to skin a snake?'

When the fire was dead, he fished out a black splinter of charcoal from the ash and said, holding it up, 'One of nature's best medicines. Eat it and it will cure your stomachache.'

I said: 'After eating the snake, you're going to need it.' My voice carried further than expected.

Eddie McGee turned to face me and said, 'And what exactly are *you* going to be doing in the jungle?'

I told him.

'Pheweeee! How long a journey is that?'

I told him.

'Pheweeee! What do your parents think of the idea?'

'They say they're worried that I'm going alone.'

'*Alone?*' Eddie McGee, that tough, weather-beaten man who used cobwebs instead of linen to bandage his cuts, appeared stunned. 'Do you mind me giving you one more bit of advice?'

I said, 'No. Of course not.' But I was sure he was leading up to say that I was an idiot to attempt this journey, like the man who had been flattened by the hippo.

'Just remember this simple rule. *Never bluff. Always know your stuff.* If you abide by that, you'll pull through.' He smiled. 'With luck anyway.'

'Thanks,' I said. 'I'll bear that in mind.'

▲ An 18th-century drawing of a British settler in Guyana directing the skinning of the giant anaconda he has shot.

A painting by the Peruvian artist José Effio (1840–1917) showing the foundation of Lima in 1535 by Francisco Pizarro, leader of the band of conquistadors who conquered the Inca empire.

A golden mask of the sun god. Tens of thousands of golden artefacts such as this were wantonly melted down by the conquering Spaniards.

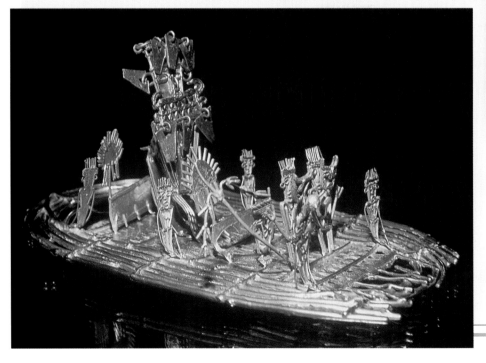

The figures on this golden raft, discovered in a cave in Colombia, appear to represent El Dorado and his attendants setting out to pay tribute to the sun god.

The Search for El Dorado

ONE OF THE MOST POWERFUL legends to grip the imagination of 16th-century Europe was that of El Dorado—'the golden' or 'gilded man'. It told of a South American Indian chief who made offerings of gold to the sun god (or a water monster, according to some versions) by covering himself with gold dust and washing it off in a lake. His subjects would then throw jewels and golden ornaments into the waters. To the gold-hungry European invaders, this legend conjured up images of a fabulous land of hidden cities rich in gold, jewels and plunder.

El Dorado was the spur that drove Francisco Pizarro and his small band of conquistadors deeper into the continent from Ecuador, where they landed in 1531. And for decades afterwards, numerous expeditions followed them in an ultimately fruitless quest. From Spain, Portugal, Holland, Germany, Ireland and England, adventurers set out to search the valleys of the Amazon and Orinoco Rivers. But El Dorado was always over the next hill or around the next bend of the river, and all they found were more legends, equally unrewarding. Many expeditions were disastrous, especially that led by Sir Walter Raleigh up the Orinoco River in 1595. Others, however, led to significant discoveries. After crossing the Andes in 1539, Francisco de Orellana and a group of conquistadors were swept all the way down the Amazon to the Atlantic, thereby becoming the first westerners to appreciate the river's immensity.

There certainly was gold in the Andes and the Amazon basin, for the Spaniards found several tons of golden artefacts in Inca tombs and temples, most of which they melted down and shipped back to Europe. But the fabulous El Dorado remained undiscovered, a myth kept alive by man's greed and love of adventure.

Sir Walter Raleigh in a portrait of 1602. After two disastrous voyages to Guyana in 1595 and 1617, Raleigh returned to England in disgrace and was executed in 1618. ▲

▲ Lake Guatavita in Colombia has long been associated with the story of El Dorado. A few golden relics were found when it was drained at the beginning of this century, suggesting a possible basis of truth to the legend.

▲ A 16th-century engraving showing the Indian chief, El Dorado, being sprayed with gold dust prior to his ritual bathe in honour of the sun god.

CHAPTER 2

Delta Village

ACCORDING TO THE MAPS, the town of Tucupita was perched on the very edge of the Orinoco Delta. So when I arrived in Venezuela I headed there straight away. From Caracas I bussed through a series of messy towns, and when these ended I caught a lift in a car. We drove along straight red dust roads in the open heat and through swampy grasses.

As we neared the delta I expected the air to become sticky, but instead the swamps dried up into bald, cracked, earth patches. As we passed through Tucupita's suburbs, the driver said that if it was the delta I had come to see, then I'd better take a look on the other side of town. There was no shortage of it there.

There was dust on the trees when I arrived. The Orinoco was low, judging by its banks, and the locals said that at this time of year the rain came only in light afternoon showers.

Life here centred on the town square, the Plaza Bolivar. It had trees with whitewashed trunks, sloths in the branches, concrete benches and courting couples. If there was a way through the forests to the sea, the real start of my journey, I'd find it here.

▲ Three-toed sloths are painfully slow in their movements and have such a low metabolic rate that they have been known to survive after being submerged in water for 30 minutes.

I took a stroll along the riverside and stared across the water to the forests. I practised my Spanish on a leafsweeper and two teenage schoolgirls with books under their arms. Then I sat in the shade of a tree in the plaza and wondered how I was going to find a passage through the delta forests to the sea.

I had read of only one Englishman who had passed through the midst of the forests and that was Sir Walter Raleigh, in 1595. The delta almost killed him. In the library of the Royal Geographical Society there was a book all about it. Raleigh was on his way to find the elusive 'great and golden city' of El Dorado, but got lost in the delta's complex channels. Driven to despair, Raleigh nearly executed his incompetent guide. In the nick of time, another guide came along. They might have wandered a whole year in that labyrinth, Raleigh said.

I spent days waiting in the plaza, asking how I should go about travelling through the delta. Old men used to press coins into the palm of my hand and say I should buy myself a drink.

The Indians had always seemed the best bet. I was sure they would know the delta, if anyone did. One of them was a boy with a pair of tatty shorts on. He stared in awe at passers-by from behind the mango trees and ran when he crossed open spaces in the town. One cool morning I left a bolivar coin at my side for him to take, and as I pretended to write my diary entry he sneaked up,

took it and ran for his life. That afternoon he was back and grabbed another one, without glancing at me.

This went on for three days and in all that time he didn't say a word. He watched me from the other side of the plaza, waiting for another coin.

On the fourth day I managed to get across to the boy what I wanted him to find out. And on the fifth, after a soft yellow sunrise, the boy came and from a distance of about twenty yards beckoned me to follow.

He took me away from the paved roads, down a dusty track, along an alleyway of bruised-faced Indian women with children crying around their feet. This was a different Tucupita to the one I'd seen. We were walking along the waterfront where naked Indian children with jaundiced skin and brown teeth pleaded for money.

We dropped down to the riverside beach, into the shade of the acacia trees. There were plenty of Indians there, but no shacks to house them; just hammocks strung between trees above the river jetsam. These Indians were irritated by my intrusion and I kept close behind the boy. They looked as if they wanted to get out of their hammocks and beat me up, but were too weak. The air fizzled with flies and stank of the putrid fish washed up along the shoreline.

Amongst all this was a white man. He was inspecting the hull of a dugout canoe. His trousers were rolled above the knees and his feet were in the surf. A fisherman, I thought. The Indian boy nodded at the man and ran off. In all the week I had known him he had never said a word.

The man asked me in Spanish what I wanted. I told him that I needed a lift through the delta forests. He laughed and said we could talk about it over a meal, perhaps, but not out here in the stink and heat. He made a living trading with the Indians, he said. *They* caught the fish, with the help of his brother and his modern fishing tackle, and *he* kept a storehouse where the fish was salted and prepared for market. His name was Juliano. He walked me to his storehouse,

Fishing is a way of life in the Orinoco Delta, where every waterfront is crowded with boats.

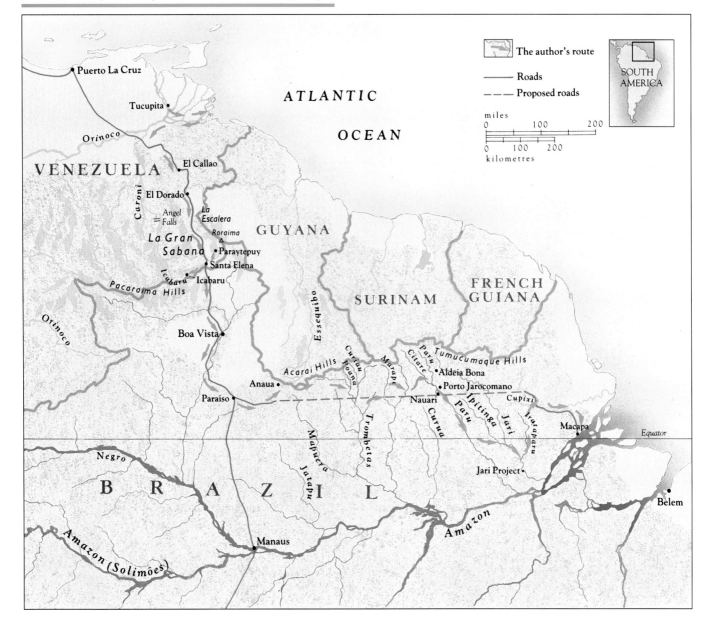

miles
0   100   200

0   100   200
kilometres

▲ Benedict Allen's journey is traced as well as he can remember it. He travelled at great speed, lost most of his notes along the way, and became very ill towards the end.

snatched stiff dried fish from the top of a pile and later, back at his hut, ordered his wife to prepare it for us. Juliano looked about sixty and his teeth were few, but large, like tusks. His wife beat the fish soft over a log in the back yard.

Juliano listened to my plans while we gnawed at the fish, and said he would get some Indians to take me the very next day. He was sending some men out to collect some fish from a remote village by the sea.

I asked him to show me the village on the map.

'You make fun of me, *señor*. The village doesn't even have a name.' He said he would scribble a letter of introduction for me to give to his brother Alfredo at the village. The Indians were uneasy about strangers, and it would pave my way considerably. I was to come back at sunrise.

As I was leaving, he said, 'You know, it's a wonder that you got that boy to bring you to me. He's deaf and dumb, and an orphan. You're the first person to have communicated with him for years. That's why I'm helping you.'

Towards the Delta

We slipped away from the riverbank before the sun was high. I had carefully added two baskets of bread rolls to my baggage, as presents to the village. Two of Juliano's Indian fishermen piloted the canoe. They had a good knowledge of Spanish; their eyes were sharp and their bodies thick and muscular. Their skin was shiny, as if it had been polished.

One of the fishermen sat at the bow, trailing his legs in the spray; the other was at the helm, steering. The motor pushed us along in jerks, and for a while we passed riverside huts, and banks of open grassland with crocodiles sprawling in the sun. Some lay with their mouths gaping open and small birds with beaks like pliers hopped in and out, picking food from their teeth.

The river narrowed, the trees closed in and there were no more riverside huts. We were alone.

The Indian at the bow yelled at intervals to divert us away from approaching snares: 'Rock to the left!' or 'Shallows to the right!' We continued weaving along like this, startling birds from branches, until darkness fell. Then, just as the fireflies rose, pricking the sky with darting lights, we turned up a narrow creek. The engine slowed and I saw the orange flames of lanterns. Dogs started barking at our approach. This was a village. A greeting was exchanged. The words were sung, rather than spoken. Warao is a light, sweet language and lends itself to lullabies.

We moored up by the roots of the bank and two heavy Indians clambered in. The motor started to judder and again we were moving. Later I understood that the two new Indians had come on board to guide the canoe through this part of the maze of delta channels. The first two Indians had been left behind. During the night we stopped three times and each time swopped two more Indians. Each pair knew every turn, every rock and every sandbank of their neighbourhood. Sometimes we had to get out and walk in only ankle-deep water and drag the canoe over shelves of soft mud.

That was how we managed to navigate the delta where Raleigh had almost failed. It pleased me, for we had done much of it in the dark, with not even a torch to guide us.

By daylight I could see the occasional Indian camps: palm shacks; thin, silent children gaping at us from doorways; women bent double over tin cooking pots; men lolling in hammocks.

That night, as cold as the last, I was woken by a new, fresh tang in the breeze: salt. We were in mangrove swamps and must be nearing the sea.

▲ An Indian fisherman paddles his canoe along the Orinoco River.

We arrived mid-morning the next day. Coming out from the trees, a seascape spread out before us. It was not the clear green water I'd hoped for, but a thin brown soup. And there, in the middle of that sea, was the Indian village: a line of huts, built on stilts. It must have been much the same view that the first Europeans had, coming along the South American coast for the first time: simple wooden structures, shimmering above the waves. In a fit of nostalgia they saw in them a 'little Venice'. So they called the new land Venezuela.

Children sighted us first. When they spotted me, my pale skin, they yelled and skipped the length of the village. In the wind I heard the creaking of the planks and poles that were strung along between the huts as walkways. The huts were opensided and roofed with palm leaves. I could see inside some: no sign of adults, only empty hammocks and untended cooking pots.

We came nearer. The tide was low and so the village was perched high up out of the water. We looped a mooring line around a pole. A rope was let down from above and I attached its end to my baggage. A chain of boys hauled up the rope in a series of jerks, chanting as they heaved. Seeing no way up for myself, I took off my canvas shoes and shinned up one of the stilts. It took several attempts to reach the village platform; each time I failed, the children burst out laughing. Later I learned that even the oldest members of the village had the strength to swing themselves up with their arms.

Once up, the two Indians in the canoe tossed up my shoes and yelled '*Adiós!*'

The Mangrove Swamp

▲ **Mangrove tree roots. Among the tangle of roots that anchor the mangrove, small finger-like breathing roots (pneumatophores) stick up through the mud.**

MANGROVE SWAMPS are home to the remarkable mangrove tree, an evergreen that thrives along the shores of coastal river deltas and estuaries. It is noteworthy for its ability to grow in waterlogged soil that is poor in oxygen, and to survive partial submersion by sea tides.

Mangrove trees have adapted to their watery habitat by developing roots that can absorb oxygen from the air. Sometimes growing outwards from the tree's main trunk and sometimes growing up through the mud, these roots give the mangrove forests their characteristically tangled appearance. Amazingly, many mangrove trees give birth to live young: instead of scattering their seeds, which would be washed away by tidal waters, these plants germinate their young on their own branches. The seedlings grow into large, dangling sprouts about 2 feet long, which eventually fall heavily into the mud, where they lodge and quickly take root.

Mangrove swamps are a unique ecosystem.

They are the breeding-ground for many varieties of birds and fish, and are home to endangered and exotic animals, such as the manatee. This makes it all the more tragic that many of these swamps are being cleared for their trees, which are often turned into paper or charcoal.

They revved the motor and pulled away. By now the children were fingering me, yanking my clothes and pointing at my white feet. While I was fighting to keep my shirt, I saw a girl on the edge of the mob examining my shoes. She peered inside them, giggled, tugged out the white laces and spun the shoes out across the water. As they splashed down, she wrapped the laces around her forehead, sweeping back her raven-black hair. This girl was one of the few to be wearing any clothing: an orange skirt, which was clean but threadbare at the back. Two other girls seemed envious of the laces; they pinched the girl's arm and attempted to swipe them. She kicked them fiercely.

When I tried to move, the poles of the village floor pitched and rolled under me. I looked at the children and noticed that they had a way of gripping the poles with their feet. Their toes were long and supple, like fingers.

In Spanish, I asked where Alfredo was. The crowd hushed, but there was no reply. 'El blanco? The white man?' I asked more loudly. The crowd edged back and looked threatened. I said 'sorry' in Warao, one of my dozen words in that language, and they stepped forward again. The truth was they couldn't speak a word of Spanish.

I pushed through the crowd and gingerly walked through the village. The poles buckled, and the knots in the wood dug into my feet like barnacles on a rocky beach. The children followed at my heels, in a pack. Ahead I caught glimpses of women scattering. Most wore tight cotton dresses.

The children sometimes squeezed ahead and walled off certain shacks from me. The ones they allowed me to enter were dark and empty; they were floored with reeds and smelt dusty and sweet, like haylofts.

I returned to my baggage, picked off some boys who had already shared out the two baskets of bread, and sat down. The crowd swarmed on to me again. I looked down at my feet and saw that the soles were red and raw. For the first time I noticed that, when standing, the children reached up for low roofbeams and hung from them to take the weight off their feet.

Looking down between the poles of the village platform, I saw that the tide was now well out. Instead of sea water, there was a grey, custardy mud, dotted about with animal tracks. In places the mud was bubbling, as if on the boil, and large hidden creatures churned around.

I wondered what they were, so I pointed to the mud. Eels, maybe?

The children craned forward, stretching their necks, and peered down through the gaps between the poles. A crab scuttled by. The eyes of the nearest children widened. Two pushy girls at the front looked startled. They spoke excitedly to the rest of the group, who became flustered. What exactly had scared them? I didn't know, but it was too late to calm them. Many were shrieking. They backed away, still staring down at the mud with gawping, open mouths. The girl with the shoelaces around her head was the last to vanish.

The sun was white and burning. My mouth was dry from the salt and heat. I ambled over to a tin barrel, which had been placed to catch rainwater from the palm roof. A green parrot sat dozing on its rim. When I came up to it, it flew away. I cupped my hands and drank. The water was warm and smelt of the

▲ The Warao village at which the author stayed. Villages on stilts such as this reminded early European travellers of the city of Venice.

parrot, but it was sweet. I unbundled my hammock and hung it in the shade.

I lay there, gently swinging backwards and forwards, fanned by the cool wind. I listened to the rush of the incoming tide against the stilts below, the water swishing and gurgling over the mud. The softness of the sounds and the rhythm of my swinging fused and I sank into a deep sleep.

When I woke the sun was still high, the tide still rising. Not much time had passed; maybe two hours. The men of the village would still not be back—they'd be away for a full day's fishing. I got to my feet just in time to see a procession coming in my direction. Some of the people were clothed, unlike the children I had seen earlier, so at first I took them for a returned fishing party. But no; as they came up, I saw that they were the same village children. They were walking along the poles and walkways in a slow march, heading for me.

I saw now that it was not clothing that most of the children wore. It was decoration: metal necklaces and bright beads hung from their necks and waists. The procession came to a halt in front of me.

A girl moved forward from the back. I recognised her immediately by the white laces in her hair. She stepped up lightly to stand at the head of the line. Whatever was about to happen, she was insisting on playing the lead part.

Something was being passed down the line from the back. When the girl at last received it, I saw what it was: a wooden platter with some sort of roasted meat on it. She handed the platter forward to me, extending it on her upturned hands. I had the feeling that she was taking care that our eyes didn't meet. I reached for the platter and took hold of the underside. Our fingertips touched. Then, as I pulled the platter away, she scurried off.

The crowd didn't seem to notice her go. They saw I had the platter and gathered around to watch me take the first mouthful.

The meat tasted rich and creamy. It was crabmeat; overcooked and dry, but still good. I'd hardly eaten for three days and scoffed it down as fast as I could, using my fingers. The ceremony baffled me. What was it all about? I couldn't wait to ask Alfredo when he came back.

A Village Meeting

Alfredo came that evening. He looked much the same as his brother: skin tanned brown, blue eyes and strong white tusks for teeth. He stormed up angrily to me and in Spanish demanded to know why I had forced the children of the village to wade around in the mud. All afternoon they had been chasing a crab just for me, he said, racing to capture it before the incoming tide swamped them. Why had I done it? I told Alfredo that I didn't know what he was talking about.

'If you *really* don't know, I'd better explain. Visitors to the village, by custom, are offered the food of their choice. Within reason, of course. Usually it's a fish that's already been caught. *You* ordered a crab. The prospect of having to catch it must have scared the living daylights out of them, as the tide was already on the turn. Why didn't you stop them?'

'I was asleep.'

His face was red. 'Asleep? *Then*, not content, you capped your performance by accepting a present from that girl Zorola, who's just coming of age. She's not meant even to *see* a man, unless he's to marry her.' He whistled air through the gaps between his tusks. 'By the way, what are you doing here, anyway? You're the first white man I've seen in years.'

I handed him the note from his brother. 'He sends his best wishes,' I said.

'In that case, why does he send me an imbecile as a visitor?' He said it with a heavy sigh, but by his eyes I could tell he was smiling. He wore a scraggy shirt, with a broad chest of grey-tinged hair beneath, and a pair of jeans held up halfheartedly with creeper twine. He asked if I was by any chance English and when I nodded, he rolled his eyes: 'Could have guessed!' Then he smiled and said, 'Sorry, I'm just not used to strangers.' He took my hand and gripped it tightly in his. 'How's Juliano? Has his hair all fallen out yet? *Hombre!* You look parched. Come and have a cup of coffee in my hut. No tea here for you, *inglés*,' he added.

While the coffee was brewing, Alfredo read the note. '*Ave Maria!* That's a hell of a journey you're about to make!'

Alfredo said that he'd better call a village meeting right away. The whole village came, leaving pots of freshly caught fish on the boil. The children ran ahead; then came the men, some with tangled rolls of fishing net. Afterwards came the women, silently. They tagged along behind, as if prisoners. They never looked up. All were assembled in Alfredo's hut.

I stood beside him while he made his speech. He said it first in Spanish, just for my sake. Although the assembly listened patiently, hardly a soul understood.

'My brother,' Alfredo began, 'has sent us an important person. He is from a country many miles away and my brother asks us to look after him. He asks something more besides. A very special favour. Your village has a long tradition of helping white people. Well, this white man is about to go on a long journey, starting here, then through the *selva*, the forests, to the mouth of another river far away. You can help by teaching him all you know about the forest: how you prepare meat, how you fish, paddle a dugout, and how you hunt. He knows nothing of these things. His land is cold and barren. The sun hardly rises at all sometimes; for half the year, everything dies.'

I nudged Alfredo. 'That's laying it on a bit thick, isn't it?'

▲ The interior of a Warao home and two of the children who taught the author the ways of the forest and the delta.

'I went to Britain once and that's exactly what it was like. Now, when we get to the end of the speech, look humble. Got it? Bow your head and look meek.'

'Why?'

'Something important has happened. I'll tell you later.' He turned to the crowd. 'As I was saying. I would like you to teach him, but *you* must decide. He was discourteous when he first arrived. But please remember that he does not understand our ways; he must learn them. He has told me he is truly sorry, and we are both pleased that none of your children was harmed.'

I bowed my head and looked meek. There were a few grunts from the crowd. The grunts told me who in the village could speak Spanish: a handful of men, who'd probably picked it up trading fish in the delta. One man in particular caught my attention. He stood at the back with his arms folded. He wore his hair in two long plaits, the only man in the village with it like this. The plaits were tied at the end with two long shreds of green polythene, knotted in a bow. He held himself stiffly and was obviously the headman.

The whole speech was said again, this time in Warao, punctuated with bickering as each point was clarified by the villagers. When the speech was over, the bickering continued, and it grew wilder and wilder. One man began cuffing his wife. Another woman kicked out at her husband. The rest joined in, yelling and hissing at each other.

Alfredo nodded at the seething mass and said: 'You'd better sit down. This could go on for hours.'

As we sat crosslegged, waiting, the sun set. Alfredo told a boy to light an oil lamp. Finally, the headman spoke up.

He began in a slow, stammering Spanish, ground to a halt, then slipped into Warao. I waited, watching Alfredo's face. In all the speech, the only word I could recognise was 'Zorola'. When the end came, the audience cheered.

'You're in luck,' said Alfredo, as the villagers trooped out of the hut into the dark. Men who passed slapped me on the back. 'I don't know what you'd have done if they'd voted you out of the village. Can you swim?'

I didn't reply. Instead I said: 'Tell me, what happened to that girl Zorola? She wasn't here tonight.'

'I said that something important had cropped up. The important something is about her. Remember I told you she is just coming of age and is not supposed to see men? Well, she not only saw a man, but she formed a relationship.'

'That sounds bad,' I said. 'Who with?'

'You,' said Alfredo, pointing a finger in my face. His expression was grave, but underneath he was smirking. 'Taking those laces from you was tantamount to accepting a gift, as you didn't object to her having them. And by being the person who presented the food at the welcoming ceremony, she got you to accept a gift from her. Those gifts are like bonds linking you together. Or so she hopes. She probably thinks you're immensely wealthy.'

'Bonds?' I said. 'You mean she wants to *marry* me?'

'I don't imagine she's thinking of anything *that* bonding. Not yet.' He grinned. 'But anyway, you're too late now because she's been taken away from here. After all, these people can't have strangers popping into their village every now and then, pilfering their women, can they? So poor Zorola won't be allowed back until you're well on your way to the Amazon. That was what the headman was announcing to the village. It went down well with the men. Meanwhile she will be in disgrace for showing herself to you. She'll be left in isolation, somewhere in the forest. The women have probably beaten her. The only reason why you were permitted to stay is because you accepted the gift in innocence. They'd have pushed you off the platform into the sea if they hadn't been convinced of that. There'd have been nothing I could've done about it.'

He'd meant it when he asked if I could swim. He paced over to the edge of the hut and peeped out into the night. I heard him mumble, 'Wonder if you'd still be afloat out there?'

Learning the Ways of the Forest

They were dreamy, summer-like days, the ones I spent in the village; long, sweet and carefree. The hazy salt air was a balm. The people adopted and nurtured me. During this time, I learnt of their ways and shared their life. These people lived gently. I knew that I would be sorry when the time came to leave.

The headman, Undo, was keen for every member of his village to play a part in coaching me. Not a moment was to be wasted. I was never to be left alone.

I was given my own space in the village, beneath the wooden racks used to dry out salted fish. Palm leaves were spread in wands over the racks and my quarters were the shade below.

My first task was to equip myself with a basic grasp of Warao. Four little girls, who spoke not a word of Spanish, were detailed to assist me in that. This was the day after my arrival. They squatted on their haunches, pointing at objects about the village, and I repeated the words after them, trying to capture the way the words rolled off their tongues. I jotted down the sounds as best I could into a notebook: rope = *becatti*; hat = *yassi*; net = *tarria*; hut = *hanaco*. And we worked on into the midday sun, with the white pages dazzling us.

In the evening, still listing words, they took me for a ride in a dugout canoe. The girls were aged between only six and eight years, yet they headed deep into the delta without any fear of it. A yellow snake swam by, but they didn't fluster. They merely pointed it out and told me its Warao name.

When it was getting late, the canoe was turned about, but the children were in no hurry to return. They thrust the paddle into my hands; to prove that I had been noting how they worked it in the water, I was made to paddle all the way through the moonlit forests, back home.

At dawn two boys of about the same age as the girls took me bird-hunting. Their names were Narru and Camahu. Alfredo had said that Zorola was their older sister. I decided not to mention her unless they did.

We took a dugout into the ash-grey mudlands at low tide. When we reached a bank of shrubby marshland, we beached the canoe and stepped out on to the mud. It was like putty on the top, where the sun had baked it, but my feet dropped through that layer to another of sticky goo, which squirmed between my toes as I sank deeper. Narru instructed me curtly to take off my clothes. Alfredo had already warned me that this was necessary. 'If you get yourself jammed in that mud, your garments will drag you under. A clumsy way to die.' I flung the clothes into the dugout.

Being stripped of Western trappings should have brought me closer to these people, but instead it distanced me. The children had never seen so much white skin at once. They gaped at my body. I felt awkward and embarrassed. Together, the boys smeared pats of mud over my back to protect my skin from the sun. As they spread it, using their palms, they seized the chance to study me close-up, dabbing and staring as they worked. The boys were less than half my age, but their skin was thicker than mine. At the elbows it was calloused, and their hands were wrinkled and scarred. While the sun cooked the mud on my back into a stiff cake, we each slapped some on to our fronts. This was a camouflage— so that, as predators, we should not be distinguished from the mudflats.

▲ Indian boys are taught to hunt from an early age and soon become expert with bows and arrows.

The boys were equipped with bows and arrows, armed with jagged metal tips; when I felt the sharpness of an arrowhead, I pricked my thumb and bled.

We slid across the mudflats on our stomachs, like alligators, closing in on the birds. Most were waders—scarlet ibis and white egrets—which pecked mudskipper fish from the shallows. Whenever pelicans were to be seen, we headed for them first. They were white, round birds, like heavy seagulls, but slower, and easy prey when they sat in the water, scooping fish into the back of their baggy throat-pouches. That day we shot three pelicans and nothing else. We returned with one each dangling from a reed strap we had fastened around our middles. I had killed nothing, but Narru said it was important that we each had a trophy hanging from us to display to the village and so each could return with pride.

While I was attaching the bird, I noticed my front was severely lacerated. The cuts were in streaky lines, from my knees right up to my chest, where I'd been slashed by seashells as we crept along. I looked back and saw a trail of blood along my tracks. The Indians' tracks had none. Camahu, the younger brother, took my hand and led me to a pool where he instructed me to wash the cuts

The Mudskipper

THE AMPHIBIOUS MUDSKIPPER is one of the most distinctive creatures of the mangrove swamps. It can often be seen either sitting half out of the water, or hopping and skipping around on exposed mudflats. This unique, frog-like fish has no true lung, but has gill-chambers that trap water and so allow it to breathe for considerable periods on dry land.

The mudskipper also has highly specialised, muscular pectoral (frontal) fins, which it uses for swimming, walking, and even climbing. It can hop along on these fins faster than a man can walk, and can propel itself even more rapidly, if necessary, by flicking its powerful tail. At high tide it generally returns to its burrow in the mud, but if it has no burrow it will climb into the branches of a tree to escape the predatory fish brought in by the tide.

▲ **The mudskipper often keeps its tail submerged as it absorbs oxygen through blood vessels close to the surface of its skin.**

clean. While the sea water was still stinging, he sat me down and plastered mud along my body, delicately working the mud into the slits with his fingernails to halt the bleeding.

The mud we were on that day was treacherous in patches, but to the Indians the only real fear seemed to be the mud immediately below the village, where I had sent the children looking for the crab. A collection of scavengers lived there, mainly carnivorous fish which had grown fat on the village debris. Very common were mudskipper fish—*patero*, the Indians called them. They had black glassy eyes on the crown of their heads which stared up like marbles from the mud. The *bagare* was another fish, a three-foot-long creature with trailing whiskers. A pet dog had fallen from the village once and got caught up in the mud as the tide water raced in. But the dog did not drown: it was saved from that by the scavengers which ate it before the tides arrived. This was one of the bedtime stories circulated to the children to keep them from the slurry beneath the village. But there was some truth in the tale.

After the day on the mudflats, I dressed my cuts under my shelter in the village and some blood dripped down into the water. It drove the mud animals into a frenzy. The water simmered and splashed and crabs scaled the stilts up to the village level and began to pick at my feet.

I spent the remaining days at the village with the men. Sometimes we were out fishing, dragging nets through the pools, wading with the birds. Sometimes we harpooned the fish, silver-flashing streaks in the murky water.

The nights were cool and mosquito-free. We often went out canoeing through the mangrove tree roots. I learned to tell many creatures just by the way they splashed through the swampy water; or by the distance between their eyes, when a torch was shone to dazzle them; or by the way they frolicked, brushing through the trees. After our return to the village we would sit talking by the fireside. The women would seldom join in, but would listen to our experiences, lying back in the gloom of the night, picking lice from their children's hair and eating them.

I had been in the village, engulfed by the community, for two weeks. It was time to embark on the journey. These had been easy, magical days and I knew they had to end. Undo and Alfredo arranged for me to slip away quietly, without a send-off, at dawn. They thought this would be best.

'After all,' said Undo in his best Spanish, 'you part of family, no longer guest. Come and go without fuss, like us Warao. Surely you come back soon anyway?'

Alfredo added: 'And when you return, you'll remember crabmeat isn't on the menu, eh, *inglés*?'

I wondered what had happened to Zorola. Was she still out in the forest?

Alfredo read my mind. 'If you come across her, give her a kiss for me!'

I settled into the canoe. We carried an Indian pilot, plus Narru and Camahu, who had insisted on coming to see me off. Alfredo and Undo waved. Undo's eyes were red and streaming. He mopped his tears away, using the ends of his plaits.

As we cast off, a white cloud of pelicans rose heavily into the sky ahead, beating a fine spray of salty mist into our faces.

The journey to the Amazon mouth had begun. That was my only thought as the pelicans swirled in the yellow dawn sky. I did not look back at the village on stilts. I kept my eyes forward, into the forests. What would come next?

Into the forest the canoe went. The sea sank out of sight behind, and we wound through the trees, through alleyways of calm chocolate water.

What *would* come next? We four would cross the delta forests until we reached their southern edge. From there I would go on alone. I would find the road leading south out of the Orinoco jungle and up on to the dry grassland

Sunrise lends a spectacular beauty to the Orinoco delta. ▶

plateaux and then I would face Amazonia. I couldn't picture what the jungle would look like, but I could feel it waiting, a thousand miles away, a looming black cloud. Maybe it would take two months to get there. I hoped it would because, shrouded in its mystery still, I feared it.

The spray that drenched my face was no longer salty. It no longer hardened my hair, it softened it. We were in fresh water again and the trees pressed in on us, their branches stretching above our heads and blackening the sky.

Up one of a thousand creeks we saw a lone hut on the riverbank. We steered towards it, passing brown thornbushes which spread along the water's edge like coils of rusty barbed wire.

No one appeared to welcome us. I thought the hut was empty, but as we got nearer an Indian girl came to the doorway, pulling a grubby cloth around her waist when she saw me. She looked sleepy and her eyes were raw, as if she'd been crying. I recognised her. The girl's face was bruised, her fringe chopped away untidily, and the hair at the back hacked off so that it no longer hung down to her shoulders. It was Zorola.

I wanted to apologise somehow for what had happened to her, but the canoe pilot held me down. We weren't meant to be here at all, he said. If Undo found out, we would all be severely punished. Alfredo had secretly arranged for Narru and Camahu to come on the journey and smuggle in some food to their sister. After being beaten, she'd been left to fend for herself for the whole two weeks I'd been in the village.

I watched Narru and Camahu talk softly to Zorola. Both brothers stayed at arm's distance from her, and when she reached out to touch them, they stepped back. She never turned to look at the canoe, where I was sitting.

The boys handed over a parcel of fish, then scampered back down to the river in tears. They crouched in the canoe with their heads down. Zorola went back indoors without waiting to see us go.

Our journey was to take us across the delta to the nearest southern mainland; an easy route, less than a day.

Narru and Camahu cheered up as we came towards the mainland. They were going to see something new: shining cars, paved roads, concrete. As we paddled along, they put on shirts—their first ever—and shorts. The material was clean and the clothes fitted well. But seeing them dressed up proudly in Western clothes saddened me. They looked ridiculous. Wearing clothes excited them, but I knew their first glimpse of the town was going to thrill them even more—the steel boats along the dockside, the fruit stalls, the cranking cranes. Not wanting to see the bright-eyed look of admiration on their faces, I decided that we should part before we reached the town. They dropped me off at a quiet beach, bordered by forest, on the town's edge.

Narru and Camahu waved and smiled at me for a while, as the canoe carried on. Then the grey town smog wafted over them and excitedly they breathed in the acrid fumes for the first time.

▲ The water's edge is home to a huge variety of bird life. Here a great egret waits silently for fish.

In the Orinoco delta, a flock of scarlet ibis gather on the stilt roots of a mangrove tree. The tree uses these roots to support itself in the tidal swamps of the delta, and also to absorb oxygen from the air.

The Orinoco—'A Place to Paddle'

ONLY A FEW MILES NORTH of the vast Amazon basin lies the source of the Orinoco River (over 1,300 miles long) and its basin, 366,000 square miles in extent. Rising on Venezuela's southern border with Brazil, the Orinoco flows in a great arc north and east into the Atlantic Ocean. At its mouth is an enormous delta which is constantly expanding into the sea from the tons of silt washed down from the uplands.

The name 'Orinoco', derived from the local Indian language, means 'a place to paddle'—in other words, 'a navigable place'. Early explorers, however, found it anything but that. In the 16th century several Spanish expeditions failed to penetrate the maze of its great delta; and in 1595 Sir Walter Raleigh found himself at first hopelessly lost, and then unable to make much headway against the force of the river.

At that time it was believed that both the Orinoco and Amazon Rivers had their source in a single enormous lake. This was conclusively disproved in the early 19th century by Alexander von Humboldt, the great German scientist and explorer. Yet, amazingly, there is a connection between the two rivers—via the Casiquiare Canal, a 150-foot wide natural channel that

funnels water for 220 miles into the Rio Negro, the Amazon's largest tributary.

For most of its length the Orinoco flows through dense rainforest and immense grass plains known as Llanos. Then, near its mouth, it enters tangled mangrove swamps and becomes a veritable maze of intersecting streams. Here it is the home of many spectacular creatures such as the scarlet ibis, the Orinoco crocodile—the largest crocodile in the world—and the docile, friendly manatees, which reminded early explorers of mermaids.

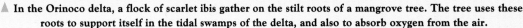
Growing to over 20 feet in length, Orinoco crocodiles are the largest in the world. However, very few of these magnificent creatures remain, since they have been driven to the very edge of extinction by indiscriminate hunting.

Rainclouds gather and deluge the great Llanos or grass savannahs that lie east of the Colombian Andes. The Llanos occupy three-fifths of the Orinoco basin, and for six months of the year they are inundated by floodwaters to become one of the world's largest wetlands. For the remainder of the year they are dry, dusty plains.

The great Cachamay Falls on the Rio Caroni, one of the Orinoco's tributaries. In 1595 Sir Walter Raleigh attempted to negotiate the Caroni, but found his way impeded by rapids such as these.

A pair of manatees float lazily in the water. These gentle giants can grow up to nine feet long, and weigh over 1,000 pounds. Their numbers have been severely reduced since the arrival of Europeans, and even now very little is known about them.

CHAPTER 3

The Hermits

T HE RIVERSIDE TOWN was sticky and hot. Next day I bought a new pair of shoes and stood by the roadside for a lift.

'Where are you heading?' a youth in a blue Ford asked in Spanish, pulling up in front of me.

'South.'

'Then step in.' And away we went, the wheels spinning into the gutter water.

The driver's name was José. He had stringy hair down to his collar and a gold chain necklace. He was on his way to a farm in the hills. It was in the sticks, but he'd take me as far as he could.

My twenty-third birthday had come and gone in the delta. None of the Indians had known about it, but I still felt I had celebrated it with them. Now that I was away from the Warao family, I felt lonely. It was the first week in March and at home it would almost be spring. Here it looked like the autumn you get after a long, parched summer. The reddish soil had cracked into squares, the grass was tinder-dry. The air shimmered like rippled glass in an old window.

Coming away from the river, the forest had been scrubbed out and the land worked into farmsteads. Goats trotted along the gutters and pigs strayed in and out of the mud houses, grubbing in the earth yards and in the shade of the mango trees. Some huts were roofed with rust-blistered iron, some were thatched with palm; all were crumbling.

For a time the road was smooth and flat. We drove straight on, southbound, with forests carpeting rounded hills in the distance.

José took one hand from the wheel and produced a half-bottle of rum from under his seat; by the time the road was rising to the hills, he had finished it.

The road twisted and turned. Boulders lay in front of us like sleeping sheep. José's eyes became glazed and shiny. We rode straight over one of the boulders and lost the exhaust pipe.

'Why don't you let me take the wheel for a bit?' I said.

'No, no, *amigo*,' he said. 'Certainly not. These roads are dangerous. They need experience.'

The car horn was operated by a chain hanging from the roof. I reached for it and kept my hand ready to jerk.

Later we pulled up suddenly by the roadside, swerving as if we had hit a pedestrian. José ran to the bushes to be sick. He had to lie down in the back seat after that, and so I took the wheel.

We pottered along the only road leading to the south. The huts became more

sporadic, the trees less frequent. We passed a road-gang of men in white cotton trousers, stripped to the waist, their backs sparkling with sweat. They were beating the roadside creepers with picks and clubs, swinging them heavily.

Off to the right was a smaller road. A sign read 'El Callao'. I stopped, just as José was coming round.

'Where are we?'

'A place called El Callao,' I said. 'Are you going on south?'

'Yes, just a bit more. Near to the prison at El Dorado.'

I got out of the car.

'Perhaps I'll see you around sometime. *Buena suerte!*' He accelerated away, grinding the gears.

I walked into El Callao. It was a sleepy town, snuggling in the forest of the hills, on the gold-rich alluvium of the Cuyuni River. There were mules in the streets, standing tied to wooden posts while their leather-skinned owners drank and spat in the bars before starting out for the goldfields. Much of the gold had been worked out. The town was past its best, people said. The gold fever had gone, the barmen no longer raised their floorboards to sweep up spilled gold dust and no one carried revolvers any more.

I spoke to a tall, lean man with a Groucho moustache. He had come to the town from Sicily, leaving his home on the lava slopes of Mount Etna and arriving alone with two bolivars in his hand, had found his fortune mending prospectors' boots. The miners came in from the hills after a month or two panning the river silts and he used to run up to them as they rode into town on their mules, with toes showing through the soles of their shoes, before they blew their money. Now he had a farm and twenty brown, coarse-haired pigs, which he fed on

Storm clouds gather over the Gran Sabana, the great grassland plateau of Venezuela.

mangoes. He also had a family: one son at university in Merida, two pretty and eligible daughters—he brought them out to display them—and a new baby. The town had grown poor, the young were leaving and the Sicilian's crop had failed with the drought. He told me this in a worn, husky voice, wearing a leather apron, while tapping studs into a shoe. 'You see? I'm back to being a cobbler after twenty years.'

Over spaghetti he said the history of the town was written on the gravestones on the hill outside. I left the table after the meal and climbed the hill.

The light was a soft yellow. It was dusk.

The graveyard was maintained by a donkey. It idled away its life wandering untethered between the wooden and metal crosses, rasping at the palms, nettles and acacias and stamping to get rid of the flies. The English had flooded over the border from Guyana in the first rush for gold. Some stayed for ever, and their epitaphs were stencilled in English: 'In memory of Alexander Jefferson. Died April 24, 1934. Aged 53 years. RIP.'

Most of the inscriptions had rusted into obscurity, but the Sicilian had been right. The history of the town was here: Fernandez, Cortez, Hernandez, Marcano—none of the newer graves had English names. The English had departed as soon as most of the gold was exhausted. They had left in a hurry: on the way down the hill I passed the shell of a Vauxhall Velox. Other relics were the grey-haired Negroes who'd come as workers for the English from Guyana. They sat on doorsteps and called out to me in an English I didn't understand. One showed me a wrinkled, black-and-white snapshot of Prince Charles and asked me if I knew him. Another recalled the day the first motor car arrived.

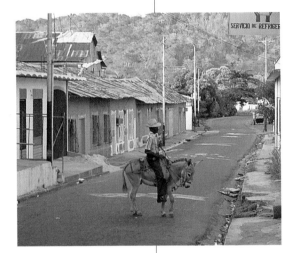

▲ A goldminer enters El Callao on his mule after weeks of panning for gold in forest rivers.

On the Road

At dawn the next day the Sicilian took me up the road to El Dorado in his buckled red jeep. He said he couldn't give me any advice for the expedition. He wished he could, but there it was. He had seen much in his life; he'd panned gold with the miners, seen them die—'mainly floods and tumbling rocks'. Most of all, he had seen what gold had done to people, to his friends. His one bit of advice was to keep my wits about me when gold fever was around. 'Will you promise me that?' 'All right. I promise. If I can, I'll keep clear of anywhere with gold fever.' That seemed to please him.

El Dorado was also on the banks of the Cuyuni and in goldmining country. It was a far cry from the El Dorado that Raleigh had sought, but someone had had the idea of attracting trade to the town with the name; there was some gold in the soil and so it stuck. The town was assembled carelessly along the forest road, a string of mud and tin huts in the shadow of the prison, the *cárcel*.

The Sicilian saw me off. 'Send me a postcard to let me know you're all right. Go to the *padre* in the church over there. He's a good man. *Ciao*.'

I went to the church and found it empty, but an Indian girl in a blue silk dress with an ornate silver cross pinned to her chest led me to the *padre*.

He was a Belgian. He had cropped, silver-grey hair and blue eyes, and spoke textbook Spanish. He'd been here for only three years. 'I am sorry. I am in a hurry. Soon it is time for holy Mass and I must take down the washing of my children before it commences.'

He led me to an upper-floor room and began unpegging large men's clothes from the line. I said, 'These are your *children's?*'

'Yes. The convicts are my children. Two men are about to be released and will need something to wear.'

While folding up the clothes, he told me more about the prison. There had been only two escapes ever. One man had been imprisoned for trafficking drugs. He was a Colombian, and fortunately his father was a rich and sympathetic general. One night he scrambled over the prison wall, made it through the bushes to the river and sped away in a launch to the airport. While he was still changing out of his prison clothes, his father's plane came for him.

The other escapee, a mild-mannered man who was afraid of spiders, had committed murder. It was an accident—no one doubted that—but the victim's family wanted vengeance and achieved a sentence of twenty-seven years for the killer. After he'd clocked up ten years behind bars, he had become part of the prison institution. Sometimes, when the warders were occupied with a good round of poker, he did them the favour of locking up some of the inmates for the night. One day the guards arrived for work and found a note waiting for them: *Many thanks for your hospitality. I am sorry but I must leave. Bye, friends. All the best.*

The Belgian said: 'Nice touch, eh? Leaving a note, I mean. You don't get prisoners like that any more.'

◀ **Miners often work in the most squalid and unhealthy conditions.**

The *padre*—a man I warmed to the closer I came to know him—drove me to an army checkpoint the following day. It was where a steel bridge crossed the river by the prison. The soldiers looked dopey in the early morning sun, leaning on their rifles as if they were brooms. The *padre* asked the captain of the guard whether he'd possibly stop a lorry to give me a lift. 'Si, *padre*. Of course we'll do that.' He smiled. 'Is your companion a man of God also?'

'Just a good friend passing through.'

The captain nodded. 'Passing through, eh?' He offered his hand. 'Pleased to meet you, *señor*.'

When the *padre*'s car was out of sight, the soldiers tucked their thumbs inside their belts. They surrounded me and stuck the barrels of their rifles into my face.

'OK, gringo. Tip your baggage out on to the road.' I did as they asked. 'Now step back against the wall.' They started rummaging. I had to act to stop it. Soon they would come across my jungle knives, and worse, the explosive flares I'd brought along as firearms for the jungle.

I took out a sealed envelope from my shirt pocket. I had hoped never to use it. 'Look, captain. I know you're doing your job—and very well if you don't mind me saying so—but you'd better read this.' I held the letter out.

When he saw the letter, the captain's face went red. He took the letter slowly and felt it over with his fingertips. On the outside were rubber stamp marks and counterstamp marks; it was sealed with red sealing wax, and embossed with a crest. Inside was a message from an 'official' of the British government of considerable standing, apparently, with friends of even more considerable standing in Venezuela. The essence of the message was that the bearer should be allowed to pass freely. It had taken me hours to concoct.

The captain hadn't broken the seal. 'What is it?' he asked, looking at the paper's watermark in the light, and running his thumb over the sealing wax.

'It's from the minister.' I indicated the rubber stamp.

'Hey, Chico! Stop what you're doing. You lot get back to your posts.'

But it was too late. 'Sir! Look at these. What could a gringo want with all these knives? I think we've got ourselves a spy from Guyana. Must have sneaked across the frontier.' He handed them to another soldier and picked up his rifle. 'You, there! Put your hands against the wall!' I looked at the captain and the captain looked at the knives. Then his eyes went back to the letter.

The soldier and I waited.

'Gringo! Get that stuff cleaned up off the road at once. There's a truck coming!' I pulled a face at the soldier as I bent over and stuffed my equipment away.

The captain slowed the pick-up truck just enough for me to climb aboard, then waved it on. In the distance I saw him slap the soldier across the cheek.

Beyond El Dorado, the forest was advancing on the road. Ground creepers edged out across the dust. On my map the road faded to a weak, dotted line as we went south, without junctions or settlements.

The slope steepened and the truck jogged and swung, manoeuvring through the ruts and water channels. Slowly we were coming out of the Orinoco water

basin, but there was still a long way to go. The engine screamed as we pulled up higher. The air became chilly. We went up into a white sky of mist, which thickened, and the world became white and dead. This was the escarpment. We were climbing out of the Orinoco forest and up on to the savannah by La Escalera, the Staircase.

We levelled out, and the air cleared. What I saw was a new world—one of grassland; no insects; no birds. It was like prairie farmland after harvest, fenceless and stark.

The breeze became warmer. It smelt of cattle. We dropped down off a ridge, seeing the Gran Sabana plateau before us. Now we were down there, crossing it in the truck. The soil was red—even redder, I thought, than at El Dorado.

The grass ocean rolled and dipped. The road was hilly and the wind licked waves into the grasses. We crossed rickety wooden bridges and the planks creaked and split. Here there were palm trees, little oases of parrots and monkeys. This was the *verano*, the dry season. Cows clustered in the shade; they were white cows with a hummock of fat, large bony hips, with rib cages like barrels and shrunken stomachs. Birds hopped on their mud-capped haunches and eased insects from their hides.

I hadn't yet spoken to the driver. It was possible that he didn't know I was aboard. At the checkpoint I'd just jumped up into the back amongst some reeking petrol drums. There was only one road and one destination, so I'd had no questions to ask. But now I had seen something, a name scribbled in the red dust on the window between myself and the driver.

'Peña'. The name rang a bell. Lucas Fernandex Peña, soldier of fortune, had

A forest road cuts through the jungle, which constantly threatens to close over it again.

The waters of the Angel Falls, the world's highest waterfall, cascade 3,212 feet onto the plains below. These falls are a staggering 19 times higher than the Niagara Falls. ▶

set out in the early 1920s from Valencia, a thousand miles away, near the coast by the capital. He walked to the end of the last paved road and continued on through the jungle, up into unexplored terrain and across this Gran Sabana plateau. The Taulipang Indians sheltered him and taught him, and he lived from day to day with their succour. A few seasons later, in 1924, he arrived at the lip of the Orinoco basin, the end of the savannah, the beginning of the Amazon jungle basin and the beginning of Brazil. There he stopped.

The Indians helped him build a house; he took an Indian for a wife, and then settled down, having noted a glint of yellow metal in the streams. He fathered twenty-seven children, with the help of a second wife. Then he found diamonds as well. He hit the jackpot on the River Surukum. Before long the rest of the world knew about it; 1933 was the year of *la fiebre del diamente*, diamond fever.

This was the stream of thoughts the name Peña generated. I looked through the glass and saw a clean-cut man with greying, thick black hair and middle-age spread. The old Peña, I thought, must be well decayed by now. For the moment, I assumed this man was one of the offspring.

We drove on, the red dust clogging my throat. The backdrop to the grasses was the Tepuys, the jutting peaks which lay along the horizon in blocks. They had yellow walls in the setting sun and streaky silver quartz veins, with rich herbaceous borders of dark, dank vegetation. One mountain, to the east, looked much like a thumb. Another to the west was the grandest, a soaring peak in the dust of the setting sun. Off its other, hidden side spilled the world's highest waterfall. It was named after a man called Jimmy Angel who flew a plane too low over the savannah, hoping to take his share of the diamonds, and discovered the waterfall moments before the crash. To the east was a range of vertical tower-block plateaux, the Roraima range. Their walls were straighter and sharper than the rest and their tops were crowned in cloud.

The truck came to Santa Elena in the dark, with the flickering white lights of the town ahead. I gave two raps on the metal of the cab roof. The truck stopped, but the driver did not turn his head.

'*Señor* Peña?'

'*Sí. Qué tal?*'

We began talking about his father, there in the road in the darkness. He could not see my face and I could not see him. His voice was smooth, groomed. He asked me what I was doing here and I told him.

'Well, certainly you're giving yourself a task. Come to the house tomorrow and eat with me. I can give you advice.'

'Where's your house?'

'Ask anyone. Till then, *adiós*.' He drove away towards the street lights, and I walked back into the night to find some trees from which to hang my hammock.

The house was a large, white, barn-like structure, capped with a steep roof of decaying *moriche* palm. It lay midway between the gold dealers and the mission.

Gilberto Peña had an intelligent face, with a pair of heavy spectacles mounted on his nose. He said his father was still alive, but with one foot in the grave, deaf and living in another village which he had founded nearby. It was named Santa Teresa.

'Just how old was your father when he left Valencia for here?' I asked.

He tapped his spectacles, thinking, and said, 'Seventeen, maybe less.' I asked how he had survived in a land with scarcely a fish in the river. 'He did the journey *poco a poco*, little by little, living with the Indians and eating monkeys. Not bad for a teenager, eh? Along the way he discovered he had the knack of tipping over rocks and finding gold nuggets lying like pebbles underneath. Now, let's hear more about your journey, then I'll give you the advice you need. My father has told me enough for me to know.'

I told Gilberto how I would journey on down the road and then face the Amazon jungle, and that I would have to cut east through it, though I did not know how. I was sure there was a way, but I hadn't yet found it. The Indians would be the ones to help.

'That's it, *señor*. You must use the Indians, as my father did. You must journey light, with a pack on your back and nothing more, and journey *poco a poco*, like him. You must not look back. Papa always told me that. "Keep moving," he said, "and look ahead to the horizon. On the horizon, somewhere out there, you will find your gold waiting for you." ' He looked me straight in the eyes. 'For you, *señor*, the gold will be the mouth of the Amazon.'

'A nice thought, Gilberto,' I said.

'It's got to be more than that. It's got to be a conviction. *Poco a poco* you will be there. It may take time, but what is time? In the jungle it means nothing. The Indians don't count the years as they go by.'

'Thank you,' I said. 'Who would not be inspired by what you've just said. Any suggestions as to how I'm going to start?'

'Fritz. You must seek out Fritz. Ask for him in the town of Icabaru—I'll ask the *padre* at the mission to give you a lift. He's travelling to Icabaru, in the Pacaraima hills, for the Easter service.'

Gilberto said the journey from Icabaru would be three days. Fritz lived the life of a hermit, panning for diamonds in the jungle. There was no one who could help me more.

Into the Jungle

The *padre*, who had red shiny cheeks and thinning grey hair, drove in his heavy brown cassock, forcing the jeep over the ruts and potholes and spouting phrases of Taulipang for me to digest. We slipped into the jungle bordering the Amazon basin. Being perched on its very edge gave me a warm feeling of excitement and apprehension. Once again I could not wait to get started, but I knew I couldn't afford to rush things.

▲ Prospectors sluice the river for alluvial gold. Thousands have come to the Amazon in search of gold, but few have become rich.

Founded in times of gold and diamond fever, Icabaru was gentler now than it had been, the *padre* said. It was indeed quiet as we drove up. The schoolteacher was dizzy from cocaine, just out of prison for peddling. The *padre* drooled with excitement over the Easter cock-fight and the men cheered and spun their hats into the pit when two knives were drawn. The Indian policeman watched the men lunging at each other: he tilted drunkenly against a tree with his arms folded and his pistol snug in its leather holster. Interest in the cockfight gave way to the fighting men and the crowd egged them on.

I walked a day from the town through scrubby savannah and white sand, greeting broad-shouldered men along the track as they dug for gold as happily as children at the seaside. One man shovelled sand into a tray, another added a bucket of water, another swished the water round in the tray and another leant on his spade, watching the brown water make its way through a framework of pipes and trays. The pipes were hollowed-out trees and the filter, which trapped the gold grit, was a hemp sack. The Ancient Greeks had used sheepskin instead of a hemp sack, and the resulting golden fleece was the object of Jason's quest. So the technique had not advanced in all these centuries.

I went on. By nightfall I was by the side of the Los Caribes River and on the true edge of the forest. There I met a Frenchman, who lived with his wife by the riverside and ran an operation sieving the Icabaru River. Any day now they were going to strike it rich, he said. 'Any day now. Just you wait and see.'

His wife boiled up some rice and beans for me. '*Bon appétit!*' She had a pet, squirrel-like monkey that lived on her shoulder. I hung my hammock in a shack of theirs, which housed a parrot. The bird chatted to me all night and stopped me sleeping.

The Frenchman directed two of his brawny Indians to take me down the Icabaru River to the Hacha tributary, where I could ask for further directions. We sped along in a large canoe, whose tail had been amputated to fit a Japanese outboard motor.

The Icabaru River had sparked the dreams of thousands. It had been the centre of the diamond rush, and its gravels and silts had been worked and reworked by pumps and spades to the point where it dribbled and choked along in confusion. After Peña had attracted interest in the area of the Surukum, the fever had spread here. The Taulipang Indian children used to play with diamonds like marbles, they told me in Icabaru town. Then the news of the 'diamond river' broke, and a stampede of miners began. The Indians were caught in its path, and were trampled out of recognition. The Indian women were seduced by the miners, the Indian men by their bottles; and the Indians took to calling the white men *racionales*, 'the rationals', because they thought their own life in the jungle had been so backward.

We ploughed on through the water, along the jungle walls. I had forgotten the rich smell of the leaf-trapped air, its musky warmth and stillness, and how it clings to the skin and stifles, smelling all the time of mature compost.

Our approach flipped dinner-plate turtles off their log perches and into the water. Ahead we saw a forest hen, pecking its way along a riverbank. One of the Indians took a pot shot at it and, without slowing the engine, we swung towards it and scooped it up. We plucked it on the way. The feathers flew behind, curling in our slipstream, then settling on the water. They were gobbled up, then spat out, by little brown fish with clean white teeth. Piranha.

Occasionally we passed Indian families slaving for gold dust in the shallows, giggling and cross-eyed from *cachire*, a purple mush of distilled cassava and sugarcane, which they sipped from nutshell cups. These people were clothed in rags. They were skinny, scarecrow people, cast-offs from the gold rush.

We came to the Hacha settlement and found the inhabitants much the same. They had just stepped out of the river from work and they shuffled forward to greet us in black rubber wellington boots. As soon as I was ashore, my transport

▲ **Yellow-spotted sideneck turtles, the size of dinner plates, sun themselves on a log. Butterflies are feeding on their tears in order to obtain essential minerals and salts.**

turned back. The headman of the village, an Indian with skin tightly stretched over his frame, welcomed me. Frail children hung from the arms of two women behind him. Neither of the women was dressed with any pride. Though mainly of Indian stock, one woman had blue Scandinavian eyes.

'Here we one happy family,' the headman said, gesturing at the group. 'We find gold in day and drink at night. So guess what?' His face glowed. 'We no longer servants of forest.'

I said that, no, I didn't suppose they were, and remembered how like slaves the Indians had looked, digging for the gold. 'How far is Fritz?'

'Two day up Hacha River.' He drew a map in the sand. 'That get you to Loco Man for sure.'

'The Madman will know the way to Fritz?'

'For sure, he know.' He took me by the arm. 'Now we drink.'

A Meeting with Loco Man

Wrapped up in bed one winter's evening at home, I had read all about the 'diamond river' and the unexplored Hacha. In a few decades it hadn't changed. It was still a 'miserable little stream, full of dead leaves and silted up with mud'. The Hacha was even less navigable; this was the dry season and its banks were thickets of dead canes. This was the darkest jungle I had seen yet. The sky showed only through the leaves above, in white freckles. Walking up the stream

Piranha

NATURALISTS CLAIM that the piranha is much maligned, and that stories of its hunting in packs and falling voraciously on human victims in a feeding frenzy are greatly exaggerated. Certainly, many varieties of piranha are meek vegetarians, and most of the others supplement their diet with fruit. Few will tear pieces of flesh from passing animals, though they will nibble at the fins and scales of other fish. Even when a 'feeding frenzy' does occur, it is only in very shallow water during the dry season, when groups of piranhas are forced together in muddy, congested areas where normal food supplies have been reduced or exhausted.

There are no verified reports of any human ever having been killed by these animals. Injuries do sometimes occur, but usually out of the water, when the fish are carelessly handled. Looking in Amazonian fish markets, it is clear that many more piranhas are eaten by men than men are eaten by piranhas.

▲ A black piranha with daggers for teeth: the stuff of nightmares. Yet this monster is in fact mainly a threat only to other fish and to creatures smaller than itself.

was like walking through a mountain tunnel, with no light at the other end.

I sloshed along in water the colour of nicotine, not able to see my boots on the brown boulders of the stream bed. Spiders' webs bridged the stream and peeled away like lint in my face. Where the water flowed slowly, small dead leaves floated by like cornflakes; my pack kept snagging in the overhanging branches and bringing nests of ants down my back.

I rested where the water was only a trickle and rubbed soap into my trousers to drive waterbugs out. Toucans clacked up in the higher branches and slender fishing birds dive-bombed the stream to extract brown, prickly-skinned fish, which I'd flushed from the muds. Some fish skated over the water surface to escape the jaws of other fish; the leaves of the riverbank rustled in the waves of surf I was creating. Once, my wet boots slipped as I crossed over a deep stream channel on a fallen tree. I clung from the trunk, digging my fingers into the chinks in the bark, my feet dragging in the peat water. A rat the size of a guinea pig ran over my hands, scratching them with its toenails. That was how I met most animals, when they scampered by in bursts of panic.

After two or more miles of journey like this, I came to Loco Man. He lived alone in a ghost settlement of miners' huts, in a glade by the stream.

I slopped out of the water, shaking off like a wet dog, and stood for a while baking dry in the warm sunlight. As I walked into the settlement, there he was, marching across a yard of foot-smoothed earth, singing loudly. There were no words to the tune; it was just 'La la, la di la, la la la'. He wasn't startled to see me; he didn't even turn his head. He said, in a rough, screeching voice, 'It's the quietness I can't stand,' and kept walking. 'La la, la di la.' His eyes were black and protruding and wild, his hair was in mats to his shoulders, and he wore a pair of brown trousers made of sacking, which had grey mudpacks on the knees. He was bare-chested and his thin ribs stuck out like the bars of a birdcage.

'*What* quietness?' I said. The jungle was screaming.

'That's what I mean. There's nothing to hear. That's why I'm pleased to meet an old friend. Someone to talk to.'

I said, 'But I've never met you before in my life.'

'Never too late.'

'Can you tell me where Fritz lives?' I asked.

He grinned. 'La la, la di la. No.' He beckoned me into a hut. 'You're lucky, my friend,' he said, as we ducked our heads and entered. The hut smelt like a cave. It dripped cold water, and a layer of algae flourished on most surfaces.

'Why am I lucky?'

'Didn't you see a woman in Icabaru?'

'Plenty. So what?'

'Do you know the last time I saw a woman?'

He pointed at a log. I sat down. The log was the height of a stool. He sat the other side of a table that was a treetrunk split in two, with the splintered inside

The brilliantly coloured toucan uses its huge, serrated beak for defence, as well as for biting into tough fruit. The bill is supported internally by a web of bony struts, and so is much lighter than it appears.

uppermost. A green snail with a shell the size of a golfball was gliding silently over one of the beams, leaving behind a silver smear.

The man slapped the flat of his hand down on to the tabletop. 'When was the last time I saw a woman, do you think?'

'Can you tell me where Fritz lives?'

'I'll tell you. The last time I saw a woman… I'll give you one more chance to guess.' Suddenly he leant forward, gripped both my arms, digging his fingers into my skin. His grip was hard and his fingers bony. I unpicked his hands from my arms and he fell back into his seat. 'You don't want to guess?'

I was not the least bit interested. I said, 'Now, please. I want to know where I can find Fritz.'

His shoulders drooped; he looked hurt. 'Tomorrow, friend. I will tell you tomorrow.' Then he sat up. 'Today,' he said, 'I will tell you about the last time I saw a woman. It was in 1962.'

I stood up, sliding the log back.

'No. Tell me where *Fritz* is.'

He began drumming on the table like a spoilt child. 'Tomorrow, tomorrow, tomorrow!' He dropped his head and rested his chin on the tabletop. He pouted his lips. He was going to sulk.

'All right,' I said. 'You tell me tomorrow.'

▲ A typical mining camp on the border between Brazil and Venezuela.

'Maybe,' he said. He sat up and started singing again. 'La la, la di di…'

Loco Man had strolled alone up and down the rivers of this forest for a couple of decades in his search for gold. In all that time he'd found no more than a pinch of it a day—enough to feed him, and no more.

If this had been a cold country he'd have died by now, he said. He took me along with him to scatter maize to the hens he kept. They were a dozen Rhode Island Reds, chasing cockroaches.

When I mentioned Fritz, he told me I should stay well clear of him if I knew what was good for me. 'He's quite mad. It's in his blood. Don't go there. Stay with me. He doesn't take kindly to strangers.'

Loco Man had calmed down now, but his screeching voice still jarred my nerves and he talked in riddles.

I produced a tin of sardines and we shared them. He licked every drop of oil from the can, working his tongue into the crevices like a cat. Darkness came; he took a match and lit a dozen oil lamps to hang in the tree where the hens roosted at night. We hoisted the lanterns up into the branches on the end of a long pole. I asked him what the nightlights were for, thinking they were to keep the night chill off the hens.

'Vampires,' he said. 'The lights scare the bats off.' I laughed. I had thought it a joke, but later Loco Man gave me a lamp for myself. 'Wrap yourself up well tonight. Especially your toes.'

I went out into the darkness to the hens' tree to see the truth for myself.

The bats had already got there. They swirled through the tree branches, pestering the hens. Their wings caused a draught on the oil lamps and set the orange glow flickering on the leaves. I watched as the bats came in closer, then a hen would give a screech each time it felt a nip. Their cries and flustering wing-beats spooked the night and kept me from sleep. In the morning there were dribbles of dark, clotted blood on the branches.

'You see?' said Loco Man. His mood was as calm as it had been the previous night, so I guessed the time was right to put the question to him again.

'Can you direct me to Fritz, please, as you promised? Here's some paper.'

He laughed and sketched the map.

But when I lifted my pack on to my shoulders, adjusted the weight and humped off up the path, he shrieked at me: 'The map is wrong. Don't you see? I lied! You *must* stay with me. I promise you the map's wrong. You'll die out there.' I didn't turn my head.

The track was thin and obscure. After an hour I thought that the madman had been telling the truth. His map *was* a lie. I wanted to wring his neck. I thought I'd have to retreat again and face his stale breath, the slimy hut with the green snails and the vampires. But then I recognised a landmark: the carcass of a light aeroplane that had crashed, a monument to the diamond rush. It was scattered over the ground in tatty chunks; a spaghetti of wires, a propeller bent as if rubber, and windscreen glass fragments amongst the leaves, like the diamonds the passengers had come for.

The path swerved, dived, then climbed through dark, dripping leaves and

---

EYE-WITNESS ACCOUNT

Vampire Bats

The English botanist Richard Spruce had several encounters with vampire bats, and made the following observations in his journal of 1852:

'SURGEONS BOAST of their painless operations nowadays, but the vampire bat beats them all. I have never yet met a person who was awakened by a vampire biting him, but several have had the vampire fasten on them when awake, and these confirm the account of the animal fanning with his wings whilst sucking. The wound is a round piece of the skin taken completely out, as if cut out with a knife. The quantity of blood lost is generally trifling, unless the vampire happens to light on the small veins. It prefers the toe ends, and next to them the finger ends or nose end.

'They cause great destruction at times among fowls, which are allowed to roost in the open air, sucking them in the head and drawing so much blood as sometimes to cause their death in three or four blood-lettings. On the granite rocks near my house the sheep belonging to the inhabitants [of São Gabriel] often pass the night, and in the morning regularly leave behind them pools of blood from the bites of vampires.'

◀ Vampire bats cluster together on their cave-top roost. Modern scientists have discovered that the bats do not suck their victims' blood, but lap it with the tongue, after injecting anti-coagulant saliva into the bite to make the blood flow freely.

▲ Dappled sunlight falls
on one of the many
streams that cut their way
through the jungle.

midges which floated in the air like dandelion seeds. Then the leaves against my skin were dry. The air cleared. I was out of the jungle. My skin could breathe again and I was in grassland.

Fritz

Seeing a footprint in the white sand, I stopped and bent down. It was fresh. Today's, I thought, because there'd been a rain shower the day before and the mark was still unsplattered by raindrops. It wasn't an Indian's—the foot was long and narrow. It had been stunted by shoes and yet was hardened. I saw other prints now. This person had a long stride. He would be tall, and with a dog.

'Unt vere do you sink you are going?'

The voice made me jump. Then the dog yapped. The tall white man was up ahead on the path. He spoke in clipped English, keeping his lips tight against his front teeth. The man had a thick beard of frizzy brown hair. His eyes were sharp and hazel. The dog was a stocky white mongrel; it scuttled around the man's legs. The man was naked, but for some clean yellow underpants. His arms were folded and poking from them was a single-barrelled shotgun, aimed at my feet.

'You are Fritz?'

'Maybe I am Fritz. Maybe I am not.' His eyes were shifting over me, noting details. I looked at the gun. Its barrel was scrupulously clean, cleaner than those of the soldiers at the checkpoint. I could smell its fresh oil.

'If you are Fritz, I've come to see you.'

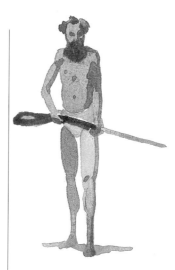

'Who told you I am living here?'

'Gilberto Peña.'

'Vhy do you vant to see me?'

'Peña said you'd be able to teach me a few tricks about the jungle. I'm heading for the mouth of the Amazon.'

'Ze Amazon jungle?' said Fritz, furrowing his eyebrows. 'Sure. Come along unt have a talk about zis in my hut.' Before we moved off, he said, 'You valked vell coming here along ze footpath. Like a deer almost, as if you are knowing ze jungle vell already. You know, Chico did not even hear you approaching.'

I followed his eyes to the dog. It was sitting on its tail, panting, with its tongue trailing from its mouth. 'Zat is goot, very goot.'

I asked him how he knew I spoke English.

'For ze first sink, you are obviously European or North American. Your fair hair unt blue eyes tells me zis. Unt ze next sink I vas noticing as you were valking along—'

'You've been watching me? How long for?'

Fritz winced at my interruption. 'Ze next sink I vas observing vas you vor ze German paratrooper boots. So I am sinking maybe you are German. But zen I am noticing your machete is made off Sheffield steel.'

'You always notice such details?'

'Do you sink I am crazy or somesink? I am alone here, and I am a diamont miner. Do you sink I can have folks strolling about in my jungle, snooping into my house vit all my diamonts? No, of course not.'

All this time he had been standing with his meaty white arms crossed, leaning backwards. Now he let his arms hang loosely. 'Right. Stick close behind me. Ve shall go to my hut. You vill stay for only as long as I sink necessary for you. Zis is not ze holiday camp.' He walked with gangly strides and the dog trotted at his heels, its head upturned towards Fritz's eyes.

'Dump your stuff zere, unt put avay zat knife. I do not feel comfortable vith veapons in range of me.'

We were standing in the porch of a small shack. It was a neat home, built with skill and precision, snuggled among a garden of vegetables—swelling melons, yuccas and avocados—fortified against the insect battalions by trenches of poisoned water. The trees in the clearing were hung with fat mangoes, decorated with orchids which spilled down the trunks. Amid all this, the hut looked like a large doll's house. It had all the permanent features that had been lacking in the Indian huts I'd seen. The Indians lived in throwaway shelters, which dissolved into the jungle a few seasons on, but this one had window frames, checked curtains, a bedstead, shelves and, by the bedside, a German book on the principles and practice of medicine. Later I found it was his only one.

Fritz rapped a beam with his knuckles. 'See zis? Made out off ze extra special hardwood. Termites cannot get zere teeth into it. Now, if I had chosen to use ze normal junky forest vood, zis house vould have been a heap off dust by now. But look. Sixteen years olt unt as goot as new. You are dying to ask me somesink, *ja*?'

'Not really.'

▲ In contrast to the deep shade in which they grow, rainforest orchids often display the most brilliant colours.

'Yes, you are. You are struck by ze cleanliness of zis place. Look at ze sand round about. All ze veeds rooted out. Unt ze house?'

'The house? Very tidy too.'

'*Very tidy?* No. You are kidding me! It is spotless. You are vondering ze reason?'

I shook my head, but he was still talking. He said that if you ever wanted to describe a person's soul, you only had to describe their surroundings. Then he turned towards the pristine clearing and looked with pride.

'And another sink: no insects. I sveep them clear off my hut, unt off all ze paths in sight. I flush out all ze vermins. Nosink can hide from me.'

Fritz didn't talk; he lectured. If I spoke, he didn't seem to hear. Unused to the strength of his own voice, he boomed it into my face, making me cringe. This wasn't conversation. These were his thoughts turning over out loud. He addressed the dog as much as me. Chico sat staring into his face, with his brown felt ears pricked and his brow wrinkled, picking up each word. The dog seemed to understand and sympathise.

I diverted one of his speeches to the subject of diamonds. I wanted to know why people got so feverish about them.

'Stay here,' he said. He dipped into the hut entrance and came back with his right fist clenched, as though he was about to punch me. But he opened his palm and there they were, diamonds the size of peas. 'You see how stupid your question vas now? Feast your eyes on zese beauties. Each von is like a naked lady.' He jiggled them like dice. 'Look at zem dancing. Now imagine seeing just von glittering in ze stream vater for ze first time. Zere is only von vord for it: fire. Zese stones have fire. Unt so all people come rushing into ze forest for zem.

'You know vat zey say? "Ze mosquito net protects against malaria, but not against ze diamont fever." So folks come in hordes to ze jungle, unt ze stupid vons, zey die. "Ze jungle is zeir glory, ze jungle will be zeir grave." Zat is vat zey

Alluvial Diamonds

THE HARDEST NATURALLY occurring substance in the world, the diamond, has been prized throughout history for its brilliant, fiery beauty. Diamonds are formed deep under the Earth's crust from carbon that has been crystallised under extreme heat and pressure. Later, seismic activity brings the diamonds to the Earth's surface, where they may either remain buried in volcanic rock, or else be gradually washed out into the sandy or gravelly beds of streams. Diamonds sieved from riverbeds are known as alluvial diamonds; the first diamonds to be discovered thousands of years ago were found in this way.

Before the modern diamond mines of South Africa began to be worked, diamonds were extremely rare and correspondingly even more valuable than they are today, both as gemstones and for industrial use. Sir Walter Raleigh, lured to the Orinoco by the legend of gold, spoke on his return of a 'mountaine of christall', and ever since then diamond

▲ A handful of Earth's more tangible riches.

prospectors have come to South America in the hope of making their fortunes.

Some rivers are still rich in alluvial diamonds, washed many miles away from their original volcanic source, but these represent only a tiny proportion of world production.

say about ze victims. Unt I sink,' he said, 'I sink zat you ought to remember zose vords for yourself.'

'Thanks.'

He clamped his teeth together and laughed through them. 'I am only taking ze micky,' he said. If it was a joke, it was the only one he cracked during my visit.

Fritz interrogated me for hours until every scrap of information I had was transferred to his memory. Was such-and-such a part of the river being worked? Had such-and-such a person looked especially happy? What about the people in the bars—was anyone in particular splashing their money around, or wearing new clothes? But, more important than anything else, had anyone asked me to see how his own mining was coming along?

Later, in the night chill, I sat bleary-eyed under the beam of the carbide lamp, batting away night wasps that were drawn and dazzled by the white light. Outside there was no moonlight and so the insects of the night were bolder and screeched louder. Every now and again Fritz would throw me a question to test how observant I was.

'How many electricity lines are hung betveen ze poles in Icabaru?' he would ask out of the blue.

'Two.'

'Zat is correct. Two. Unt zey turn ze power off at ten in evening. Ven it is staying on all ze night, it means eiser ze man in charge is drunk, or somevon in ze town is dying. Ven zere are dyings, zey alvays leave ze lights on.'

Mostly, though, it was just one speech after another. He was unbottling himself. He wanted an audience and went on, deeper and deeper into the night, while a heap of half-roasted moths, flying ants and wasps lay kicking at the foot of the carbide lamp.

When at last I slumped over asleep, he kicked me. 'Are you not interested in vat I haf to say? Vhy haf you come all zis vay to see me, if you are not paying ze full attention? If you are not interested, I do not care. *You* are ze von needing help, not me.' Then he started a fresh spiel. After that he said, 'Vell, it is getting cold now. I am off to bed.'

I slept in my hammock, under the night sky, but for only a couple of hours.

'*Guten Morgen!* I am surprised you are not up already.'

'But it isn't even first light yet.'

'Zat is vat I mean. Take zis gun, unt go unt shoot ze animal for us to eat. By ze time ze sun is vaking up, it vill be too late. Remember: ze early bird is catching ze vorm.'

I walked through the mists of dawn and came back to the hut when the grey, damp air had lifted and the sun was out of the trees.

'Vat? Only a lousy parrot? I do not sink I have seen such a miserable specimen in all my life. How many cartridges did you vaste?' He held out his hand for the gun. 'Tomorrow I vill come vith you unt show you how to shoot properly.'

Fritz spent the day sifting river deposits in a narrow gully and I watched him bully the pebbles through different grades of sieve. 'Zese are all quartz shingles. Zey are rubbish.' He discarded the stones in heaps on the riverbank. 'Here comes another load!' He hurled a cloud of shingle through the air.

'What do you do when you get ill?' I asked that evening.

'I have been ill vonce only. Zat vas ven I vas down vith ze fever. It hung around my head for two days, nosink vorse zan influenza. But zen on ze zirt day, I vas very ill. I could not get out of ze bed. I lay sinking I vas doomed. Two days later, I knew my end vas near for certain. I had to make von last effort, othervise it vas curtains for me. So I got out ze rifle unt valked over zere, by zat tree, my head crazy vis ze fever. I vas desperately requiring nutrition. But vere from? Zen, can you imagine vat I see? Before my eyes is ze deer! Enormous, fat deer for me to eat. I shot at ze animal, unt it is dropping dead at my feet. How about zat? Ve must alvays believe in ze miracles. Does God exist? Before zis I vas sinking not. But somevone vas kind to me zat day. So anyvay, I slit ze deer open unt I took all ze most nutritious parts: kidneys unt liver. I ate zem immediately. Unt zat is vhy I am still living today.'

Fritz took me hunting. We stalked up a winding forest trail and he showed me the spot where he had been charged by a boar. He had shot it squarely between the eyes as it tore through the undergrowth at him, gnashing its yellow tusks. It was not the shot that stopped the pig, it was the tree. He made me bend to inspect the buckled treetrunk.

Further up the track, we stopped for a drink. Fritz sliced open a liana creeper that looked like a cable used for mooring a ship, and sugary juice trickled out.

On another day we walked through a grove of banana trees, their green rubbery leaves tattered and waving like battle flags. Fritz showed me how to take water from their stems as well.

On the way back from hunts, when it was midday and most of the animals were curled up and snoozing, Fritz would tell stories. 'Did I ever say how Chico's mozer died? Vell, she vas killed by a vild boar. Pigs are ze only sink zat you need

With its ears pricked for any sound of predators, a red brocket deer pauses while drinking. ▶

to be scared off in jungle. Apart from ze jaguar, off course. If you are bitten by ze snake or spider, it is your own stupid fault. You have been clumpsy or somesink. Anyvay, vere vas I? Ah, yes, peccaries. Zey are pigs zat go around in herds. I am telling: if you hear a crashing, drumming noise, you better be vatching out. It means ze peccaries are on ze move and maybe you had better start running. Zat vas von vay I nearly lost Chico, but I nearly lost Chico anozer vay too.' He stopped on the path and told me the tale.

'Von day in ze forest I am hunting ven I hear his special bark—half-danger, half-excitement. Vat can zis mean? I come nearer through ze trees, and I see Chico staring face to face with hairy animal vich is two times bigger: an ant-bear.

'I vait, and vatch. Chico is dashing forvard for a vile, prancing and teasing ze ant-bear and showing himself off to me, telling me how brave he is. Zen Chico goes up to ze animal unt starts to grapple vith it, unt immediately has it pinned to ze ground. Chico is vagging his tail, unt ze ant-bear is lying on its back. It is doomed, you might sink. But zis animal is not stupid, unt in a few moments—.' Fritz stopped speaking. He had stiffened his spine. Something was worrying him, but I couldn't see what.

He spoke slowly. 'Flick zat black ant off my arm, vill you?' I saw an ant, the length of my thumb, twitching upside-down on Fritz's elbow. I spun it off with the back of my hand.

'*Mein Gott.*' He wiped the sweat off his eyes with a sweep of his hand. 'Zat vas a *ventiquatro*. If von off zose is nipping you, you are getting a fever for a day and are flat on your back in dreadful pains.

'Anyvay, zere vas Chico and zis ant-bear, wrestling on ze forest floor, scaring all vildlife for miles around. Unt ze ant-bear had vorked its arms around ze back of Chico's neck, unt had its claws crossed over and pulling at eiser side of Chico's throat like razors. Slowly, slowly, slowly, slowly, ze ant-bear vas tightening ze claws unt ripping open Chico's neck. At zat moment I stepped in and I am bashing ze animal with ze stick until it is letting go.'

Fritz reached down for Chico's ear and scratched it. 'Now Chico is as right as rains, but he is never forgetting zat day.'

I said, 'Unt vat is happening—I mean, what happened to the ant-bear?'

'Ze ant-bear?' Fritz smacked his lips, and started off down the track. 'He vas dinner zat night.'

The Final Test

Fritz enjoyed his lectures and never excused either the dog or me from them. But I was learning.

His was a no-nonsense world, stripped of folklore and romance. The jungle around the hut clearing was his garden. He waged war against any pests or weeds that disturbed it. Everything in sight of his doorway had some use: medical, nutritional or household. Everything else that encroached was exterminated.

But there had been changes since my visit. Fritz's lifestyle was deteriorating; almost collapsing. Leaves lay scattered on the paths. Spiders hitched webs across

▲ **This three-toed tamandua or lesser anteater is equally at home in trees or on the ground, as it searches for ants with its long sticky tongue.**

the clearing. Chico sulked and went off his food.

The truth was that Fritz's existence here was on a knife-edge. Alone, he could maintain his civilisation, but with a companion to distract him, he lost all the time he needed to maintain his jungle niche.

One night something happened to change all this. Fritz, as usual, curtly muttered 'Sweet dreams', as I spread out my hammock under the sky. Then, as I bent to unlace my boots, I sensed a movement nearby, a rustle in my hammock. I fingered in the darkness for my machete and a torch. When I got close to the hammock, I caught it in the torchbeam—a black scorpion, twitching in the hammock, tangled in the threads and stabbing the air with its sting.

I clubbed it with the machete and only then saw that it had been tied down by a strand of white cotton. It was secured with a neat double reefknot, and placed in the central sag of the hammock, like a gift, where I would have lain.

'Sleep vell?' asked Fritz next morning. He looked unusually radiant, I thought.

'Yes, very well indeed, thanks.'

'Zen I am sinking it is time for you to leave for ze Amazon.'

'Sudden, isn't it?'

'No point in you staying. Nosink much more zat I can be teaching here.' He hadn't mentioned the scorpion, but we both knew that I had passed his test; for the first time he looked pleased with me.

▲ A black scorpion of the lowland rain forest. Scorpions feed mainly on insects and spiders, many much larger than themselves, which they paralyse with their venomous stings.

'You have been listening very vell to all my talkings. I have been putting ze pressure on you, but you are vinning through. Ze jungle is tough, so I vas being tough.' He released a glimmer of a smile. 'Pack up your bags. I vill show you a path back to ze River Icabaru avoiding zat crazy imbecile vith his bats.'

He led me down to a track, then said, 'Gootbye, unt goot luck vith ze Amazon.' Before I could get in a reply, he turned to his dog and said, 'Come on, Chico, let's go home', and they raced back up the path to the hut without looking back.

On the Mountain

Roraima, the tower-block plateau I had seen coming over the Gran Sabana, commended itself as a place to be alone. I very much wanted to be alone before entering the Amazonian forest, so I walked for a day through grasses and *moriche* palms to Paraytepuy, a Taulipang village of pastel-pink huts capping a hill.

The savannah was as lifeless as it had seemed through the dust of Peña's truck. The grass rustled with occasional lizards or springing grasshoppers, but otherwise moved only in the breeze. On the track there were ants building defensive turrets the size of pipebowls at their tunnel entrances and I followed the three-toed anteaters.

The grassland buckled into hills at the foot of the mountain. Snow-white mists curtained the sheer face and whirled off the plateau summit. I made a

campfire at the mountain's base and slept the night rolled up in a blanket.

Further up, there was forest. It was a mossy, cramped mess of frogs, ferns and tortured trees, fed by the cloud. It smelt of ditchwater. A diagonal fault was the path up the cliff face to the summit.

I did not reach the top until hours later. The rocks were blackened by the driving mists and shaped by them into caves and statues. Soil clung to the mountain in the shelter of nooks and ponds. The only sounds were of dripping and of lost, twittering birds swept up from the forest below. If a tree grew, its wood was deformed and twisted. The sedges looked pained when I trod on them and the succulents cracked open under my boot. Two plant species in particular thrived here—pitcher plants and sundews; both carnivorous and the colour of fresh blood.

I walked for a week in the cloud, sleeping in the caves with necklace-length centipedes, and blue and black frogs with yellow underbellies. I found my way with a skein of cotton, unwinding reels of it in a trail behind me as I went. It was a labyrinth. Without the cotton I would never have found my way down.

When I did, I felt clear-headed and sobered. But ready? I wasn't sure. Peña had said that I wasn't to look back, so I didn't.

▲ The lofty plateau of Mount Roraima towers more than 9,000 feet above the boundaries of Brazil, Venezuela and Guyana. Its primordial scenery is believed to have provided the inspiration for Arthur Conan Doyle's novel *The Lost World*.

With a wingspan of 12 inches, the Amazonian hawk moth is a giant in the insect world. Remaining inanimate during the day, it serves the forest at night as a pollinator.

Although most katydids (a kind of grasshopper) are masters of disguise, this multi-coloured specimen has obviously opted for high visibility.

The waxy-tailed lantern bug is another type of grasshopper. It has modified its appearance by growing a long tail of wax, which is thought to offer some protection by confusing potential predators.

A group of beetles decked out in a dazzling array of patterned colours.

Insects—Kings of the Rain Forest

O F ALL THE CREATURES ON THE EARTH, no group is more varied than the insects. There are only about 5,000 species of mammals in the world, compared with 750,000 catalogued species of insects. And scientists know that these are only a fraction of the total number of insect species that actually exist. Recent estimates, based on research in the rain forest, put the likely world total at a staggering ten million. For it is in the world's rain forests, and in their canopies in particular, that the largest and most diverse insect populations are found. In the case of the Amazon, insects are so numerous that scientists believe they account for 85 per cent of the total animal population, calculated by *weight*, in any given area.

The insects of the Amazon have long held a special fascination for researchers. The early 19th-century German scientific explorer Alexander von Humboldt reported on the astonishing range of insect life in the region. Then, 50 years later, the English naturalists Henry Bates and Alfred Russel Wallace subsidised their Amazon expedition by sending 14,000 insect specimens back to London for threepence each. This enabled them to do pioneering work, identifying thousands of unknown species and observing the 'mimetic' defence by which one type of butterfly imitates another that birds find unpalatable. This led to their developing a theory of evolution at the same time as Charles Darwin.

For the modern visitor, the vast majority of Amazonian insects are simply a stinging nuisance; at worst, a considerable health hazard. Thanks to their superb camouflage, many are virtually invisible. But anyone can marvel at the beauty, colours, behaviours, noise and sheer variety of the insects that occur here.

▲ Leaf-cutter ants are among the forest's busiest inhabitants. They patiently cut near-perfect crescents of leaf, which they carry back to their underground nest. There they chew the leaves into a mulch and then feed on the fungus that grows on it.

▲ Contrary to appearances, this iridescent beauty is not a swallowtail butterfly, but a urania moth. It is one of many creatures that have mastered the art of mimicry.

The bright colours of this caterpillar warn predators that it is foul-tasting, or even poisonous. As a second line of defence it also has a formidable forest of sharp spines. ▶

CHAPTER 4

Making Contact

THE BRAZIL THAT ROLLED off the Pacaraima hills was cattle land. The dust road from the frontier was fenced with barbed wire and behind it cows scratched their backs on the ant-hill pillars. Only beyond Boa Vista had the jungle been permitted to stay, for the time being.

Boa Vista was a spread-eagled town whose government clerks smelt of cheap soap. They knew little of my jungle. I drank a thousand coffees, it seemed, before I knew all I had to know of it. Now I could picture the forest for the first time: Amazonia was no longer a dark, mysterious cloud in my mind. I had done my research, but I'd still had no contact with the Wai-wai Indians of the interior. My funds were running low and I had tired of slinging up my hammock in hotels that doubled as malodorous brothels.

I sat in a bar in a small, jungle-frontier town much like all the others: men in sombreros at tables clacking dominoes, or strumming *brasileira* music; bar girls draped around them; flies and smoke; a dirt floor; bottles in clumps on the tables. Many days before, I had dyed my hair a deep mahogany to look less like a gringo. Now the dye was fading, but no matter, because I'd learnt to drink *cachaça*, a sugarcane rum, without wincing. It was taken with a slug of lemon juice, squeezed straight down the throat or sucked from the back of the hand.

The streets were washed with rain; the roof crackled under the pelting. I thought back to the Gran Sabana, thought of it breathing again and of animals hopping about in the freshened air. One day it had been the dry season, the next the wet. The change had been as quick as that.

'Mind if I join you?' A voice spoke in Portuguese.

A man was bending over me, blocking my light. He stooped and had a thin, bony face. He was wearing a black felt hat, a grey suit with dark rainsplashes down the shoulders and a white shirt with no tie. His clothes were too well cut to be a farmer's, but his skin was brown and flybitten. He was armed.

'If you keep that knife tucked away in your belt, certainly you can,' I said. I pushed a chair out with one foot. He sat down and asked if I was alone.

'Perhaps.' I shrugged. 'If you think I'm worth robbing, forget it, but I'll buy you a drink.'

He took off his hat and hooked it on to a rum bottle. The hat showered the table with water droplets, which were red from the dust. 'Thanks. Could do with one.' He flung the dregs from a glass, smeared with two different shades of lipstick, over his shoulder and I tipped out a shot of *cachaça*.

'Heard you're looking for someone to guide you through the forest to the

Storm clouds loom
over some of the last
cattle land before the
jungle begins.

Indians.' He swigged the drink down in one go. 'I think I can help.'

'Know anything about the jungle?' I asked.

'No.'

'Anything about the Indians?'

'Not any around these parts.'

'What about cooking?'

'I can't cook anything other than beans and rice and coffee.'

'Can you read maps, carry loads, anything useful whatsoever?'

'No, *senhor*. Just thought you might like to forget about your expedition for a while and spend a night on the town before you leave. I know all the spots.'

'Well, well.' I held out my hand. 'Let's finish off this bottle and get another.'

He said his name was Jorge. We clinked glasses and gulped down another bottle. 'Jorge, what do you do for a living?' But he couldn't get the words out. His cheeks looked pale and I led him outside for a dose of fresh air. The sky had cleared, the mud of the street was wet and slippery and water flowed along the gutters in rivulets. I had to prop Jorge up.

'Come on, Benedito, let's go dancing.' He was pulling me down a dark, pot-holed back street. Occasional open doorways splashed light across the street. Women in tight skirts slouched in the doorways, jangling their bracelets. We ducked inside another bar that looked out on to a river.

'This is my favourite joint in town,' said Jorge. We pushed through a crowd of men with bottles in their hands.

'Don't they have glasses to drink from here?' I asked.

'Want to catch a germ or something?' said Jorge. 'Stick to your own bottle.'

We were steering towards a table. On the other side of the room, around the corner and beyond the bar, men were stomping in the dust to a samba rhythm. Someone was twanging a guitar. We cleared a space at a table and sat down. Two women descended on our table from the crowd and snuggled up to us. My girl had heavy earrings studded with paste diamonds, bigger than any real ones unearthed in Gran Sabana.

'Are one of you two going to get us girls a drink?'

'I'll go,' I said and went to the bar. I was back a few minutes later and by then two more girls were around the table. Jorge said they'd have to share out the two beer bottles between them.

The oldest girl was a Negro, with light bones. Another had green eyes. The third had hard eyes and bad breath. The fourth was the youngest and her blood was pure Indian. They were all professionals. Smiling looked a real effort.

'Let's dance,' said one girl.

'Yes, let's,' said Jorge and the girl strapped her arms around his neck. They slumped off to the dance floor.

'Come on, then,' I said to the flock of girls and went after Jorge without looking back. The only girl still behind me when we reached the dancing space was the Indian girl. I took hold of her hand. We moved into a sweaty forest of entwined men and women.

My girl said her name was Maria. Up until two years before she had been at a

The Wai-wai Indians

THE WAI-WAI TRIBE come from the remote jungles of northern Brazil and were for years talked of as the legendary 'White Indians', famed for the beauty of their painted bodies and feather ornaments. For centuries they remained untouched by modern civilisation, and were officially discovered only in 1837 by the great 19th-century explorer Robert Schomburgk, who noted their hunting skills and love of decoration. 'This tribe particularly traps the harpy eagle for its ostrich-like feathers,' he wrote.

Today the Wai-wai live restless, nomadic lives, building a new village every two or three years. Their name for themselves is *wéwé*, meaning 'wood or forest people'; and it is in the forest that their famous hunting expertise has developed, the bowmen stalking their prey or ambushing it from camouflaged hides. Fish are caught with arrows and nets, or stupefied with poisons. Quarrelsome among themselves, the Wai-wai are nevertheless renowned as dog-lovers, unusually among Amazon tribes who generally believe that a hungry dog is a better hunter. Puppies may be suckled by a woman if their mother dies, and are washed in a special herbal infusion to make them strong. Older dogs are groomed regularly and fed on the pick of the kill.

A Wai-wai warrior decorated with ceremonial paint and feathers. ▶

NICHOLAS GUPPY, 1953

good Catholic mission school. And before that she had lived with her family in the forest. Those were the days when she was called Mawa, which was a good name to be rid of anyway. A *mawa* was a sort of frog. The missionaries had christened her Maria and to be quite honest she'd forgotten her other name completely before I brought the subject up, she said. But two years before, when she was ten or eleven, she'd run away to the bright lights.

'Why?'

'More money. More money for perfume, clothes and all the things a girl wants.' She said that soon she would be rich, richer than she'd ever dreamt, and if her family knew they would be proud of her.

'You are a Wai-wai, then?'

'Was.' She stopped dancing and dropped her arms from around my waist.

'Would you be able to take me to your family in the forest?'

'No.' She stared at her feet.

'Please. If I paid you as a guide?'

'No. I'm not seeing my family again. I don't want to go back to the forest. I have a new life. I'm not going back.'

'Please. Just give me directions. Where do they live? It's not asking much.'

'I said *no*.' She stamped her feet.

'Then, do you know anyone who can help me?'

'No, no, no!' She pushed me back and dived into the crowd.

'Please,' I said, catching her hand.

'That's the man you want,' she said, 'over there. Now let me go.'

I released her and blinked through the smoke to where she'd pointed.

'Complete nutcase, that girl,' said Jorge over his shoulder.

'Know anything about that man over there, Jorge?'

'He's a brazil-nut gatherer. Stay well clear of him. Bad sort.'

The man in question had a thick, shaven head and wore thigh-length boots. Silver spurs jutted from his heels. He looked the epitome of a thug and was too big for his stool. On the table before him was his hat. It was lilac-green, and a black-and-white spotted jaguar's tail hung from the rear. Two other men were at his table. One looked unconscious and his head was resting on the tabletop. The other had a heavy girl clinging to him. He was bouncing her up and down on his knees and she was bellowing with laughter.

▲ Brazil nuts are hard to cultivate commercially and many Indians make a living gathering wild nuts in the forest.

I bought a bottle of *cachaça* at the bar and went over to the bald man.

'Can I sit down? I'm told you may be able to help.'

The man spat at the floor. 'And who might you be?'

'Call me Benedito. I'm told you know the forests. Is that true?'

'What if I do?'

'I'm looking for a guide to take me to the Wai-wai Indians.'

'Are you some kind of lunatic? That's a month's walk, unless you know the paths.'

'How long if you know the paths?'

'Look, I'm not interested in taking you anywhere. I'm a nut gatherer. I follow

the trails and scrounge around the jungle floor picking up nuts. So I can't help.'

'Have a swig of this,' I said, placing the bottle in his ham fist.

He wiped the bottleneck with his fingers, then gulped some down. He knocked the head of the lifeless man with the bottle, who sat up and took a swig, dribbling it down his chin.

'You'll take me, then?' I repeated.

'That's not what I said.'

'Good. Here, have another drink.'

'OK, but I don't know the first thing about Indians, so there's no point in you asking.'

'I'm not asking. Pass the bottle to your other friend. Perhaps the lady wants a drink? That's right. Drink it all up.' She did, as if it were lemonade. 'Right,' I said. 'Where can we meet to discuss it?'

'Are you deaf or something?'

'That bottle didn't last long, did it, *senhor*…? I didn't catch your name.'

'That's because I didn't give it to you. It's Pablo.'

I went away, gave the drink half an hour to work on him, then strolled back.

'What time did you say we'd meet tomorrow, Pablo?'

His eyes were confused. 'Damn you. Why don't you leave me alone?' He clapped his head in his hands.

'I will in a minute. What time?'

'Ten o'clock, outside here tomorrow.'

'Promise?'

'I never promise.'

'Ten o'clock, then.' I picked up his limp hand and shook it.

On the way back to Jorge's table, I was clipped on the ear by a flying bottle.

The tables and walls were rocking with the beat of bottles and fists. A fight was brewing on the dance floor. 'Plenty of action here,' said Jorge. The music stopped. A bottle smashed. A clutch of bar girls ran to the door, screaming. Then the lights blew.

The barman had an oil lamp ready.

'Time to leave, Jorge?' I said.

'Yes, time to leave.'

Jorge stepped outside, supported by two girls. It was first light. The river was steaming and fishing boats with rattling engines chugged through the grey water.

'Sleep well,' I said to Jorge. He grinned and squeezed the girls. I said that I'd see him first thing tomorrow. Then I went off to bed.

In the morning, Jorge appeared before Pablo did. We drank coffee at a table in the bar. 'How do you know Pablo is going to turn up?' Jorge asked me.

'Because of this.'

I showed him what I'd collected the night before. 'He's sure to come back for his hat.' Jorge took the hat and stroked the jaguar's tail. He repeated that he thought Pablo was a bad sort and he didn't want to be here when he came.

'What's your job, Jorge? I never asked.'

'I'm a missionary.'

I snorted. 'No, come on, tell me.'

'I'm telling the truth. A missionary.'

'Prove it. I don't believe it. A man who drinks in a seedy place like that, who frolics with women, tells me he's a preacher! What sort of religion is that?'

In a deadpan voice Jorge said, ' "God works for good with those who love Him." ' He said it was from Romans 8:28.

I gaped. 'You really *are* a missionary, aren't you?'

' "Repentance and forgiveness of sins should be preached in His name to all nations." Luke 24:47.' He nodded, with knitted eyebrows, as he said this, then he smiled. 'You see, Benedito, to survive here, you must modify your principles, take account of local values. Bend with the wind, that's my motto, bend with the wind, or else'—he clicked his fingers sharply—'you snap.'

'Is that what you were doing with those girls? Bending with the wind?'

'Look,' said Jorge. 'This is my home. It's where I let my hair down. When I'm refreshed, I'll be back to work in the Amazon, preaching God's love to the Indians. You know there are people out there who haven't even heard of the Lord?' Jorge thought I was mocking him, but I really was interested. He had changed overnight. It was fascinating.

Pablo came dead on time, before Jorge could get away.

'You got something for me?'

'Ah, Pablo!' I said. 'Sit yourself down. I've already got you a drink.' Pablo grabbed the hat, and scrutinised it. Then he sat down heavily and took the beer bottle in his hand. He felt the coolness of the glass and smiled.

'I'll be going, then,' said Jorge, getting to his feet, 'if you two are about to discuss business.'

'I didn't come to discuss any business. Just to pick up my hat.'

'Well, I've got things to do anyway.' Jorge extended his hand to me. He wasn't inviting me to shake, he was giving me something. 'A present for you, Benedito.' It was his knife. 'It'll come in useful. Hide it in your boot.'

'Thanks, Jorge, that's very kind,' I said. I was glad we were still friends and asked him to slip 5,000 cruzeiros to the Indian bar girl I'd upset. Without thinking, I used her Indian name.

'Mawa?' Jorge shouted.

Pablo let out a curse as his beer bottle chinked on his front teeth.

'*Mawa?* How did you know that was her name?' Jorge was leaning forward on his knuckles, like an ape, rocking the table and fuming into my face. '*Maria!* That's her name. A good Christian name. *Ma-ri-a.* What right have you to come along and remind her of her primitive upbringing? Just tell me that.'

The veins on Jorge's neck had risen into blue electric flexes. 'Let's all just hope you haven't done too much damage. It's unlikely, but who knows? Now she may think of going back to the forest to live. What then, eh? What then?'

I couldn't think of anything to say.

Jorge stomped off. Pablo was cackling with laughter. 'You know what, Benedito?' he said.

'What?' I was still watching the dust cloud behind Jorge. He hadn't said goodbye.

'You might have earned yourself a ride into the forest.'

'Why is that?'

▲ A missionary priest conducts a service in a Brazilian Indian village.

'You see,' he said, 'Jorge and I are not what you might call friends. He did something unspeakable to an Indian tribe I knew, on the far side of Amazonas.'

'Unspeakable?'

'Yes, he Christianised them, that's what he did. Flew into the jungle, spotted a village, built a church overnight, told the Indians they'd be damned if they didn't pay it a visit every day of the week. Handed out T-shirts. Told them they'd be on their way to Hell if they didn't cover themselves up. Jorge taught the village a shortened version of the Lord's Prayer and told them to recite it every day before going fishing or hunting. Then he decided it was time to spread the Word elsewhere, so he handed out Bibles and flew away in his aeroplane, on to the next tribe. He had told the headman to ostracise anyone who didn't obey these rules.

'Five years go by and that's when I turn up. I was just passing through, looking for better brazil nuts, but what do I find? I find a handful of puny, bony people, amid a junkyard of huts and burial mounds. Why? I'll tell you why. Their clothes had worn through and they'd been naked and, because of that, ashamed. Others had died of starvation, because the need to go to church meant the village couldn't be moved on to fresh fertile land and they wasted valuable hunting time in front of the altar.'

Pablo emptied the bottle. Had I read any Mark Twain? he asked. '"Soap and education are not as sudden as a massacre, but they are more deadly in the long run."'

Pablo, the shaven-headed thug, had, it turned out, been to university in Brasilia. There he'd specialised in English literature. He had grown up poor, on the forest edge, where his father scratched a living from the land. He had kept the forest life in reserve, if all else failed with his city career. It did, so now he was a brazil-nut gatherer.

'You'll find I have a soft heart underneath—if I'm handled right.'

'Does that mean you are going to help me?'

'You'll have to show me your plans first. But I should be able to. Ten minutes ago I wouldn't have helped if you'd offered me a fortune. Thought you were something to do with that priest.'

I unpacked my maps and flattened them out on the table, weighting the corners down with beer bottles, but Pablo pushed them away. The cartographer's interpretation of the forest—a web of vague gullies and tracks, dreamed up in air-conditioned offices, he said—made him laugh. He would take me to a bunch of goldminers, *garimpeiros*, deep in the forest. They knew the Indians well. From there it would be up to me. We agreed a price for his packhorses.

'And terms of payment?' he asked.

'I'll divide each note in two,' I said, 'and give you the left halves now. You'll have the right halves once we get to the *garimpeiros* and we're within reach of the Indians.'

'Suits me,' said Pablo.

I split the cash with Jorge's stab-knife, a double-bladed instrument which carved through the wad as though it were lard. Pablo reached for the money, thumbed through the notes and packed them into his breast pocket.

I needed only one day for final preparations, but Pablo said he needed a dry day before entering the jungle. The going was treacherous and he couldn't afford one of the horses slipping in the mud and breaking a leg. He gave me three days from now. If by that time it hadn't stopped raining, he could not ferry me through. 'So you'd better start praying for sunshine.'

We were to meet on the first cloudless daybreak, in the village of Paraiso.

Waiting for the Sun

South from Boa Vista, down into the Amazon basin, the main road split; this was Paraiso, two dozen huts by the road.

Most of that road went on south to the city of Manaus, an Amazonian river-port which had been the vanguard of the rubber boom in the 1900s. Rubber barons had milked the forest for its latex and achieved such opulence from the trade that they erected baroque mansions in the jungle; they cobbled the streets with imported stones and mosaic pavements and sent their linen to Ireland to be laundered. That was Manaus, where the main dirt road led. The other road spluttered east from Paraiso for a few miles, then stopped. That was the frontier of cultivation and the beginning of my jungle, a dark wall of one-hundred-foot trees. Seven hundred miles to the east lay the mouth of the Amazon.

I was ready within a few hours, but the sky billowed and swelled with slate-grey cloud and sluiced the streets with rain, splattering the huts with red blobs of mud.

I had my supply stacks waiting. Everything had been thought of: flour, rice, coffee, sugar, beans; enough food, even without jungle meat, to last three people for four months. The sacks had been heaped, unheaped and heaped again on the dirt floor of my room in Paraiso, but still the skies were thick with cloud. On the medical side my strategy had been based on a defence against jungle fevers. I had brought most drugs from home, but topped them up with a few local tonics. I'd reinforced my stock of presents for Indians with trinkets. I'd memorised the maps, and I'd sealed up my survival belt—an emergency bag that would be strapped around my waist, stuffed with fishing lines, a compass, hooks, matches and so on.

There was nothing more to do but wait. Still it rained.

I sat on my pile, the size of a cot, and stared at the dark sky all that day. The next was as wet. The dozy hotelier said he'd never seen it so wet at this time of year and it was incredible. Still the rain fell. The drumming on the tin roofs was driving me mad. I could barely keep still. I paced the bar or drummed my fingernails on the counter.

The following day was no better. The streets were awash, the sun blocked from the sky. The rain pummelled the roof without a break, all through the next night. I could not sleep and lay damp in my hammock. If at dawn the rain had not cleared, I would not be going at all. This was my last chance. I looked through the dark to my stores. Why was I making this journey anyway? I could not think of a good reason and then I asked myself who would mind if I turned back and went home. The answer was no one. I wanted to express all this in my notebook: the rain squalls, the clattering of the roof, my stores waiting beside me. I opened a fresh page and wrote: '2nd April. Lonely.'

▲ A typical modern highway cleaves its way through the rain forest.

Later, I did sleep, and later still I realised why: the roof was no longer rattling.

At dawn I swung from my hammock, unbolted the wooden shutters, and looked out into the street. The road was lit gently. The sun was still below the treeline. Blue mist was steaming from the walls, street and roofs. The air was sharp and bitterly cold, but the tinbox houses looked magical, veiled in pale wisps of mist. I felt like skipping through it, down the street. There was not a cloud to be seen. The sky was a smoky blue and quite clear.

Before long I was sitting in the street with my stores beneath me in the dawn sun. Soon Pablo would come with the horses and we would be away. I paced the gluey mud of the road. Where was he?

Hacking Our Way

Another brazil-nut gatherer called Raimundo came with Pablo to manage the horses. Raimundo had small eyes and a small mouth that hardly ever opened. He had a monkey face with thick eyebrows that met in the middle, and a bristly neck.

The jungle was a full day's walk from Paraiso. Along the way, the forest had been bruised by small farmsteads, whose crops were all failing. The road ended at a small river called the Jatapu; shortly after, there was the jungle wall.

We slept at its foot, on the land near one of the last farms. We were embraced by a farmer who showed us his children's rib cages, and ran his fingers over their bones as if they were xylophone keys.

The next day we had another look at the jungle wall. Pablo seemed to dip into it at random. He probed about, forcing the lead horse ahead of him, batting it from behind with a stick and shoving its head into the leaves. Each time, the horse refused to enter. Its eyeballs rolled, its nostrils widened and it whinnied and stamped, with its nose in the air. 'The path has grown over a little bit, perhaps,' said Pablo. The truth was that the jungle had sealed it up completely.

'The jungle is fighting back,' said Raimundo, nodding at the charred remains of the field behind, the farmer's latest assault. 'But it'll lose in the end.'

Eventually, we penetrated the wall. It was warm inside the jungle, as choking as a hothouse. The air was still; it pressed against the skin and its moisture clung to the back of my throat. Light came in splashes for a while, but as we entered deeper none of it broke through. The sound of our knives hacking was sponged up by the leaves, and the insect buzz muffled the crunch of our boots. Deeper, the undergrowth had mostly given up hope of light and the horses nosed their way without prompting.

Pablo said we were northward-bound for a while, following the Jatapu River.

Cattle pasture is cleared by felling and burning the rain forest. However, without trees the land soon becomes infertile, leading to yet more forest being cleared. ▼

Not far from an Indian village called Anaua, we were to swing east. I stayed close to Pablo, keeping my eyes on his green hat, and on the black-and-white jaguar tail, which flapped from it. We moved at a trot to keep up with the horses, slicing at the creepers with our machetes to trim them back. If we came across birds or monkeys, Pablo blasted at them with his shotgun, but we were moving too fast to take hunting seriously.

We stopped only once, during a cloudburst, when we pulled banana leaves over us as umbrellas and crouched under the horses in their steam.

That night we drank *cachaça* by the fireside. Pablo said he was off to find some brazil nuts for our supper and later he came back, hugging casks that looked like cannon balls. Inside there were the nuts, lying snugly like orange segments. We cracked them with our molars and roasted them dipped in sugar. Pablo said we had made very good progress and should reach the goldminers before the next nightfall. They lived in a decrepit shack nicknamed the Palace.

We stoked up the fire, tied up the horses next to it and fenced them in by hitching up the hammocks in a large triangle around them. Pablo said the jaguars knew him well in these parts and had been craving his horses for years, and this was why he wanted them on the inside. I was not to worry myself, he said; he would be wide-awake and waiting for them.

Later, I heard a purring and was scared out of my wits. It was not a jaguar, only Pablo snoring, and I got up and cuffed him.

Forest Monkeys

New World and Old World monkeys have different heritages. Evolving in isolation after the separation of the Earth's major continents, some New World monkeys have developed the unique advantage of a prehensile or 'grasping' tail. Of these, the noisiest are the howler monkeys, which have also evolved bony and greatly enlarged sound boxes for their voices, so that the roars they produce can be heard over distances as great as a mile.

Most agile, however, are the spider monkeys, whose tails function very much as extra hands—immensely strong and yet so sensitive that their tips can pick up objects as small as a pea. In fact, their tails are better at delicate tasks than are their hands, which have little stumpy thumbs and curved, awkward fingers. Spider monkeys often 'hold tails' instead of holding hands, and young ones entwine their tails with those of their mothers. Largely vegetarian, and confined strictly to tropical American rain forest, spider monkeys congregate in bands of between 20 and 30 members, foraging for nuts and fruit, lingering in an area for several weeks and defending their territory fiercely against all intruders.

Spider monkeys are the acrobats of the forest canopy. ▶

We were on the move before dawn. Raimundo potted a spider monkey, and as it tumbled down he muttered, 'That's one less person after our brazil nuts.'

The *garimpeiros* were Negroes, but their skins were palish from lack of daylight. There were three of them and they were excavating a pit. Their Palace was a palm lean-to which stood in a clearing paved with dead leaves and stunted cottongrass. They blinked like moles when they came out from the trees in answer to Pablo's hallooing. One took the monkey away to prepare it; another—who looked identical to the first, with the same fleshless body and limp wrists and neck—asked if we had any alcohol. The third, Antônio, was hairier, but otherwise much the same, and ran up to Pablo to hug him. He whisked off Pablo's hat, patted his smooth, fat head and laughed. He asked what month it was—surely Pablo had made a mistake coming at this time of the year?—but it

▲ The Amazonian pink-toed tarantula. Originally known as wolf-spiders, tarantulas were once thought to cause a disease known as tarantism—so called because its victims leap about in a frenzy as though performing the Italian *tarantella* folk dance.

was wonderful to see him so soon and by the way, unfortunately their dear mutual friend Jamarillo had drowned last week; it was most strange because the water had been only as deep as the bottle he'd had in his hand at the time, but there you are.

A tatty bird skipped into the clearing and pecked at my boots.

'Ah,' said Pablo, 'the Palace turkey.' The Palace turkey had a tarantula, hand-sized and kicking, in its beak. It dropped the spider on to my boot. Pablo stepped forward, sniggered, and smeared it into the dirt with his foot.

But the tarantula pulled itself back together again, reassembled its crushed black fingers and stroking down its bristles, like a cat its whiskers, hurried away.

We ate the monkey boiled. Dinner was a heap of limbs in fatty yellow water. They tasted rubbery and chewing the fingers made me cringe. Nevertheless, I piled my bowl full so as to avoid eating the monkey's head.

The Negroes came from Guyana, whose border was only a stone's throw away to the north. They bragged they knew the jungle by heart. When they heard where we were going, one of the two identical ones said, 'You ain't never wanting to go near dem Injuns, man. You know, dem folks have tails. Dey swings just like monkeys.'

Pablo laughed at this.

'It's true, man. And somethun else. Dey got skin as white as bone.'

'Dat's true, Moses,' the other said, shaking his head. 'I ain't approachun a million miles near dere.'

'Funny you should say that,' said Pablo. He winked at me.

We had to use up a lot of *cachaça* to persuade them to take me to the Indians. Once they had agreed and were flat on their backs snoring, Pablo and I talked.

Pablo said he would wait here with Raimundo while Moses and Joshua were taking me, and leave for home only once they were back and he had a sign from me saying I was safely with the Indians; the jaguar's tail from his hat would do fine. He plucked it off and pushed it into my hand. I said I thought Joshua and Moses might not turn out to be the best guides in the world and he agreed. He'd been thinking the same thing. The trouble was that both he and Raimundo had

had a slight misunderstanding over some gold they'd come across near the Wai-wai village and they weren't keen on being seen. But he would persuade Raimundo to accompany us part of the way. If Raimundo dropped me off with Joshua and Moses just short of the Indians, everything should be fine.

Later I bought two fistfuls of gold dust from the *garimpeiros*, as extra currency for trading with the Indians. I paid with five bottles of São João, and 500,000 cruzeiros. That gave me four ounces of gold at a rock-bottom price.

Antônio was supposed to be Pablo's best friend. He had poky eyes and a hooked nose; even when he smiled, he reminded me of a vulture. He also dabbled in medicine.

'Hey, man, I got somethun for you,' he said, while the others were packing the horses. 'Come wid me.'

'Where are we going?' I said.

'Just you wait un see.' We were walking towards a straw house made of freshly cut and dried grass. 'Step right inside.'

The little house was murky. It smelt of spring cow-parsley. The grass walls were still green and sprouting shoots. They were stacked with sheaths of dried herbs, barks and nuts. This was a jungle medicine cabinet.

'I got potions for you. Dey will help you good. Dey is magic.'

On the wall was the head of a toothless alligator, grinning. It was dried solid, but Antônio wrenched open its jaws to see if there were any back teeth left. There weren't. It was a crying shame, he said, because if you sucked one like a lozenge it would cure almost any bladder problem.

I said I didn't have a bladder problem. 'What else have you got?'

'Dis is what I wan you to take along wid you. For true, man, dis will give you good luck.'

'What is it?' I said. It was a hard, scaly, bony thing; a trumpet, I thought.

He said it was an armadillo's tail. 'Dis give you de hearing of a jaguar. You grinds it up and you drinks it in hot water like cocoa. Mark my words, man, you gonna need dis ting good.'

'Got anything else?' I was eyeing some purple berries, which looked like over-grown bilberries. As a medicine they looked more promising.

'Dat's my supper,' said Antônio. He put out his hand to say goodbye. I took the hand; it was hard and bony and had long, crusty fingernails. It was lifeless and cold. When Antônio moved away and I still had his hand in mine, I almost screamed. He'd left the thing behind.

'Dat's a monkey's paw,' he said. 'Now, dat give you plenty of breath when yous needin it. Makes your lungs strong. You gonna need both dese tings good. De armadillo tail let you be hearing danger and dat monkey's paw helps you run good from it.' Antônio clasped my arms and shook me. 'Now you be lisnin careful.' His eyes were bulging at me. 'Bad luck walks wid you, man. Any folk ever told you dat before?'

I scoffed, but said I was sure the monkey's paw and the

With its bony armour plates, this yellow armadillo resembles a reptile but is in fact a warm-blooded mammal. Because its burrow is likely to be flooded during the rainy season, the armadillo needs to be a strong swimmer. It can even increase its buoyancy by swallowing air. ▼

◀ A white uakari monkey resting on its paws. Sometimes called 'the Englishman', this animal gets its extraordinary red face from an extensive network of blood vessels that show through its near-transparent facial skin.

armadillo's tail would come in useful. I backed out of the hut and hurried up to Pablo. 'Your friend Antônio,' I said. 'Is he, er… mentally sound?'

'Not really. None of my friends is.'

'That's all right, then. But it's strange—I've had an unlucky run on madmen so far on my journey.'

I stuffed the gold down my boots, trouser linings and saddlebags, stashing it away in cigarette-lengths. I then gave Pablo the remainder of his money. He said he'd already spent the left halves, by gluing them together. The people he mixed with were too drunk to notice.

He wished me luck and I promised to send back the jaguar tail to show I was safely with the Indians. 'Come out of the jungle again, won't you, Benedito? I admire your pluck.'

'Thanks, Pablo.'

'Know what they used to say to me in Venezuela? "The jungle is an eternal prison." Prove them wrong, eh?'

The others came without a word. Raimundo flapped the reins. The two horses we were taking with us lifted their heads reluctantly, wrenching away last mouthfuls of grass and savouring them. Sunbathing lizards rattled the twigs strewn over the clearing as we moved off. The last of the scorched leaves crackled under our boots and then we were back in the jungle, in the dark again. Our hair was once more wringing wet and we wiped perspiration from our eyes.

Contact with the Wai-wai

Three days on, an hour after the morning mists had lifted, Raimundo said we were nearing the Indians. He was walking at the back horse's tail; Joshua and Moses were at the front; I was wedged between the two horses. After a long silence, plodding on like this, Raimundo said, 'All right. We'd better tie up the

A hyacinth macaw, a species of parrot, at the entrance to its nest. Usually noisy birds, macaws remain quiet during the nesting period so as not to attract potential predators.

horses now. From here, we go on by foot.'

'But we ain't nearly dere yet,' said Moses.

'Near enough for my liking,' said Raimundo.

Joshua said, 'Yeah. Dem Injuns is bad people. Dey got monkey tails. Dey got skin as white as bone.'

'So you said,' said Raimundo. 'Now, you stay put with the horses, Joshua, and don't make a sound. I don't want the Indians ever to know I was here. They might not be too pleased about you two either, you being goldminers as well.'

We tiptoed forward, leaving Joshua trembling alone on the track. I could dismiss Joshua's fear as ignorance, but Raimundo's worried me. I knew only that he had had a 'misunderstanding' with the Indians over the gold. That was what Pablo had said; knowing Pablo, it meant something far worse. The 'misunderstanding' had probably included eloping with the headman's most precious daughter and the Indians were dying for revenge. It would be something like that.

Raimundo jerked to a standstill and stiffened. Neither Moses nor I had heard the sound, but sensing something wrong we listened with him on the track, not daring to breathe.

I caught it the second time—a crack of a twig that came from ahead.

There were the usual jungle sounds: whistlings, chirpings and clickings; and far away a crash of leaves—monkeys passing through the canopy, yanking branches. Bird sounds, too—the squawks of parrots and the twitterings of smaller, hopping insect-eaters.

What did the other two think? Should we run? I wanted to see Raimundo's eyes, read his face. But both men were ahead of me on the track and I could see only the backs of their heads. They still seemed to be waiting for the sound to come again. Or perhaps they could hear it plainly and were thinking out our next move. Both men knew the jungle. They could hear the false notes; I couldn't. This thought made me feel small.

The air was steaming with the sweat of leaves and branches. As we waited, yellow wasps darted about in the stale air around us, trying to settle and lick the salt from our skin. The silence and the waiting were unnerving me.

Raimundo bent backwards to Moses. He was taking care not to move his feet and so snap a dry leaf. He cupped a hand around Moses' right ear so that he was speaking away from the direction of the noise. They were a stride away at the most, but I didn't hear the whisper.

The rust-freckled barrel of the shotgun came down from Raimundo's shoulder. He cradled it in his arms, gave it a smile as if he were cuddling a baby and signalled us to follow. We slunk forward. The forest had gone dead. The only sounds were our clumping boots. Were we going to be ambushed? I tried to prepare for it, holding my breath and bracing myself for the whooping shriek of the Indians. I pictured the leaves sprayed with blood and prayed I wouldn't show myself up by jumping with surprise when the attack came.

Nothing happened for a time. When it came, it was the others who jumped. We were crossing a stream bridged by a fallen tree, swaying in single file with our arms outstretched for balance. We couldn't have made ourselves more vulnerable. The bushes ahead crashed open. I stopped dead, with my mouth wide open, halfway across the log. Raimundo and Moses spun around on the spot, while I stood petrified in mid-stride. They shot past me in a blur and sprinted along the treetrunk, with their hands reaching out for the forest.

Still tottering over the stream, I saw the Indian—only one and he was small, with a short red loincloth and a knife. He had no bow and arrows. Joshua had been right; his skin was pale. I knew it was too late to make a run for it. I could hear the boots of the others pounding back down the track behind.

The Indian looked at me for a second. His skin was a milky caramel, but his hair was jet-black, cropped into a fringe at the front and plaited into a tail at the back, which ended in a heavy clump of silvery egret feathers.

I put the handle of my machete in his hand. He took the knife and eased it into his loincloth.

There was blood smeared on his face. I breathed out. No, it was paint; greasy smudges of it across both cheeks. I noticed that his hand, still on the knife, was shaking, his knuckles white with the pressure he was putting on the handle. We stood there, eye to eye. I could not read his intentions. His face wasn't hostile, or curious, or kind. He looked me over. I tried a few phrases in Portuguese. His expression didn't alter. I tried Warao, but when he still looked blank, it didn't surprise me. The Wai-wai are of Carib stock and belong to a different linguistic group. Now what?

The Indian pointed the knife at my stomach—not threateningly, but carelessly, as if the consequences of stabbing didn't matter. I kept talking, trying to establish a relationship, while that knifepoint pricked me like a blunt needle.

'*Tushau*,' I said, gesturing for him to lead me on. Pablo had said the word meant 'headman', or 'chief', in Wai-wai. The Indian grunted, then prodded me up along the track.

On the way, I remembered another of Pablo's words. I turned my head, still walking. '*Kiriwanhi*,' I said, pointing at my chest, '*kiriwanhi, kiriwanhi*. Me good, me good.' He spiked my shirt with his knife and we continued in silence.

The path split and thinned. Walking in front, I took too many wrong turns, so the Indian took the lead. He became agitated if I lagged more than a pace behind and when I did, he would wave the knife in my face.

The forest became darker, the path veered, then we broke into dazzling light. I had to cover my eyes. Still blinded, and wondering where the Indian was, I heard the lapping of running water a couple of steps ahead. A girl screamed; a dog barked.

I opened my eyes and saw river water thrashing with running women. They were naked and ran with cloth bundles and kicking babies tucked under their

▲ **Wasps gather round their nest in the rain forest. As the author discovered, they sometimes settle on humans to obtain salt from their skin.**

arms. They were sprinting for a group of palm huts, high up on the far bank. The huts were round and simple, with loosely plaited walls of leaves and drooping roofs with even looser thatching—I got the impression the huts had been thrown up in a hurry. These people weren't nomads, because they weren't practised in the art of making speedy tents. So maybe they were refugees; either that, or being drenched by rain didn't worry them.

I took off my hat. Beyond the village some children were mucking about in the river. They hadn't seen me. Some were diving into the water from an overhang of soft fawn rock. Others were cartwheeling down off tree vines, holding their noses and screaming as they dropped. When they did see me, they ran like the women, yelling across the water. When we came to the village, the women and children were a wall of waving arms, legs and bosoms. My Indian bawled at them and they backed away into their huts.

We walked into an empty central area of bare earth. The ground, as smooth and hard as concrete, reflected the sounds of gossiping in the surrounding huts. In the doorways were hot ash heaps and pots with blackened bottoms. A slender hand came out from one of the huts and whisked the contents of a bowl with a stick. The steam smelt of boiled ham.

NICHOLAS GUPPY, 1953

▲ A Wai-wai hut. The Wai-wai build a new village every two or three years, abandoning their old homes in order to move on to new hunting grounds.

The Indian stopped me and jabbed his knife through the doorway of a hut much smaller and more tightly woven than the rest. I went in.

I had to stoop, because of the lowness of the roof. The light coming through the door was blocked off behind me. The entrance was being stacked with spiky palm fronds, the spines along the mid-ribs like black hatpins. The walls were woven like a wicker basket. I leant against them, but they didn't give. This was not a hut, it was a cage.

I waited an hour by my watch, wondering when I was going to be allowed a drink. I was not worried, not as much as I might have been. The palm door wasn't fastened and I didn't get the impression I was a prisoner. But where could I have escaped to? I wearied of squinting through the wall chinks and so I listened to the women jabbering in their huts or walking by, scuffing their feet, tired in the heat.

Later I heard men talking and felt the earth vibrate under a stampede of feet. A hunting party had returned, I guessed. Through the hut walls I could see only the backs of children hopping up and down to get a better view over a crowd. The men must have had a good morning's hunt. As they distributed the meat, I heard one word repeated time and time again: 'Atchi, atchi, atchi'.

Two people with heavy steps were approaching. The doorway was cleared and two men stepped in. They had short, thick legs, compact torsos and hair cut into clumps above their ears. One had a pigtail—he was the one who had put me in this cage. They were talking loudly to me. I smiled, nodded and listened patiently, but I couldn't understand a word. They became more and more

◀ **River bathing is a favourite pursuit for all ages.**

worked up. All I could do was put up my hands and say I wanted the chief. '*Tushau, tushau, tushau.*'

The newer Indian bent down and joggled my arms. '*Garummmpppooo!*' he said. The hand on my arm was quivering. He pushed me back against the wall. He reached for my throat, but I ducked in time. This was getting nasty. Then I caught the word he had said before. *Garimpeiro*; he meant 'goldminer'.

I shook my head. 'No, no, no. *Não garimpeiro!*' I said. I beamed at them. I thought this had done the trick. The Indian was no longer bearing down on me. We would soon have this little misunderstanding straightened out.

He took a small package out of his red loincloth. I frowned. They had been rifling through my supplies. Then I saw what he had got and almost fainted. He held out his palm and sprinkled out one of my phials of gold. I watched it spiralling down and began to fidget. After he had emptied every grain out, he brought the gold up in front of my nose. He sniggered and blew it into my eyes. Before the sting had worn off, the thick wrist of the Indian made another grab for my windpipe. The situation was so frustrating and so stupid, and the grit in my eyes was so painful, that I lost my temper and exploded in English:

'Get your lousy hands off me!'

The Indians stopped the scuffle. Something had happened. The nearer Indian said, 'You talk *English?*'

I was stunned with surprise and relief: I could hardly breathe. I wiped my eyes and blinked out the gold. They were waiting.

I said, 'As a matter of fact, I do.'

They slapped their hairless thighs. 'Golly God. Dat make three of us!' And they both fell about laughing.

▲ The ever-changeable chameleon can hide itself among the green leaves of the canopy just as easily as on the brown floor of the forest.

A brown-throated three-toed sloth asleep in the branches of a cecropia tree. It relies on its immobility to remain hidden from harpy eagles. This specimen also shows the greenish hue of the camouflaging algae which grow in its fur. ▶

The false-leaf katydid relies primarily on camouflage by imitating a dead leaf on the forest floor. However, when danger threatens, it throws up its wings to reveal bright red undersides with 'eye' spots, which it hopes will frighten away an aggressor. ▼

▲ The horned frog also relies on camouflage to disappear among the leaves on the forest floor.

△ This caterpillar has a panoply of poisonous spines for protection, and warns off potential predators by clothing itself in lurid colours.

◁ The massive spines on this tree are thought to have evolved at a time when giant animals roamed the Amazon basin. Their purpose would have been to prevent such creatures from pushing the tree over to feed on its fruit or leaves.

Jungle Defence and Counter-Defence

FOR MOST PLANTS AND ANIMALS in the rain forest, life is a complex and dangerous game of survival. Animals need to eat without being eaten, and have therefore evolved a number of stratagems to succeed. For many, the simplest ploy is to stay motionless, or near-motionless, during the day, while relying on camouflage for protection. The sloth and the chameleon have perfected this technique, the sloth even allowing green algae to grow in its fur so that it is better hidden among tree leaves.

Conversely, some creatures make a virtue of being seen, having evolved lurid colours to warn predators that they are unpleasant or even poisonous to eat. The caterpillars of some butterflies, for instance, absorb chemical poisons from the plants they feed on and are consequently avoided by birds, which have learned that they are inedible. Many insects mimic poisonous ones, or even other menacing creatures. The owl butterfly

and the false-leaf katydid, for example, both have large 'eye' spots on their wings, which are intended to scare off predators.

Plants, amazingly, are no less inventive in finding ways of ensuring their survival. Some use only the simplest techniques—for example, growing protective thorns or oozing sticky substances like latex, which gum up insects' mouth parts. Others have developed complex chemical poisons to ward off browsing animals and insect larvae. Many trees are actively hostile to their neighbours, some actually littering the ground with toxic leaves that kill competitive seedlings.

Most remarkable, however, are those instances where symbiosis or cooperation takes place between plants and animals. Hummingbirds, for instance, will nest among dangerous, but sheltering, thorns. And several species of plant encourage fierce, biting ants to protect them by secreting nectar from specially located glands.

△ The tiny nest of a hummingbird, cunningly positioned among fiercely protective thorns.

A pair of ants feed on drops of nectar exuded especially for them. They will attack and eat the eggs and grubs of any insect that appear on their host plant. In some cases, ants such as these will even drive off browsing animals. ▷

CHAPTER 5

The Pig Duel

▲ **Among Amazonian Indians, bright decorations are very popular with men.**

IT WAS NOT A HUNTING PARTY that had returned to the village, but a luggage party. The two men, still wheezing from the laughing, let me peep out of the hut. I saw all my bags spread out and scattered. The Indians had flocked to them, and were picking through my things. One man was wearing my hat. He had tipped it to one side and was mincing across the clearing, showing it off. I tried to run forward to stop the rummaging, but I was held back.

'For now you wait. When headman come, you talk good why you have gold. If you no explain, then bad for you.'

'Yes,' said the Indian called Anarau, who had escorted me to the village. 'If you no explain, too bad for you!' He flourished his knife.

We watched the looting of my stores. Some of these people, like the Warao, wore a smattering of Western clothes. I saw a pair of shorts and a nylon miniskirt. But these were relics, so threadbare they were see-through. All the newer garments were red and from a rough cotton: aprons for women, short loin-cloths for men. Beads and tassels of soft breast-feathers swung around nearly everyone's necks, though those on the men were heavier and brighter.

Now, sitting in the white, mid-afternoon sun, my machetes were being used to slice open the food sacks. While dogs and children pattered in the spilt rice, two women were carving my trousers up between them.

'*Atchi*', the word I'd heard earlier, seemed to mean 'What is it?' They picked up my thick woollen socks. '*Atchi, atchi?* What is it?' The women shared the socks out and tried them on until they could find somewhere they fitted. One was stretched over a husband's head. Another pair was squeezed over a woman's breasts and my two men laughed so hard they had to clutch their stomachs.

The headman was every inch a king. He walked majestically and the villagers dispersed from what was left of my luggage to trail behind him as he strutted into the village. Two men walking humbly behind him were bearing between them a bristly pig, which hung upside-down with its trotters tied to a pole. It was the size of an overweight goat and it was alive: I saw it blink.

I was left alone, sitting crosslegged on the dust, while my two captors reported to the headman. He had a fringe and the rest of his hair was in a plait, which hung stiffly down his spine in a sheath of animal skin. Cotton wool covered his earlobes in white puffs and his short neck was ringed with beads. He wore a white armband that pinched into the muscle; a machete with a muddy brown blade projected from his loincloth. He looked over towards me and stared. He came nearer, still staring. His face was old and withered, but below the neck his skin was firm and young. The entire village trooped up two paces behind, squinting at me.

'You take Wai-wai gold?'

'No. I'm just journeying through.'

'Through where?'

'To the Trombetas,' I said, naming the first major river to the east.

'You want gold in Trombetas?'

'No, I'll move on east and east. I want to go to where the jungle stops.'

'If you go to end of jungle, you go wrong way.'

'Mmmmmmmm,' said one of the hunting Indians, nodding. He had a shotgun balanced on his shoulder. 'Only way home is way you come.'

'No, I want to go east.'

'*You* not going anywhere,' he said suddenly. '*You* staying here. Where your present to me?'

'I have brought many presents. Look over there.' He looked, I looked and the crowd turned and looked, but all we saw was the dust clearing and a few scattered grains of rice. Everything had gone.

'You bad man. You lie.'

'Your people have borrowed them. I'm hoping they are about to bring them back. If you ask your people, they will bring the gifts. Then I can present a special gift for you.'

'No. I will have *everything*,' he said. He barked a few orders and the villagers

A hunting party sets out on a river expedition, armed with spears, bows and arrows. ▼

went away sulkily to bring back the spoils. A few men stayed on and stood around with their arms folded, their eyes on the survival pouch around my waist.

'What else you got?' asked the headman, who seemed to be called Maipuri. He made no mention of what he had in mind, but his eyes were fixed on my survival pouch as well. I pulled a couple of picture postcards from my breast pocket. I'd been entertaining Joshua with them that morning. I put one in his hand. It showed the Queen smiling in state, with Windsor Castle as a backdrop.

'What this say?'

'It says, "Greetings from London".'

'Your chief sent *greetings*? But she a *woman*.'

'Yes, she's a woman.' I showed him the other card. 'This shows her house and there's a picture of a big village called London, where she lives. That red thing is a bus. And that's Tower Bridge, and that's—'

'Mmmm. Your chief has big hut.'

'That's Buckingham Palace. She is the most rich person in the world. She is waiting for me to come back safely.'

Maipuri scratched his navel, and looked down at the dark crescents of sweat spreading from my armpits. Two other men peered over his shoulder to look at the photos, but he flattened them against his chest as though they were a hand of cards.

'But she a *woman*?'

'Yes.'

The chief coughed uneasily, turned to his men and muttered something in Wai-wai. The villagers began to laugh, but it was the women who were laughing most and also clapping their hands. When they didn't stop after a while, the men turned on them and waved their fists.

'When this woman coming here?'

'After I've got back home safely.'

Maipuri frowned. 'What her name?'

'Elizabeth.'

'Lizbet,' said Maipuri to his men. To me he said, 'Lizbet like gold?'

'Very much.'

'Then you take gold from Maipuri to Lizbet? You agree?'

The Indians were standing looking at me on tiptoe, holding their breath and very still. I basked for a while in their gaze.

'All right, I agree.'

The men gave heavy, whistling sighs of relief. The headman glowed at his coup and the men looked at him with admiration.

'On one condition,' I said. There was a heartbroken silence.

'What you mean?' said Maipuri, slowly.

'You must help me on my way. With my baggage, of course.'

Maipuri mumbled to himself, flexing his fingers at his sides. Then his arms stiffened. He marched right up to me and said, 'Baggages *mine*. I want baggages.' He stepped back again, folded his arms and nodded triumphantly. 'I keep baggages. You my prisoner. So you make you quiet for now.'

'Mmmmm,' said the men. 'You quiet for now.'

They put their heads together for a good think.

My luggage was now back in a heap by my side. The Indians looked it up and down longingly. I felt stronger with it near again.

The Challenge

'I make decision,' said Maipuri, raising his right hand with his fingers to the sky for silence. 'My decision this. You prisoner, so you in trouble deep. You in trouble deep, so you need Lizbet. We also in trouble deep and need Lizbet. You talk that Maipuri is a friend.'

I said that the arrangement seemed satisfactory. Maipuri grinned at the men either side of him. One of them said that I looked pretty weak and might not make it out of the forest anyway. Maipuri said he had already thought of that.

'You strong?'

'I can do a hundred press-ups. Shall I show you?' I began to bend down.

Maipuri said he had a better idea. 'We watch you kill pig.'

'You do what?'

'You kill pig with bare hand.'

This was just the sort of predicament I had dreaded ever since first setting foot in South America. Imprisonment by hostile natives, interrogation in a foreign tongue, decimation of all my stores. Today, all my nightmares had cropped up in real life; all except the test of skill and daring. That was coming now.

'Fetch pig!' the headman yapped, and two bulky youths loped off.

How do you go about killing a pig, I wondered. As a boy, I'd earned holiday pocket money on a turkey farm, executing turkeys for the Christmas market. But a wild pig? That was different. I thought of Fritz's wild boar, the one that made a mess of a tree even after it had been shot through its head.

The crowd was stirring. A pathway was being made to let the pig through. It was causing quite an upset and must have been kicking out wildly. I imagined something the size of a horse, breathing in grunts, with yellow teeth jutting out like chisels. But what I saw was more moderate: a peccary, the fat, goat-sized animal I'd seen earlier, fresh from the forest. It was screaming and the scream

▲ **The wild pig, or collared peccary, of the Amazon has curved tusks and can fight ferociously when threatened.**

was a lonely cry for help. Never say die, piggy, I thought. Look who you're up against.

I took a couple of steps closer to the pig, into the centre of the village. The crowd encircled me; only twenty-five or so Indians. We could see each other in the open for the first time. My view was of soft tawny skins, feathers, glossy black hair and rainbow hoops of beads. Some women had babies resting in the crooks of their arms like handbags. Their view was of a man a foot taller than anyone they'd ever seen alive, with blue eyes and green, sweat-blotted khaki. They were lusting after my clothes and confused by the colour of my eyes.

'What you waiting for?' said Maipuri.

The pig was forced to the ground, as an act of generosity. The Indians were blue in the face, struggling to maintain their grip. Seeing me over it, the pig squealed again and humped and flopped on the ground like a seal. The crowd was swaying for the best view. The noise was of the cockfighting crowd of Icabaru: jeering, taunting, daring. I felt as apprehensive as the pig, crouching in the middle of that crowd. Neither of us wanted to fight, but like the cocks we were going to have to.

I decided I'd go for a throttle hold. That was my best chance. First, I'd hold the beast down with my weight, then I'd go for its throat, which was as thick as a mule's. I hadn't heard of anyone wringing a wild pig's neck, but I thought that in the Bible Samson had strangled a lion once.

I took hold of the pig's ears. They were rubbery and damp, like bacon rind.

The Indians leapt back. The pig and I were alone in the ring. Neither of us moved. I was on my knees; the pig was on its side, blinking its white eyelashes and blowing up dust with its snorts. The pig wasn't trapped, it was waiting.

'He clever,' said a man in the crowd. 'He know how to fight.' Who was he talking about—the pig or me?

The pig kicked out. I rolled on to its stomach and flattened it to the ground. I began to walk my fingers up through its bristly hair, against the growth, in the direction of its throat. The skin was dry and hairy, as well as prickly. The pig rolled its eyes when it realised my fingers were slipping towards its neck; it buckled and jolted to dislodge me. Soon I was winded and had to bring back my hand to keep the animal under me.

The crowd crept in and roared, thinking the pig was gaining the upper hand. I could feel the strength of its lungs under me. A man's foot stamped near my nose and sprayed sand into my face. I thought it was deliberate. The crowd roared as I winced. Were they for me or against me? I had no way of telling. One girl at least was egging me on. Our eyes met, as I was winded again by a loose trotter. She grinned—her teeth were brilliant white—and nudged a girlfriend. But now the pig was working itself free.

It was slippery with perspiration and my fingers were numb. I lurched back on to the animal to give my fingers a rest. The crowd swelled forward in a tide. Now they thought I was moving in for the kill. I had heard the same gasping roar a second or two before the end of each cockfight; but this crowd was wrong. I was weakening and the pig was strong. The men at the front of the crowd were again flicking up dirt in my face. One foot trapped my hair. It *was* deliberate this time. I was so annoyed that I thought, right, if *they* are going to cheat, then so am I. I loosened my grasp on the pig. It twisted itself up on to its hindquarters and took a deep breath. Before it was away, I butted it into the crowd. We were right into the forest of legs. The crowd tried to back off, but several men and women toppled. In the confusion I hunched up, tugged Jorge's knife from my boot and smacked the blade up into the pig's throat.

The pig's screaming stopped. The roar of the crowd stopped. I hid my knife away. Had anyone seen? The blood was spouting everywhere; it made my fingers stick together.

The crowd was stunned. It had missed the kill. It had been cheated. The girl who had been egging me on smeared the blood on her cheeks in bold stripes and laughed. That was the only sound. Perhaps they had all been betting on the pig to win. I got to my feet, wiping my face on my shirtsleeve.

'You got strong teeth,' said the headman. 'You bite deep into pig.'

I smiled and touched my teeth. 'Mmmm-mm. Sharp,' the crowd agreed.

'He kill like jaguar kill,' said one man. 'He dangerman.'

'You stay for ever if you like, Dangerman,' said Maipuri.

I asked Maipuri not to call me that. It might lead to trouble. 'Call me Benedito.'

'I call you Mad Benedito, because you mad to leave forest the long way.' I said '*louco*' meant 'mad' in Portuguese, and so I became Louco Benedito.

I went for a dip in the stream, leaving the men behind to poke at the pig carcass. A very long way downriver I threw off my clothes and dived in. The cool bite of the water was invigorating. It was smooth as a millpond here and as green as the overhanging leaves.

I had wanted only a short bathe, but I was kept in the water by the appearance of the girl with red smears of blood across her cheeks. She came skipping along the bank while I was up to my neck amongst some ropy tree roots on the other side. She came to my pile of clothes and stood looking around for me, smoothing back her hair. I kept still and her eyes missed me, so she bent over and began sorting through my garments. It was the boots she was interested in. She tipped them out, one at a time, rolling back their tongues. I knew that she was after the knife. She must have seen me use it. Was she going to tell the others, or just keep it for herself? She shook the boots, but nothing dropped out. She hurled them down, looked about her and sprinted off.

The knife was tucked into my survival belt around my waist.

I passed her on my way back along the riverbank. She had stepped out of her red skirt and was splashing water over her face.

An Indian woman removes her beaded jewellery before bathing in the river.

Her nose was touching the water and her hair streamed down like weed in the current. She must have heard my footsteps, but she didn't open her eyes.

It was time for presents. The pig was on the chopping stone, the fires were being stoked up and everyone was seated in family clusters at the headman's feet. My stores were beside one of the huts, in two neat mounds. The two halves of my split trousers lay on the crest of each; the beans had been mixed in with the rice and sugar; but not a thing was missing.

To the headman, Maipuri, I presented one of my Brazilian machetes. He showed me his own. It was better, tempered from Sheffield steel, like mine. I doled out ten cartons of Benson & Hedges cigarettes. They bit off the filters and chewed them, pulling faces. Then they sat dumb. Needles, fishing hooks, cotton and beads—whatever I produced was a let-down.

Maipuri eventually said, 'Lizbet. We want see Lizbet more.'

I brandished a stack of pictures: Buckingham Palace, Piccadilly Circus, Tower Bridge, the Houses of Parliament and 'Lizbet'.

Hands snatched them away. The men and women sighed with heads together. 'Mmmmmmmmmm. She beautiful.'

The Godman

That night I squatted with Maipuri by the fireside and drank soapy cassava beer from a gourd, while we ate some of the richest cuts of the pig. I reminded him that he had said the group was in trouble and needed the help of my headman. What had he meant?

Not many rainy seasons back, Maipuri said, they had lived in the land called Guyana, on the other side of the Acarai Hills. They had picked up scraps of English there, on the upper reaches of the Essequibo River, from a 'Godman', a Christian missionary. The man had been good to them in many ways, but he had evicted the witch doctor, sending him off into the forest. 'But *more* terrible,' said Maipuri, 'he say is wrong to take two wives.' That was the final straw. They decided to lose the Godman in the jungle. The plan was less than half-success-ful, though, because most of the tribe had drifted back in dribs and drabs. The Wai-wai's weakness is that they like decorating themselves. Some had got hooked on wearing clothes. Anyway, Maipuri's group of five families had walked on into the forest. Unfortunately, the government had also decided it was development time for the Indians and sent a junior office clerk off on their trail to do the job.

'Well, dis poor boy arrive. He never seen Wai-wai before and he very afraid. His knees quaking. He think we going to eat him. But we calm him. We sets him drinking cassava beer. After one moon go by we gets him sleeping in a special hut with woman. We ask him if he want to join us and live wid trees. He says he can't do dis. "Orders is orders." Den we break de news. We not hanging around no more. We going many moon into forest. He say, "Please don't leave me here alone. My career die." He been sent out to tame us. "Well," we says. "Sorry,

▲ A group of Indians sheltering from the rain under an enormous banana leaf.

mister, can't do dat, we gotta go." So dat night we disappears and next morning he wakes and we all vanished, Louco Benedito. Mmmmm, he all alone. Maybe he die out dere wid his career. We dunno. We walks to here. We here now, but we always keep moving. Soon we go to River Mapuera. Mmmmm, Louco Benedito, *dat's* why we here.'

This group of Wai-wais were on the run, as I'd originally thought. That was why they built their huts like flimsy tents.

Maipuri said that one of his two wives had died. She had been struck down by a jaguar while strolling back from bathing a few sunrises ago. It was a shame, but she was an old woman anyway, and he had taken another woman when she had lost her vigour and was not able to satisfy him.

'Didn't she mind you having an extra wife?'

'Mind? Why she mind? She *like* it. Now she more important wife. She get second wife to do all work. Mmmmm… she happier dan ever, Louco Benedito!'

My hut was downwind of the fire. That night I slept in its warm, woodsmoke sparks. I slept late. When I came out into the morning sunshine, my hair smelt of smoke. The women were already milling around the pots, and the fires were hissing with dripping pig-fat. The ground was sticky from a night shower and my boots were clumsy. But I kept them on. I had grown sick of having to dig parasites out from under my toenails with a needle. Most were planted there by jigger fleas, which left the eggs tidily under the skin to incubate.

I took a stroll behind the village to a scrubby patch of jungle. I had to beat through what I thought was a thicket of bamboo to get there, but suddenly I realised it was a garden and I had wiped out a tract of sugarcane. The plants which told me this was a garden were the cassava and yams swelling in the soil like oversized potatoes. I walked along their furrows, whistling, then came to some cotton plants, with the white woolly puffs fixed on to their twigs. Three women came by, buckled up under the weight of banana leaf stacks propped on their backs. They smiled at each other when they saw me, but kept on walking.

I went to see where they'd come from and, through a bed of trumpet-flowered plants, which I knew were tobacco, saw the girl who'd tried to steal my knife. She was beyond what looked like a gooseberry bush, with her head up in a banana tree, cutting down leaves and laying them in a heap by her feet. Her skin was caramel-coloured and paler than I remembered, but perhaps that was because I was comparing her in my mind to Zorola of the Orinoco Delta. This girl was older, fifteen or sixteen, with a fringe right into her eyes.

She shifted the tarpaulin-sized leaves as though they were feathers. Her body was so powerful and she moved with such finesse, I couldn't help but gawp.

I ducked my head and crept away, back to the village. I wandered around the huts, stalked by children, and afterwards lay in my hammock daydreaming. All I wanted to do was go back to the garden and take another peep at the girl.

The cassava or manioc root is a staple food in the Amazon and requires lengthy grating, straining and roasting to remove its toxins. The roots can also be fermented to make beer.

▲ A group of Yanomami Indian children in north-west Brazil, with their *maloca* or communal house in the background. The boy in front is carrying an enormous bow and arrow.

▲ A Yanomami woman preparing vines for basket weaving. She is wearing traditional adornments: leaf armbands and slivers of wood piercing her nose and mouth.

◀ A group of Amahuaca Indians in Peru preparing an alcoholic drink for their banana festival. They chew the fruit and then spit it out into bowls, where it ferments with their saliva to become a potent brew.

Life in an Indian Village

I N THEIR SCATTERED VILLAGE SETTLEMENTS, many Indians of the Amazon rain forest follow a way of life that has remained unchanged for centuries. The communities of 60 or more people are wholly dependent on the forest for their livelihood. They build their houses out of wood and thatch them with palm leaves; cultivate crops of maize, gourds and manioc in clearings; catch fish and turtles in the rivers; and hunt game in the forest with astonishing skill, using bows and arrows, snares, spears and blowpipes. The vast treasure chest of the forest also provides them with drugs, medicines and poisons.

Life is generally a communal affair, and many villages have at their centre a huge communal hut, known as a *maloca*. This is often an elaborate structure made of palm leaves, and sometimes with a large opening in the middle of the roof. The *maloca* houses many families, each with its own space to hang hammocks and keep belongings. Clearly, privacy is not a leading concern here. Rather, cooperation and sharing are what matter, and what survival depends upon. So the men collaborate to fish and hunt, while the women remain behind to cook, weave, and tend the crops and children.

Under these conditions, and in such isolation, social activity is very important. Neighbouring clans will regularly exchange festive visits, at which everyone is decorated with body paint, feathers and headdresses. Alcoholic drinks may be specially brewed from fermented fruit, and hallucinogens taken for heightened pleasure. On special occasions, such as harvest festivals, the dances and songs tell of the cycles of nature that are so important to village life.

▲ **An Indian woman suckling her baby and a tiny monkey. In many communities, animals are virtually members of the family. Pet monkeys can often be seen grooming their owners.**

Boys of the isolated and fiercely independent Txikao tribe in the Mato Grosso. They are dressed and painted for a ceremony to pay respect to the spirits of the dead. ▼

▲ **Arrow-making is a highly skilled occupation that requires hours of careful labour. Note how the feathers on this arrow are spiralled to give it greater stability in flight.**

CHAPTER 6

Hunting the Tapir

IN THE VILLAGE I WAS PLAGUED by flies and children. The flies came from the forest, the children from the huts. Peering into these, I saw floors of shredded bark and straw, and babies being rocked in hammocks. I usually caught a muggy whiff, even at midday when the sun had burnt up most of the smells outside.

The children often had dogs under their arms: happy mongrels with brown-and-white splodges. Dogs were everywhere, perched in hammocks, snug against the babies, snoring on shelves up in the palm roofs, or diving into rock pools down by the river with the children. They were part of the family.

Maipuri said he knew some Wai-wai Indians on the Cafuini, a tributary of the Trombetas. He would let me take two of his best men. Whether the Indians there knew anyone further away, over to where the sun rose, he couldn't say. I would have to take a gamble.

Maipuri said he wanted me to go off hunting with some of his men for the day. I must pick two of them as my guides for my expedition. He hoped one would be his son. It would be an honour for the boy and for himself. He squeezed my shoulder and looked up into my eyes.

A father relaxes with his children and a favourite dog. ▷

'Maipuri be mighty sad, Louco Benedito, if my son not chosen.'

'Maipuri must not fear,' I said. 'Any son of yours will be strong and brave, I'm sure.'

I hoped his son wasn't too much of a fool, and thought it shouldn't be too difficult to fix up. I'd find out who the son was and make sure he was honoured; a piece of cake. Everyone would be as pleased as Punch.

'To make justice good, I telling my son not to be telling who he is.'

Damn.

'He sleep with another family.'

Maipuri sent a boy to fetch the men from fishing, clouting him on the back of the ear to make him run at the double. I waited by his hut, in the black shadow of the roof's eave.

The women were spinning cotton, twiddling fluffy balls of it with their fingers and stretching it out into thread with their toes. Little girls fed it to the women's hands. The children looked bored. They watched me swatting flies and tweaked the dogs sitting on their laps. The women's faces were creased up with concentration; they drew out the cotton without ever glancing up. A pair of small, dark birds, with stumpy rounded wings and turkey wattles, flew over, croaking.

'*Hannaqua!*' screamed a child, pointing at the birds, which looked ungainly and prehistoric.

'*Hannaqua! Hannaqua!*' the stupid birds called back.

The earth was baking to a dust pan and the cotton spinners got up to move out of the sun's glare. I suddenly wondered why I had seen no old people here; not a single grey hair.

A train of boys ran into the village, whooping. They dived into the huts and bounced out again with parrot feathers speared through their ears and white bands around their arms and legs.

'This your hunting party,' said Maipuri. 'You choose guide from these.'

'But…but they're only *boys*.' I simply had to put my foot down here. I required skilled guides, not children.

'They *good* boys.'

I closed my eyes.

'And you take Tautau, if you like,' said Maipuri, jabbing a finger at a man who was striding up from the river with a fistful of arrows. Maipuri explained that this man Tautau would be the lead guide and I was to choose one boy and have two other porters.

Tautau was a brawny man in his mid-twenties. His hair was plaited into a tail interwoven with white duck feathers. He wore shorts, leftovers from the Godman, he said. They looked it; he must have been given them as a child. They had worn away between his legs and there was a cotton loincloth beneath.

I went to get my machete. When I was back, Maipuri put a shotgun in my hand. It was also a 'leftover' from the Godman, along with all the cartridges, a canvas bag for them and a tin crucifix, which was kept in the bag as a lucky charm. The Indians said it was the very one the Godman used to wear around his neck. They took it from him while he was asleep the night they fled.

▲ **This Wai-wai warrior shows off his magnificent pigtail plaited with beads and feathers.**

Arrow Poisons

FOR THE AMAZON INDIANS, bows and arrows and blowpipes are essential equipment for hunting the birds and monkeys that live way out of reach in the forest canopy. To increase the effectiveness of their arrows and darts, they smear the tips with poison so that even a small nick will bring an animal crashing to the ground.

Curare, the most commonly used poison, is derived from the *strychnos* vine. Water is filtered through shavings from the bark of the vine, then reduced by boiling to a thick brown paste containing the agent turbocurarine. When this powerful nerve toxin enters the bloodstream, it paralyses the muscles and causes death by suffocation when the lungs cease to function. Another poison used for hunting is the sticky resin extracted from the bark of the virola tree, a muscle relaxant which causes animals to drop from their branches when hit. The deadliest poisons of all, however, come not from plants but from a number of garishly coloured frogs, which secrete lethal toxins from glands in their skin. They are all appropriately known as arrow-poison frogs.

▲ These cane arrows have been tipped with nerve poisons wiped from the backs of arrow-poison frogs.

The arrow-poison frog protects itself from predators by secreting powerful toxins. ▶

The shotgun barrel was sprinkled with dirt. Maipuri tutted when I said it wouldn't do and snatched an arrow from Tautau, which he rammed up and down the barrel from both ends. The barrel looked spotless, but now needed a good wipe over with oil. Maipuri was looking at me with disdain and I didn't dare mention it. I had ruined a perfectly good arrow, he said.

The arrows were made from 'grass', like the canes you use for running garden beans along—taller than Tautau, but a lot shorter than me—and they were smooth and balanced. They had flights of feathers, which were curved to set the arrow spinning to its target. The tips were poisoned and kept safely in a separate quiver. The poison must be brewed for many days, Maipuri explained.

It is a secret process and the brewing is done in a special little hut, well away from women. Some of the poisons are from the worst snakes, like the fer-de-lance, and a bark, a vine and a leaf. All are pounded and mashed up in a pot, brewed and brewed for days, and kept on the boil until the mixture hardens into a treacle. Then the tips are dipped in it. That was all Maipuri would tell me. Later he confided that other Indians, the Wapishanas, had made this batch.

They had swopped the poison for a Wai-wai cassava grater.

The four boys were ill-disciplined, over-eager and noisy. Tautau ordered them to tag behind, which meant they kicked my heels and shunted me along the riverbank path at jogging pace without letting me pause for breath. I was in a huff. We were not going to catch anything. I had never known such a riotous hunting party. I did not want a boy guide for my expedition and I didn't know how I was going to select the headman's son.

The boys knew they were being watched and were all desperate to be chosen as my guide. But they were also under observation by Tautau. They were being initiated into adulthood. Today's hunting was one of a series of tests. So why on earth were we setting out when the sun was high, just as the forest animals were tucking themselves into their nests and burrows? It seemed stupid.

We walked upstream. The boys kicked through the water, upsetting the birds from their nests miles ahead. I asked why Tautau didn't tell them off.

He laughed. 'We go on and on.' He pointed through the branches to the sun. 'When he strong, we at home of *maipuri*.'

Maipuri? But we had just left him in the village.

'We go and kill him, Louco Benedito.'

This was certainly going to be some initiative test. Kill the headman?

'*Maipuri* taste good.'

I decided the headman shared his name with an animal. 'What is it, this *maipuri*?'

Tautau instructed the boys to imitate it for me. They giggled helplessly.

'*Atchi?*' they squeaked, scuffling through the riverbank grasses, pawing the roots with hoof-shaped fingers. They showed how it cocked its head to listen and scratched off ants from its back.

It was a tapir. I guessed that from the way it smelt the air with its rubbery trunk-nose.

We were still on the river when the sun was high, but the river was only a trickle. We were at the tapir's home. The boys had gone silent; they stepped delicately through the water as if they were herons.

The forest was fast asleep. Tautau spoke softly to us. Then the boys stood to attention and pleaded silently with him for the bow and arrows; they were given to a boy with a garish red feather in his ear. His name was Ak-ak, the sound of a frog. He gave a snide smile at the three other boys, who pulled sour faces.

Tautau waved them away and they merged with the forest on the left bank. We crossed over to the other side, scrambled up the steep rock and looked back down, almost from canopy level. The river swung lazily around this rock, and here it was deep and had a duckweed smell. The four boys were worming up through the undergrowth. Above them was the tapir, mottled black and white and lying back dreamily in an open patch; to get to it undetected was not going to be easy.

We loaded our shotguns. As their test of skill, the boys

Many tribes use enormously long arrows. Here a young bowman takes aim at a quarry in the branches of a tree. ▼

▲ The vegetarian tapir is an ungainly combination of rhinoceros and horse, with a short, flexible trunk which it uses to search for food. It can often be found near the banks of rivers.

would each have to touch the tapir before Ak-ak fired his poisoned arrow.

'Ak-ak must touch it as well?'

'No. Ak-ak job easy. He just shoot *maipuri* here'—he tapped his neck—'and best not shoot a boy either. Poison kill easy.'

They were closing in from the rear. Ak-ak was crouching in front, where the animal would run to. He looked small, waiting by himself behind a bush. He was fumbling with an arrow, slotting on the poisonous tip and hitching the arrow on to the string.

Tautau's instructions to me were simple: if something went badly wrong—if the tapir charged and crunched up a boy—there was nothing much we could do. We should fire our shotguns only when the tapir was in full view. The animal was the size of a heifer and we had to score direct hits on its head.

Tautau began to strum his fingers on the rock. The boys were taking too long. They'd lost their nerve. We watched the four, white, scared faces. From here we could almost see their trembling.

Then the tapir lurched in its sleep.

One boy jumped. The two others thought he was making a dash forward and sprang out. The tapir rolled to its feet, snorting. The two boys got to its rump, tapped it and took to their heels. The third boy arrived just in time to catch the eye of the tapir. They were face to face, the tapir with its nose trumpeting and its jaws wide open. It bent its head and charged. The other two boys weren't watching; they were on their stomachs clutching their heads, ducking the arrow. But the arrow was still in Ak-ak's bow and he was waiting for a clear shot. We watched the tapir crash into the first boy's legs and a frail shriek echoed up.

Tautau was screaming, 'Ak-ak! Ak-ak!'

But Ak-ak's target was blocked by the mangled boy, who was draped across the tapir's neck. The tapir dived for the water, still jockeying him along.

'*Ak-ak!*'

The arrow flew. It struck between the tapir's front legs. The animal bellowed and pranced, snapping the arrow in two.

The boy slithered off. The tapir plunged into the pool and, hampered by the water, made an easy target. My shot missed. The tapir cantered on upstream, streaming blood from Tautau's shot, with Ak-ak at its tail. There was blood on the wounded boy also. He was lying head down in an inch of water.

Tautau got there first. He hoisted him into the air and beat on his chest to get some life into him. The boy groaned. Tautau laid him on riverbank reeds, propping his head on a green boulder.

Once we had crowded round, the boy began to writhe and contort his face. Tautau held his head tight on his lap with the grip of one hand. Upriver there were high-pitched yells.

'Ak-ak catch *maipuri*,' said Tautau, but didn't look up. 'This boy called Yakka-yakka,' he said, in a broken voice. 'This boy my only son.'

I said I thought Yakka-yakka wasn't too badly hurt. One of his shinbones might be cracked; maybe a rib or two. I glossed over what really worried me: Yakka-yakka was clutching his sides and trying to curl up like a loop caterpillar. I thought his kidneys or liver might be punctured.

Ak-ak came back running. He jabbered away to us about his fine shot. Tautau said that the women of the village would be coming shortly to heave the *maipuri* meat back to the village. Ak-ak was to stay and fend off the vultures until then. Ak-ak scuttled off upstream without looking back. I flushed Yakka-yakka's cuts with water. Tautau sent another boy off to find a special herb. He returned with a sprig of silky-leafed plant, which we strapped over the bruises with a stringy sapling. Knotting it up tight, we made the boy convulse.

I wanted to stretcher Yakka-yakka away, but Tautau scorned the idea and simply folded him over his shoulder. That was too much for the boy, so he was borne piggyback. To keep Yakka-yakka hanging on, I had to bind his wrists together with a vine, so they were locked around Tautau's throat. He hung like a hunk of meat in a butcher's shop window.

We met the women wading upriver after about an hour. Tautau wouldn't let anyone touch his son. He pushed away his wife and stared blindly ahead.

'He my only child. He my only son.' He said it again and again as we went lumbering on. 'He my only son, he not die.' When we got to the village he was still mouthing the words, 'He not die. He my only son.'

White Man's Magic

Maipuri was thunderstruck by the news. The village had no witch doctor to heal the boy. Ever since their flight from Guyana, they had had no one to administer medicine. 'My people dying,' moped Maipuri. 'Each new moon, one more die.'

The village was wrapped in stillness. Children stopped romping with the dogs. The dust settled. Leaves fluttered into the yard and rattled in the evening breeze through the empty village. Yakka-yakka lay on a shelf in Tautau's hut. His bad leg was blue. I tied it in a splint of arrow grass, and I gave him a dose of morphine. The bone looked straight, but the boy was sweating, so we dabbed him with cold water. Tautau sat perched in a hammock, holding Yakka-yakka's hand. Maipuri ordered a boy to fetch the Godman's crucifix. It was a last resort and stooping this low grieved him. He hung it around the boy's forehead, as he'd seen the priest do to an old woman who had been gripped by coughing fits. She'd died, but Maipuri thought it worth a try.

I left the hut for some more cold water. The village was a liverish yellow in the setting sun and it was so quiet in the yard I could still hear Yakka-yakka's throaty breaths.

On my return up the river-path I met a cloud of tobacco smoke. I traced the smell back to Tautau's hut.

Yakka-yakka looked very hot and his groaning was desperate. Maipuri had been chain-smoking cigarettes and puffing the smoke into the boy's face. It was a trick they had learnt from the witch doctor, to clear off bad spirits. I pretended I thought Yakka-yakka was suddenly on the road to recovery and they stopped.

But his eyes stayed red and swollen long after the smoke had cleared.

'He cry,' said Maipuri, peering at the boy's eyes.

'No. He no cry,' said Tautau. 'He man. He my son.'

I said I'd watch over Yakka-yakka for a while, if they liked. Both men left me alone in the dark hut. The boy murmured something. I tilted a cup of cool water towards his mouth, but he shrank back from it. I tried to insist; he clamped his lips together, his face tightened and he held his whole body stiff. I put the cup down and heard him say 'Mooder'.

'Mother?' I said into his face, and he smiled. The effort made him wince.

'Mooder.' He wanted his mother. He had been afraid to ask in front of the men.

I knew Tautau and Maipuri would be furious if I let his mother anywhere near him, so I just said. 'When you're better. Then you see your mother. Tautau wants you to be strong.'

'*Mooder!*' he choked. He pulled my fingers to his face. I felt the wetness of his cheeks and the weak quavering in his lungs as he sobbed. 'Mooder! Mooder!' There was nothing I could do, but squeeze his hand: I told him he would be better soon.

Maipuri and Tautau came back in. 'You working good magic?' I released the boy's hand, but Yakka-yakka snatched mine back and wouldn't let go.

Tautau grinned. 'You working good magic, Louco Benedito.'

An hour later, when the night was lit with silver moonshine outside, the boy suddenly closed his eyes and his face slackened. Tautau sank back into his hammock and moaned. Maipuri ran from the hut without a word. But I had Yakka-yakka's hand in mine and I knew the boy had only gone to sleep.

A Farewell Feast

The tapir was brought into the village in chunks, late that night. We heard the procession miles away and the warbling songs of the women were louder than the night bats and river frogs. Maipuri was celebrating Yakka-yakka's recovery with cassava beer; he wandered out with an empty gourd in his hand to greet them. The dogs ran out with the children and came back ahead of the women. Everyone wanted to carry a piece of tapir. They came running, clutching wicker baskets of offal and casks containing the liver and heart. Ak-ak danced at the front, holding up the tapir's head.

The meat was smoked in the night fires, wrapped in the banana leaves I'd seen cut that morning.

When I awoke at daybreak—the fat had been spitting in the flames all night—the meat had been stuffed out of reach of the dogs in the roof eaves and Yakka-yakka was able to raise a smile. Tautau looked worse. He hadn't slept a wink. He kept tweaking Yakka-yakka's leg, even though the boy screamed, to see if he would be able to dance at my farewell feast that night.

I was called to Maipuri's hut. Maipuri lay in his hammock and his wife in a lower one, within arm's reach of the fire.

She didn't look up. She was weaving a basket and breastfeeding a boy of three or four years old, with little white stumps of teeth, round eyes and thick knots of beads through his ears.

'You chosen guide for journey?' said Maipuri.

I coughed. 'Er…'

'Well, you tell people tonight. You choose my son. He proud to be chosen by you. Tonight big feast. Tonight you happy. Tomorrow you leave. Then you come back after many moons with Lizbet. Mmmmmmmmm. Maipuri like you very much.' He gave a child's smile.

'I like you too.'

'Mmmmmmm. You like stay many, many moons?'

I said I couldn't. I just had to get home again.

'Maybe you want better hut. I make for you. It take only two suns.'

I had to decline the offer, but I walked into the sunshine smiling, with children stalking out behind. In a couple of days I had become completely at home here.

'Or maybe you seen girl you like.' Maipuri's head was poking from the dark of the hut. 'Anarau, he got daughter who say she like you. She watch you. She say you strong. You make good husband, she say.'

I was not in the least surprised to find out who Anarau's daughter, Yimshi, was. And now I knew why she'd reminded me of Zorola when I spied on her in the garden. It was because circumstances were conspiring to bring us together in the same way. And what was more, Maipuri had a lot to gain, he thought, by adopting me. I was a man strong enough to bite through a pig's neck, a man with a woman chief, the richest chief in the world.

In the milky dawn sunshine the women were wrapping up the last of the tapir in parcels of rubbery green leaves. The men were shaping arrows. They twirled the arrow grass in the smoke of the fire, to iron out the curves. Then, sitting on logs, they rolled the arrows along the length of their arms, squinting along the shafts; five feet long from the flight feathers, through their fingertips, through their toes to the wood shavings in the dust. Other men sat on their haunches, shaping feathers. Maipuri said that the only time women squatted like this was when they were giving birth. It was more becoming for them to kneel.

The children were dressing up the dogs, weaving yellow parrot feathers into cotton and fixing them on as collars.

Tautau and Anarau were out in the forest, putting the initiate boys through another test of manhood. This time they were stealing honey from a beehive, which was lodged in the crown of a coca tree. Yakka-yakka had been dragged along to stand at the foot of a tree and watch the other three boys knock out the nest. Maipuri said he couldn't risk me going to watch. 'Bee get angry. Bee hate thieves. Bee go killing.'

'What about Yakka-yakka? He should be lying down, taking some rest. Besides, he won't be able to run.'

Maipuri said, 'Even dead men run when bee coming after them.'

And the bees did come. They flushed the Indians through the trees—they ran

▲ Meat is wrapped in banana leaves before being hung over a fire to smoke overnight.

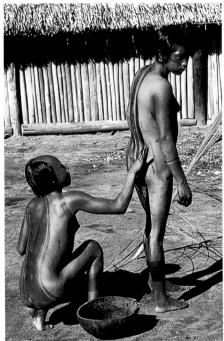

▲ Women assist each other in applying festive body paints.

▲ The urucu or annatto plant is the source of the bright red dye used for body paint. Its seeds can be rubbed directly onto the skin, or boiled to produce a sticky paste which is also an effective insect-repellent.

like stampeding forest pigs, then dived into the water and stayed under. Maipuri was right; Yakka-yakka could sprint quite easily, even with a broken leg.

The bees smelt honey in the village and pestered all of us. They became more and more irritable as the sun began to burn. They made the dogs whine and two babies had to be dipped in the river and then swaddled in a poultice of leaves.

Later a burst of rain drove the bees away into the trees.

From the hammock where I was dozing, I saw the men begin to paint themselves. The camp now smelt of incense instead of hair and dogs. I traced the smell to the red greasepaint they were wiping over their faces, chests and legs in stripes and spots. They highlighted their doodles with charcoal-black paint. Maipuri came from his hut with red macaw feathers arching from his nose. His pigtail was cobalt-blue with toucan plumes, clumped at the end with a parrot's yellow-and-green flight feather and the electric-blue breast feathers of humming birds. He had combed palm oil into his hair to give it a blue sheen.

'Louco Benedito, what you think?' He smoothed his thumbs along the length of his nostril feathers. 'Beautiful?'

'You look magnificent.'

He puffed himself up and strutted around the camp, while the men studded their ears with mother-of-pearl and hung last-minute tassels over their buttocks.

The women took less trouble. Even the dogs were better dressed than they were. The few who bothered were the nubile ones and they merely smudged red paint in lines over their cheeks and slung a few beads over their breasts.

There was one exception. At the other end of the village, Yimshi was twirling like a model in front of her girlfriends. She was too preoccupied to notice me and I was glad, because of what I had gathered from Maipuri about her ambitions in my direction.

I sat with Maipuri as the food roasted on stakes in the fires. He said he hadn't seen so much meat for ages; the jungle was a hard place in which to live—that was why the initiation ceremonies were taken so seriously. Every man had to prove he could support a wife. And for the women it was just the same; they also had to prove they could endure discomfort and at puberty were sometimes sent off alone to bring a queen bee back alive, which meant cracking open the nest and rummaging in its core for her.

He said he would never forget the time when Yimshi was ordered to do this as a little girl. She came back with the whole nest in her hands. The bees were so angry they almost wiped out the Indian village.

I asked why Yimshi hadn't been married yet. Maipuri said it was the woman who chose whom she wanted to marry, and when she fancied a man, all she did was sling her hammock in his hut and start cooking for him. Simple as that. Usually the girl's father persuaded him to move into her family hut. And, the very next day if possible, he would start cutting a field for crops. But not Yimshi.

An Indian girl, suitably
decorated for the
occasion, enjoys herself
at a village feast.

She was biding her time. No one had seduced her, though many had tried.

In the twilight, as the mosquitoes droned up from the river to the village for their night feed, fresh banana leaves were laid at the entrance to the huts. Maipuri's wife joined us, and one of Yimshi's girlfriends set down a gourd of stew in our midst and some mashed banana pâté. Before we had started on those, a girl came up and dangled ropes of tapir meat for us to cut off with our hunting knives. We were brought slabs of pig-fat and more stews. We worked from dish to dish. It wasn't enjoyable; it was a tortuous marathon of sweet and bitter concoctions which, apart from the meat, all tasted like boiled rhubarb.

The four initiate boys were alone in a quiet circle, nursing their bee stings and gobbling down the food. I had no way of knowing which was Maipuri's son. It wasn't Yakka-yakka, because he was Tautau's, so I plumped for Ak-ak. Maipuri was bound to have done a sneaky thing like arrange for him to take the shot at the tapir. No one gets to the top of a community without knowing how to fix the odds.

After nightfall I wandered among the family groups. I was sitting between two men, Cheroobé and Anarau, by the side of one of the fires, when Yimshi jumped down beside me. When I saw who it was, I groaned. I heard Maipuri suppressing a snort behind me. Yimshi looked into the heart of the fire. She looked hot. Her brow was damp.

'She want kiss you, Louco Benedito,' said Maipuri loudly.

The girl turned her head to Anarau and whispered close up to his ear, as if she was nibbling it.

'She say, how many moons to your village, Louco Benedito?'

'Tell her it's too far to walk.'

Yimshi leant towards Anarau, waiting to hear the reply. She stared into the flames, her arms down by her sides, while he told her.

'She wants to know if it's true your chief is a woman.'

I said it was.

'And does she really have more riches than anyone else in the world?'

As I said yes again, I saw ambition kindle in her eyes. Anarau had noticed it too. He said that Yimshi's name was a shortening for 'baby', but that really she was more like a jaguar.

'Not!' she shouted, and glowered at Anarau.

'See? She even understand a little English. You see her face? She got cat's eyes.'

I said, 'So you're a jaguar, are you?' Her eyes darkened and she shook her head. But she couldn't stop her lip curling in anger and her sharp teeth showed.

I nodded. 'You *are* a jaguar.'

'And *you...*' she said, 'you are...' She pondered, looking me over. 'You are...Mad White Giant.'

Immediately the whole village burst into an uproar of laughter.

Maipuri, at the fireside of his hut, began the singing. He drawled a soft chant, with his arms outstretched to the village. Anarau said he was calling his people to dance. The babies were bundled into the huts and the children ordered out of their hammocks to watch. The chant was slow and it was a dull sound, so that while everyone sat in silence I heard the night: a low murmuring howl and the river chattering.

Jaguar Culture

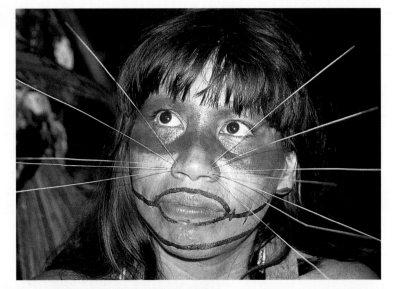

In 1552 a German naval gunner employed by the Portuguese was captured by the Tamoio Indians of southern Brazil and spent several months with the tribe. Discovering that their chief was a cannibal, he protested that even wild animals did not eat their own kind; to which the chief replied that he was a jaguar, different from humans and therefore entitled to eat them.

It is now known that many Amazon tribes of both forest and highland have claimed jaguar ancestry. Pelts are still worn for ritual dancing in the Andes, and some forest hunters mimic the jaguar's natural camouflage with blotched face paint. Most famous of the jaguar-cult tribes are the 'cat-people' of the Mayoruna, who tattoo their faces and pierce their lips with spines to represent whiskers. Until recently the tribe was thought to have been wiped out during the rubber boom which claimed so many Indian lives; but they were discovered in the late 1960s by the photographer-explorer Loren McIntyre, who later went on to find the source of the Amazon. Living in the forest with no reliance on agriculture, the remarkable cat-people hunt with cudgels studded with jaguar teeth, and file their own teeth to accentuate their feline appearance.

▲ This Mayoruna woman from the area of the Javari River is wearing elaborate spine-whiskers.

◀ Kayapo Indians, who live near the banks of the Xingu River, perform a ritual dance after killing a jaguar.

The men of the village, only five of them, got up from their logs and formed a line, swaying to Maipuri's drone. A woman served up beer to the men, each in turn, putting the gourd to their lips as they listened side by side, facing Maipuri across the yard. After the drink, the men answered Maipuri's song with a slow chorus. They wailed, as if they were in mourning, and their bodies began to arch and writhe, their torsos rippling. I didn't know what the song meant, but it brought tears to the men's eyes. Later Tautau explained it was to do with paying respects to the spirit of the dead tapir, which, after all, had put up the feast.

Five women formed another line, standing to attention facing the men across the firesparks and darkness. Maipuri turned aside and led his men off in a shuffle. They encircled the women, who stood rigid with their eyes tightly shut.

The children began drumming a rhythm on the logs and one of the men in the line blew on a flute. The beat quickened. I tasted dust in the air. Just as the rhythm began working, seducing the women to open their eyes and look at the men, it stopped. The dancers dispersed and settled back down on their logs. Maipuri shouted that Louco Benedito should now get to his feet.

I got to my feet.

'You tell Maipuri who you choose as guide into forest.'

'What, *now*?' I was standing in the centre of the village, where the pig-fight had started and ended, and the same hungry faces were looking me over. Into the darkness and silence, I gulped and said:

'I choose Tautau.'

The silence continued. The crowd was waiting to hear the name of the chief's son. I screwed up my eyes and breathed in. The four boys braced themselves in a dim corner.

'And Ak-ak.'

The men whooped and tossed Ak-ak into the air, and Maipuri thumped him in the chest when he landed and paraded him around the village. The other three boys ran off into the night and I never saw them again.

As the fires faded, the dancers became only pale shadows in the dark and I caught the rhythm from the trembling of the earth.

Ak-ak, with fresh red feathers in his ears, was dancing with the men. They were circling, with their hands resting on each other's shoulders. Ak-ak couldn't reach, even on tiptoe; his voice was weak and it piped clear above the others.

For the first time the women began to sing. They answered the men's chant by throwing back their heads, winding their necks around like courting swans. The men paddled the dust, surrounding the women again.

The dance was a wild reel. The men stopped dancing and faced in on the women, who opened out their circle and, spinning round, came closer and closer to the men. They teased the men by brushing so close with their breasts that the men's heads were swimming. Then the dance pace slackened. The women became limp and sleepy. Their heads lolled. The song became a gentle murmur and, with its last breath, almost a sigh of relief. The mass of dancers dissolved into the darkness. The audience of children filed away and a feather, red in the fireglow, dropped softly to the ground.

A Wai-wai Proposition

Even in the gloom of the hut, I knew I was not alone. It was the slight whiff I caught of a man's body paint. I saw the faint outline of a hammock. I tapped the hammock cords with my fingers. They were taut, but I could swing the hammock with ease, so I guessed it contained a child. Ak-ak, I reckoned, had decided to start his duties as a guide right away. He had curled himself up in my spare clothes, making a nest to keep off the cold, and positioned his hammock alongside mine. I squeezed off my boots and rolled into my hammock. Tomorrow I would be moving on again into the forest, with Indians this time. I would have Tautau and this boy Ak-ak as guides; Maipuri had said Anarau and Cheroobé would be porters. I drifted into a cosy sleep.

My dreams at first were of hunting the tapir. Then I dreamt of Yimshi. I didn't want to, but she forced herself into my dream. I could feel the warmth of her body against mine and the softness of her skin. I began to get uncomfortable. She was too tangible. I opened my eyes with the shock which usually terminates a nightmare, when you think for a second that it has all been real. This time it was: in the dark there was the creak of the empty hammock next to mine and Yimshi was in mine, hugging my neck.

I recalled what a mess of things I'd made with Zorola, accepting her gift of crab. That memory still made me wince. Outside, the men and women were

Rainforest Indians richly adorned with feathers perform a fiery festival dance. ▼

stamping out another dance, howling tunes like lonely dogs.

'Yimshi?' I said. I heard her snuffle and knew it was her laugh.

'Mad White Giant!' she said. She squirmed closer.

'Yimshi,' I said quietly in her ear. 'Yimshi must go.' She must have covered her body all over in the perfumed greasepaint very recently. The smell was overwhelming me.

'Yimshi must go,' I said again.

'No,' she crooned. 'No. Yimshi not go.'

Her head lifted like a snake about to strike. My face fell in the shadow of her breasts. She took me in her arms and drew my chest up against her. Her fingernails dug into my shoulders like claws.

▲ An endangered rainforest tortoise forages on the forest floor. Indians often capture these animals and keep them as an emergency supply of meat.

'Yimshi, *no!*' I prised her off. You *are* a jaguar, aren't you, I thought, getting my breath back. On my neck I felt Yimshi's warm tears dropping. She whimpered in my ear. It was a horrible thing I was doing to her. She would be in disgrace now that she'd been rejected. The whole village was probably pinning its hopes on her. Maipuri wasn't going to be pleased that his gesture had been rejected, either. I tipped Yimshi gently to the floor where she lay in a heap.

'Yimshi?' I called softly. 'Yimshi?'

I heard the unfurling of the empty hammock next to mine and the creak of the strings as she clambered into it; then a final soft whimper.

When I opened my eyes again, daylight was seeping into the hut and Yimshi was gone. The whole village knew that I hadn't accepted her. Maipuri wouldn't talk, except to say he'd thrown Yimshi into the cage and she'd stay there for as long as he thought fit. He turned his back to me when I said it was no good, I didn't belong here, I had another world waiting for me and I was not a Wai-wai, a 'forest dweller'.

After a drink of cassava beer he put his arm around me. 'I understand you.' He talked slowly, looking down at his feet. 'You too good to be Wai-wai.'

I said it wasn't that at all; maybe I wasn't good enough to be a Wai-wai. 'What will you do now, Maipuri?'

'We go hide. We seek place wid no Godmen, no guvment. Maybe find more Injuns. You come back, say hello to Maipuri?'

'But how will I find you?'

'If you find way out of forest, you find me easy, Louco Benedito. You come back wid Lizbet?' I promised.

Maipuri's wife presented a tortoise to Tautau, who stuffed it into Ak-ak's wicker backpack.

The pathetic village group lined the riverbank and watched us walk into the forest: the children with dogs nuzzling their faces, and the women huddled in timid groups behind the men, as if I were a stranger again. There was no waving goodbye, or movement of any kind; they had taken on the drained faces of the goldmining Negroes of El Callao, the ones left in the lurch by the miners after the gold rush.

Jungle Medicine

OR THE INDIANS, the rain forest is a storehouse of natural products, remedies, poisons and intoxicants. Apart from food, the jungle provides them with deodorants, contraceptives, and therapies for conditions as diverse as stomachache, snakebite, dandruff and diarrhoea.

Tobacco is smoked for relaxation, and the leaves of the coca bush are widely used as a stimulant, sustaining hunters for days without food or sleep. Many tribes also take hallucinogens in the form of snuff blown up a person's nose through a cane tube. One such drug is *yakoana*, which produces visions of bright, shifting colours and a sense of well-being. From the curare vine and the virola tree come nerve poisons used for hunting. These are smeared on blowpipe darts and arrowheads, and take effect remarkably quickly. Equally dramatic are the poisons that are used to suffocate fish in a river or pool.

Competent as most Indians are in the use of plant and animal products, no one knows more about healing and medicines than the shaman—the 'witch doctor' or 'medicine man'. Acting as both priest and doctor, he is a central figure in every community. This is because the Indians believe that they are surrounded by spirits, who are often responsible for various troubles, and with whom they must strive to live in harmony. The shaman's task is to deal with the spirits on behalf of his people, and he does this by entering a state of trance—often by means of hallucinogenic drugs—in which he can contact the spirit world. There he may have to fight with a malevolent being, or consult with a benevolent one, in order to end an outbreak of illness or some other misfortune.

Mushrooms, bark, seeds and other medicinal products from the rain forest are ▲ widely available in local town markets.

An Indian woman treating her sick child with a bunch of medicinal leaves. Many Amazonian Indians possess a wide knowledge of herbal therapies. ▼

▲ A bundle of poisonous vines being beaten in a river pool. They release toxins that stupefy or suffocate nearby fish.

▲ A Yanomami shaman from north-west Brazil has narcotic powder blown into his nose by his son. When in a trance, the shaman will often act out the struggle he is experiencing in the spirit world. ▶

◀ Kamayura Indians from the Xingu area perform a shamanistic dance with rattles and elaborate costumes.

CHAPTER 7

In the Jungle Deep

▲ The beautiful markings
of the emerald tree boa
provide perfect
camouflage and make it
difficult to spot, even
during the day.

IT WAS A RELIEF TO BE IN THE FOREST, though I hadn't expected it to be. The heat, the sweat and the sodden leaves were refreshing after the empty stares of the Indians. Tautau and Ak-ak went ahead, clearing a path; Cheroobé and Anarau grunted along behind, humping loads.

We went on, day after day, sleeping very little. When we did sleep, it was during the daytime, in the hours when the jungle sizzled and snored in the heat. We covered most ground at night, moving with the snakes and frogs. In the dark I tagged behind Tautau, holding his pigtail with my eyes closed, learning to move using my sense of smell. The leaves had smells and so did the barks, the flaky-skinned vines and the water trapped in the pineapple bromeliad leaves.

I had always thought that listening was more important to Indians, but Ak-ak laughed out wildly at this and Tautau put a fistful of leaves in my face and asked me to smell whether they would be bitter or sweet to taste. I said sweet and then he asked Ak-ak, who said bitter; then he made me eat the whole lot and I was sick. 'That why smell more important.'

The Indians scorned my heavy boots, mainly because with their splayed-out toes they could stalk monkeys without cracking twigs. But my boots were what kept me upright. Within them I was waging chemical warfare against skin fungi and my skin was as weak as blotting paper. What my feet needed was a good airing, but nothing in the jungle got an airing—even by the campfire my hair was wringing wet. Because one palm splinter through the heel would be enough to cripple me, I never took a step anywhere without the boots.

Five days on, tunnelling through a deep fence of bamboo, Tautau asked if I could smell anything. The smells of that moment were the raffia-basket smell of the bamboo and the warm smell of the mossy soil. But there was another and it was of bonfires.

We dropped down into a gully and by a brookside was a smouldering pile of leaves. The ground had been smoothed by naked feet. There was no one about, just ourselves and the jungle. Ak-ak tapped my arm and pointed further up the brook. He had spotted a white-and-brown-blotched mongrel on the ground. It was dead, I thought, as we came nearer and it didn't flinch.

Tautau yelled through the trees. There was no answer, but an old man pattered out after a time. He appeared from behind a fig tree that was strangling another fig tree, squeezing it dry with its roots. The man was a Wai-wai, I knew that from the pattern of his loincloth, but he was a wasted-away one. His eyes were yellow, his skin stretched and translucent over his cheekbones and gnarled like a tree where it sagged around his neck.

'He come here to die,' said Tautau, loudly. I grinned awkwardly at the man and told him I was sure it wasn't as bad as all that, he'd be better soon, but he ought to take a rest. Maybe later we could carry him back to the village.

'He *come* from village. He come here to die, one moon back. He surprise me he still alive.' He patted the old man's shoulder. 'Not long now, old man.'

The old man smiled.

I helped him to the pile of smouldering leaves. I sat with him for an hour, while the others dozed. He opened his mouth to speak sometimes, but nothing ever came out. Once I wondered why there were no old people in the Wai-wai village; now I knew.

Tautau came up and cross-examined the old man to see how long he thought he could last out. It would be bad form for us to be around when his time came, so Tautau asked him whether he thought he would peg out that night. The man shook his head. He thought he could last out that long. Tautau was pleased because we could make our shelter here.

Ak-ak was eyeing the old man's neck beads greedily. He couldn't take his eyes off them. Eventually Tautau, saying they were too valuable to waste, untied the beads from the man—who didn't raise a hand to object—and strung them around Ak-ak's neck. Ak-ak rolled the beads over in his little fingers and puffed out his chest for me to see them.

'Dog die also,' Tautau said.

◀ **This strangler fig has encased its palm tree host.**

Strangler Fig Tree

THE STRANGLER FIG is an epiphyte—a plant that depends on another plant or object for physical support. It starts life as a seed, which germinates (usually in compost) in the cleft of a tree branch, having been dropped there by a passing bird or bat. Unlike other epiphytes, however, which rarely damage their hosts, the strangler is a killer. It grows enormous aerial roots which seek out the soil far below. Once these roots penetrate the forest floor to extract its nutrients, the fig grows apace, gradually encasing the host tree with ever-thickening roots, which fuse to form a living coffin. Eventually the host tree will die and rot away, leaving the fig to stand as a massive, hollow tree towering up through the forest's canopy.

These figs may be murderous to their hosts, but they provide food and shelter to hundreds of forest creatures. Gecko lizards and frogs live within the trees' many cavities along with wasps and bees, while ants make colonies in old bees' nests. The trees may fruit as often as three times a year and are an important source of nourishment when other food is in short supply; the well-known laxative effect of the fig ensures that its seeds are swiftly and widely dispersed!

I bent over the mongrel. 'But he's only young,' I said.

'He die young, then.'

When it did not touch them personally, as Yakka-yakka's plight had done, the Wai-wai accepted death without emotion; no fear, no ritual. It was as natural as their lovemaking.

We cooked up the tortoise into soup. I gave the old man and the dog a leg. Tautau laughed and said I might as well throw the food to the eagles. The dog accepted it, but the man shied away and wouldn't even take a sip of soup. Instead, he held my hand tightly in his, so tight I thought he wouldn't die for weeks.

At daylight, hardly lighter than night in the thicker forest, we were walking again. I was the only one to look back at the old man. He was staring into his slow bonfire, breathing in the grey smoke. The dog was around my neck; I felt like a shepherd lugging home a long-lost sheep. I would take it along to the next village—it had perked up already.

After three more days I was a wreck. 'You too tall,' said Anarau, who carried two pillow-sized rice sacks on his back. 'You Mad White Giant,' he said, ducking under a tree that was across our path.

Ahead we heard what sounded like a woodpecker tapping a hollow tree, but it was Tautau signalling to us by thumping his heel against a root buttress. Cheroobé whooped back and beat a tree himself.

'We not far to go.'

'How far?' I said, wheezing.

'When sun is high, we there.' That answer was vague. The sun was hidden in the tree canopy and no one had sighted it since the village, a week ago. I listened to the cicadas, their pitch rising in the heat, and when they were whistling in my ears and the parakeets tucked their heads under their wings to take a nap, I knew it was time.

▲ A cobalt-winged parakeet; one of the smaller members of the parrot family.

Tautau slipped his pack off and dumped it lightly on the forest floor. The headband of bark he used to spread the weight had scored white stripes across his forehead. But he wasn't short of breath and he lifted my pack down with the thumb and forefinger of one hand.

We faced a sluggish stream. From what Tautau said, it was a southern tributary of the Cafuini. That meant in one week we had come sixty miles or so eastward, skirting north of the first of my six Amazon tributaries, the Mapuera. We waded through the water without difficulty.

Ak-ak scampered ahead up the far bank and jumped up and down, waving. He could see village smoke.

The huts were conical, like beehives, and had dingy interiors. There were only two of them and only one tree had been felled to open up the tree canopy. The undergrowth, which was dying from the shock of light, was the same buff colour as the palm hut roofs. If it hadn't been for the smoke, I might have passed right by.

No Indians came out to welcome or attack us. Tautau frowned and told us to wait by the river. We backed behind a clump of palms.

Tautau called out to the huts, mentioning Maipuri, but not even a dog trotted out. He beckoned us to come out from our cover. As soon as we showed our-selves, four men trickled out of the huts, squinting in the sun. The men were red with *roucou* fruit dye, their skins looking glossy and wet in the sun; snaky black lines were printed over their bodies from their throats to their ankles. They looked gormless, not hostile.

One of the men shouted at me in Wai-wai, with his head jerking forward like a threatening lizard. He wanted me to go away. Tautau flapped his hands dismis-sively. They watched us, not sure what to do next. They were as short as our Wai-wais, but none of them had pigtails. A woman with shrivelled breasts meandered through the men towards us for a better look. When she saw me, she upset her bowl of manioc tubers. They spilled over the men's toes, and the men flashed their teeth at her. They had a brief chat with Tautau, then stomped back into the huts.

In one of the huts there was a woman with a dire illness and the witch doctor was treating her. Tautau said we shouldn't disturb his magic. For the rest of the afternoon we sat on the edge of the camp, dozing.

Helping a Witch Doctor

Under cover of dark Ak-ak crawled into the village on his stomach. I gathered that there was one woman who was just about to die, and she had two husbands who were fussing over her. The woman we had seen was the only other woman, and she also had two husbands. That just left the sorcerer, who was a failure at his art and had an enormous chip on his shoulder about it.

Tautau went to see how things were coming along in the village and yelled back that I could come forward. His call woke two Powis birds—clumsy, black, turkey-like creatures with white breasts and golden legs—which almost fell from their tree with fright.

◀ **Indian women work together grating tubers of manioc, or cassava, a staple food of the area.**

The witch doctor, a sunken-eyed man with disorganised hair and bow legs, appeared and showed me into one of the huts. It reeked of black firesmoke. Tautau said special leaves had been put on the fire to clean the air of bad spirits.

▲ A witch doctor or shaman invokes supernatural spirits to drive sickness from his community.

The witch doctor ordered everyone but Tautau and me out of the hut. Through smarting eyes we saw his patient, who lay shivering, bathed in her own sweat, in a hammock. Her face was knotted up with pain and she smelt cheesy. I pinched her leg; she didn't notice and the crease I'd made didn't disappear. I said I thought on the whole she was dying, but might last the night. The witch doctor agreed. Tautau whispered that the witch doctor's future wouldn't be much better than hers if he didn't get this patient fixed up. Though most doctors knew all the jungle potions, this man didn't have a clue and had had a long run of failures.

Half an hour later we had drawn up an agreement whereby I would try my own magic on the woman (no one else need know), restore her to health and the witch doctor would get his Indians to help me to travel further east.

I wasn't left alone with the woman until the middle of the night. Ak-ak offered to work as my assistant. He ran to fetch my medicines and a gourd of cold water. I opened the woman's mouth and looked at her teeth, as I'd seen people do to horses. She had lost most of them. Apart from being about to die of fever, she looked short of all basic vitamins.

Together we rolled the woman over. A bandage of palm had been strapped down her spine. I looked carefully at the bandage. It was woven with black ants tied on with their stings projecting on the underside. The witch doctor was hoping to torture the evil out of the woman. I threw the bandage into the fire, and the bodies of the ants spat and crackled like chestnuts.

I dressed the woman's spine with calamine lotion, then gave her a general antibiotic, not knowing what would happen.

Outside, it was raining. The patter of the rain on the roof soothed the woman and her breathing slowed and deepened. We stayed the night in the hut, taking it in turns to douse her with cool river water.

The ill woman's progress was remarkable. At daybreak, whatever illness she'd had before the witch doctor treated her was well under control.

The rain gave the air a fruity smell. The leaves paled and softened to a lighter shade of green and the palm fronds of the hut roof swelled and looked like corn.

The witch doctor had the goaty, thin-lipped sort of face I had learnt to distrust, even at kindergarten age. In addition, he spewed saliva from his mouth while talking. He also hated me for delivering his patient from the jaws of death. Tautau, in a moment of absent-mindedness, compounded the situation by announcing that I had already worked a miracle on his son, Yakka-yakka. The witch doctor left under a storm cloud, spitting like an angry cat. Tautau made amends by saying he would help me force the witch doctor to fulfil his side of the bargain. He would even come with me, further into the forest. So we arranged for

him to stay on with me until the next village. It was time for the others to go.

Anarau and Cheroobé led off across the river, back to the village with Ak-ak. They began trotting with the thought of getting home. Ak-ak waved for some time through the green beams of light before the party was invisible.

'Right, let's get these people into action,' I said to Tautau.

'Into action,' he said, and nodded gravely. He walked back into the hut ahead of me. You're a real stalwart, Tautau, I thought. He was as staunch a friend to me as Pablo had been, but more civilised.

I spent the day telling the witch doctor how he should complete the woman's course of antibiotics, but he refused to understand. Tautau and I ended up staying another whole day, so that the woman was strong enough to stave the witch doctor off.

The remaining Indians worked together in completing a dugout canoe. It was a graceful craft, as straight as a pencil, light but not frail. The Indians roasted it on a fire to harden the wood and covered it in black pitch. We launched the canoe into the river, and it was sound.

Tautau made the decision about which guides to take. They were all equally unwilling. I had to proffer a third of my gold to raise any enthusiasm at all, and none of the men looked worth it. They were lethargic, measly Indians. Their teeth were fawn-coloured chips, sunk in grey, spongy gums. Tautau said it was because these Indians were part of their tribe that had come from Guyana, and like most Indians who had seen 'Godmen or guvment' they became lazy and didn't grow the right food, or drink good cassava beer.

Tautau ran into difficulties picking out the guides. He couldn't stop them bickering with each other.

▲ **Indians carve and hollow out a massive treetrunk to make a dugout canoe.**

'Can they all paddle?' I asked.

The men said of course they could paddle. Anyone could paddle. They claimed that, though they were all exceptional paddlers, each of their friends was actually even better.

'What are they up to, Tautau?' I said. 'Why don't they want to come?'

'Benedito Mad White Giant, I not know. I sorry. I think your journey end here. I sorry. You stay marry Yimshi. She powerful lady. And if you not like her now, she *make* you like her.'

'I'm sure she has her ways and means.'

'Yes, and maybe Lizbet not mind you stay in forest and not bring gold home.' Tautau was desperate to cheer me up. '*Maybe* Lizbet come out and live with Mad White Giant and Yimshi.'

I thought I was about to faint. 'Please, Tautau, just find out what will satisfy these people. I don't care how you do it. Get them drunk or something. I want to know why they don't want to come.' I stormed away, bitterly sorry I was putting so much pressure on Tautau. He was only trying his best. I went and talked to the dog, who was snoozing in the canoe. Today he even had the strength to stand, but he was not yet strong enough to cope with the witch doctor's medicine and I'd have to take him on to another village. Because he didn't have a name, I called him Cashoe, to simplify things. It meant 'dog'.

Tautau came over. He had cracked the cause of the problem. It appeared that each of the men had thought the husband with whom he shared a wife would maltreat her or wear her out. They each wanted to stay and keep an eye on things.

'Good grief. Tell the two husbands of the sick woman that the witch doctor will see she is safe. Surely the men will trust the doctor?'

'Everyone trust doctor. Life not worth living if not trust doctor.'

'I can imagine.'

The jungle is an eternal prison, Pablo had said. I marched to the canoe in triumph, because so far the jungle was not proving a prison.

The witch doctor did not stand on ceremony. There was no farewell.

'He the same witch doctor our village had many, many moons ago, in land of Guyana,' said Tautau as we tugged the canoe downstream. 'Godman sent him away.'

'Not surprised,' I said.

Deep into the Interior

Haimarha and Sipu were bad guides. Their hearts were not in the journey and I had to give them a pinch of gold a day, just to keep them from fighting. After a while I learnt that what they yearned for was Western clothes. They were much happier once they had stolen all my underpants and were wearing them over their loincloths. But, as Tautau said, 'Mad White Giant, problem is they bad Wai-wai. They seen too much Godmen and guvment.'

A moon waxed and waned and rapids came and went. Sometimes they were white, mashed-up water, other times gentle furrows as clear as glass. We went deeper into the interior. It got no darker or danker, or thicker. It didn't change.

The forest had a canopy roof, so high the pinpricks of light in it might have been stars. And the air between the ground shrubs, on the floor where we lived, was the green colour of stagnant ponds.

The Acarai hills loomed up on the left, the north; green ranges with jets of snowy white cloud streaming over the lowland in the wind. Then, one afternoon, we rounded a tight river bend. When we looked up to see the hills again after the river unbuckled, they were not there.

Soon I forgot I was beyond reach of the outside world. I lived as part of the forest. We ran through the trees below the ring-tailed capuchin monkey troops, sprinting on and on until we were ahead; then we lay in ambush ready to shoot them down; we went nut gathering; we harpooned fish, or whistled mating songs at birds to lure them.

There were days when I was taken with fevers. They were mysterious, whimsical diseases which could bring me to my knees within hours. When I was ill, I had one recurrent dream—that I was being flushed down a drain. 'That drain is my future,' I would say as I woke, burning all over, still with the image in front of my eyes. Then, as always, Tautau was there as my source of strength. I came to see him as my only hope of ever getting out.

Tautau had to turn back shortly, I knew. I dreaded being stuck with the other two Indians. Tautau said that once these had been bold, perky men. The Godman had told them

▲ **Braving rapids on an Amazon waterway.**

they sinned in sharing a wife, and ever since then they had lost their love of life and even forgotten how to laugh like a Wai-wai.

Tautau said that what the Godmen didn't understand was that everything went to the Creator. Pebbles in the rivers, ants on the forest leaves, even the fat old boar. Everything went to the Creator, because everything had a spirit. The forest spirits weren't good or evil—unless, of course, the witch doctor worked magic on them. So the world was as nice a place as we made it. It was up to everyone to make it as happy a place as possible by sharing all things. God did not bother to listen to our prayers, because he hadn't asked for them in the first place. Why should he? What marked man out from all the other spirits? 'What make us so special?' Yes, said Tautau, everything the Godmen said was silly when you came to think about it.

The jungle was neutral, Tautau told me, tough but rarely with evil intent; and I felt more content in the forest than ever before.

For a few days now we had been trying a short cut east from the Poana River overland through the forest to the Curiau. That night, however, we decided to beat a retreat and continue south on to the Trombetas, before cutting further east. The river ahead was barricaded with fallen trees from flooding. During the day it had rained so hard that the river exploded its banks and the current swelled and churned with clouds of red clay. The water was choked with straw-coloured leaves, bugs with black, spiny hairs, caterpillars of all sorts and crumpled leaves and saplings. Hundreds of spiky black ants skated on the floodwater towards us and grappled with each other for a hold on the canoe.

Sipu and Haimarha almost capsized us trying to stamp out the boarders.

'They no good Wai-wais,' said Tautau. 'Even *you* better, Louco Benedito.'

South we went down the easy northern Trombetas, where Sipu and Haimarha wore through two perfectly good paddles, east another fifty miles up the Venturi tributary. Afterwards, there was a gruelling march overland on to the Marapi.

Poling north up the Marapi, we were in a dire state. I knew I had pushed everyone too hard and Tautau's skin was greying and flaking. In the old days Sipu and Haimarha had spent much of the sunshine lying back decorating themselves with feathers and paint. Now they slept.

'Mad White Giant Benedito?' said Tautau paddling behind me one bitterly cold dawn.

'Yes?' I knew what it was.

'Mad White Giant, Tautau think he cannot go paddling much further with you. I been good. I come two moons with you. But time coming for me to leave. When I leave I cry much.' He rubbed his eyes. 'Maybe Yakka-yakka need my help.'

'You have been very good to me, Tautau.'

▲ On this floodplain a river has burst its banks and spread out into meandering loops, thick with silt and vegetation.

'You have been very good to Wai-wai, Benedito.'

Not much further up the Marapi we took a right turn east up an unnamed tributary and came to Tirio territory. We knew only because we happened across them unexpectedly, while harpooning fish with arrows. Tautau and I were spearing at a pike-like fish, which had banks of needle teeth. It was lurking in a sward of weed, passing time while a gentle *paku* fish, fat and round and the colour of tomato ketchup, swam dreamily into range.

'We being watched,' Tautau said softly in my ear. I looked up. I couldn't see anyone; only brittle ranks of sepia grass and bottle-green trees. One of the Indians moved his eyes, a glint of white that was enough to give him away. I saw curved twigs—they were bows—and next I saw their bodies, as dark as the treetrunks.

'Tirio,' said Sipu.

'Why are they hiding?' I said.

'They so scared they dangerous,' said Tautau. 'Now is time for presents.'

I decked the canoe with beads and my last postcards. The two Indians came out of cover. From the riverbank they were just like Wai-wais, but once Tautau was near them he looked like a child. They were taller, their skin ruddier, as if they lived out in the sunshine. They had no feathers, but red armbands and red loincloths, like the Wai-wais.

▲ **Perfectly balanced in his canoe, an Indian fishes with bow and arrow.**

I couldn't make the men understand my version of Wai-wai, but Tautau could with some sign language. He said the Indians had never seen someone with a long nose and so many clothes before—they were looking at me—and this was what had upset them.

The two Tirio Indians took us along to their village and we left the canoe to be guarded by Cashoe. But it wasn't a village. The Tirio were on the move, searching for a new hunting ground. We found the group raising shelters and adjusting hammocks under them. I handed out postcards. The children grabbed eagerly at them, but a man with white streaks in his hair confiscated them and fed them to the fire. Tautau said they didn't want to be burdened with too much clobber and food would go down better.

Haimarha was sent back to our canoe and brought back a tortoise we had bumped into in the river that day. We had saved it in the nick of time, because its legs were being chewed off by piranha fish. The Indians jumped for joy when they saw it and cracked it apart with two chops of a machete. Sipu rubbed his hands. He said if this was going to be a feast, he would dress for it properly. Tautau said yes, it was probably going to be a feast.

While the tortoise spun round and round on a spit, Sipu and Haimarha took it in turns to paint each other. The Tirio men, five of them, said they could do better than Wai-wai Indians, swiped our pat of red dye and plastered it over their chests as a background to more black-ink spiderwebs. Tautau spotted a

An Indian boy tends his pet macaws. Many other types of bird are also tamed and kept as pets.

small boy's pet macaw and plucked some puce wing feathers from it, which he plaited into his pigtail. The Tirios put showers of the feathers into their armbands and by nightfall the bird was bald and miserable.

We drank a sticky type of cassava beer, which was stronger than the Wai-wai brew. The headman had a drum of furry tapir skin, which he held to his ear and knocked with his fingers. We ate the tortoise around one deep red fire.

We talked until the bats went to sleep and Tautau said he had found me two good men who wanted to be my guides.

'They say they take you on towards where the sun comes up. Oyampi Injun country. Rest of the Tirio go to guvment home soon. They say they want easy life there. These two men say they want Tirio life. They want be happy still.'

'Can I trust them?'

'Mmmmmmm. They good. They say, "Can we trust Mad White Giant?" One of Tirio say he want go furder wid you. He want see where de sun come up. He say he hear from witch doctor it come from endless lake.'

The endless lake was the sea; the mouth of the Amazon. I leaped up and down, hugging Tautau. He had found someone to take me to the end of my journey. He started to hug me as well.

'Mad White Giant! You pleased wid me! Mmmmmmmmmm! Tautau very happy! Louco White Benedito Giant!' We danced around the fire, holding hands. Tautau burnt his toes, but said he didn't care.

Another Testing Experience

The mists were thick in the trees the next dawn. The Tirio said goodbye at the riverside and left us. I split the supplies into two heaps. Tautau heaved my share to me from the canoe sack by sack.

'Maybe you come back to Wai-wais?' he said.

'I hope so.'

He scooped Cashoe from the canoe and snuggled him into my arms. 'He good friend to you. Keep him till you out of forest. He good Wai-wai.'

Sipu and Haimarha said they didn't want the gold I owed them. We had been friends and only non-Indians had to have money. So I kept it. We wished each other luck. Sipu and Haimarha paddled and Tautau stared back in my direction long after he must have lost sight of me. As the canoe blurred into the mist, there was only the slopping sound of paddles. That sound fading was the loneliest sound in the world and I ran off into the forest so as not to hear it slowly die.

It was a new day and I had completed another link in the journey. I made myself think of that. On my way back to the Tirio camp I watched the skipping parrots and silent flutter of golden butterflies, which were like autumn leaves. The large, metallic-blue morpho butterflies were always bolder. They flew alone and haphazardly, like wounded birds. That morning I saw some perched on shelves of leaves, waiting for the damp to lift from their wings, and they were like scraps of wind-scattered satin.

The Tirios were packing up and about to march on. My guides squatted beside the dead fire, dragging on smouldering rolls of tobacco. I sat on my haunches next to them. We waited without a word, while the others got organised and the men led them away into the forest.

The two Indians smiled coyly. They looked me over. I looked them over. They handed me their cigarettes in turn. I drew on each and handed them back.

'Benedito,' I said, patting my shirt. They said their names were Pimi and Toeleu.

I spread out my maps and asked them about the local geography. 'Hills?' I said, pointing east. 'Rapids? What do you call that river?'

The Indians were polite, intelligent and honest. Toeleu was a quiet, ponderous sort, who smoked his cigarettes right up to his lips. His eyes were as round as an owl's. Pimi—Pim for short—was bouncy and mischievous, about sixteen years old. He was the one with the ambition to see the sun come up out of the sea.

We spent the day in a hard march through a scrubby open forest with grass lawns, more crickets, fewer cicadas and even patches of burning white sky. At nightfall we were at the Borboletas stream where the Tirio group had abandoned their dugout. We then had to tramp back again for the remainder of our supplies.

▲ A brilliant morpho butterfly stands out against a background of green foliage.

'Why you cover your body with clothes?' asked Pim, two days on, when we were waterborne. We communicated in a clumsy Tirio/Wai-wai patois.

'My skin is weak and white. My skin hates the forest.'

Pim split his sides laughing each time I said I needed my hat to deflect the showers of tree ants, or boots to keep out the poisonous thorns.

Those thorns littered the ground like pine needles some days. Other days, when the rivers were dried up into silent puddles and we had to hop overboard to drag the canoe, stingrays flapped through the sands between our feet. A slash from one of those, or a nip from an electric eel, would have made life not worth living. These things, and a few animals like crocodiles—the black cayman—made the Indians more cautious of the rivers than of the land.

Pim was convinced that I had no worries in the jungle. After all, I could smell rain coming as well as them and seemed to be as good at stalking game birds. Soon it was time to put me to the test.

I was swimming naked with the others in a rivulet of frilly green weed. We had had a bad day's hunting and had come a full day from the canoe. Pim and Toeleu suddenly ran whooping from the river, and left me behind, waist-deep. They pointed at what had scared them. I looked over my shoulder and saw nothing, and said so. When I looked back, Pim was streaking into the forest with my clothes and Toeleu was on his tail, clutching my boots.

I gave chase. 'Oi! Come back!' But they were soon out of sight. I tracked them as Tautau had taught me to track pigs. Their tracks divided—which meant they knew I was trying to follow—and I gave up.

I sat on the water's edge and stared into the water. I knew it was one of Pim's games. He wanted to see if I could survive without clothes, like any normal Indian.

The light dimmed. The mosquitoes were hounding me. I avoided them by lying in the water up to my neck. Then, as the night chilled, I caked myself in mud and lit a fire. The heat baked the mud, which cocooned me in a protective layer. I tore up palm leaves and made a bed to keep the cold off. At first light I bound my feet in spongy leaves and marched back through the forest to the north. Once I hit the river five miles on, all I had to do was follow its course to where we had left the canoe. The forest cut me to ribbons, but I hardly paused for breath. I couldn't wait to get my hands on those two Indians.

'You take long time,' said Pim when I stormed up to him.

'We almost leave without you,' said Toeleu.

'Why you not travel in dark like *good* Indian?' Pim asked.

I didn't know what to say. They were leaning on the canoe, side by side, and looked bored. 'Where are my clothes?'

'Hey. You bleed all over, Benedito.' My thighs had been ripped raw by the forest. Some leaves were like hacksaw blades, others had edges as fine as razors.

'*Where are my clothes?*'

Toeleu shuffled his bottom along the canoe uneasily. 'You almost *die.*'

'I know,' I said. 'My clothes, please.'

There was a bad scene about the clothes. They had been scattered through the jungle. Deserting me like that had been an initiation test, as the pig-killing had been to the Wai-wais. I couldn't be too angry. I had passed and I would rise in the Indians' esteem.

Electric Eel

STREAMS IN THE AMAZONIAN rain forest tend to be sluggish and thick with decaying leaves and other vegetable matter, so their oxygen content is often low. In consequence, the gills of several species of fish have virtually disappeared and they have developed instead the ability to breathe air. The electric eel (no relation of any other eel species) is one of these air-breathers: its 'lungs' consist of a highly sensitive lining to its mouth which absorbs oxygen from the mouthfuls of air it gulps while on the surface.

This eel's electrical capability—a charge of some 300–500 volts generated within its muscle system—is thought to have evolved in order to protect its delicate mouth from damage: its prey, once stunned, can safely be swallowed whole. The electricity is also used as a defence mechanism—other creatures leave the electric eel well alone—and as a navigational aid, since its eyesight is poor and the water it swims in is often murky. Alexander von Humboldt, the first scientist to describe the electric eel, wrote of accidentally touching one: 'I do not remember having ever received…a more dreadful shock. I was affected during the rest of the day with a violent pain in my knees and in almost every joint.'

▲ At times of flooding the forest floor becomes home for this electric eel.

Our dribbling stream, the Borboletas, joined up with the Cumina and we arrived there at the turn of another moon. It was hard for me to think in days or months now. It was about mid-June and I had almost forgotten why I was journeying.

On the Cumina we paddled south, then forced the canoe through the trees to bypass a sequence of rapids. That brought us to the Santo Antônio, a stream which twisted and petered out into gravy-like mud. We took to the land again, harnessing ourselves to the canoe and tugging it to another unnamed tributary. There the air hung with white gnats. Our faces had already been peppered with wasp bites from the forest hike. That tributary led to a stream and the stream to the Citare.

Toeleu said he was going to die if we went on like this much longer, 'Too much paddle, not enough hunt', so I announced that it was time for a holiday and we fixed up a shelter and snoozed flat out in our hammocks for two days.

Naked as a Tirio

It was on the second night that we met the Indians. Pim and I were hunting, gliding our canoe on the river current like a crocodile to come within reach of a paca, a beefy rodent. We often found pacas hunting like this, as they were sipping water under cover of night. We could hear their lapping in the dark and though we could not see them when we shot, Pim never missed with an arrow. They tasted best roasted.

▲ Golden sands of a stream bed shine through its clear waters as it winds its way through the dense jungle.

Just as we were drifting near, not daring to disturb the water with the paddles, I reached out to Pim in the dark and touched my finger to his ear. That was the signal for him to listen out. The noise was distant and upriver. It might have been a crocodile, but was too regular. We knew the rhythm was of dipping paddles.

Pim called out and a man's voice yelled back with the same twang. He was also a Tirio. Pim's call had been aggressive and the answering voice sounded scared; a man with a lot to lose. Pim took hold of our shotgun. I told him to put it away, but he slipped off the safety catch.

The canoe came up, as black as the water. We heard it parting waves, then it knocked against our dugout. It ploughed us back with the weight of its load. Possibly five adults, I thought, and heard the light breath of children. They were hiding in the bottom of the canoe. The man who had spoken reached out and placed a gourd in my hand. I smelt what he was offering and dabbed some on my tongue. It was a cassava beer. I took a swig, then finished it.

While Pim was being presented with his drink, all I could hear was the whining of mosquitoes. Pim said the drink was good stuff. A cheer went up and the other canoe sloshed in the water, while the children squirmed out of hiding.

We had not yet seen each other and we received a first glimpse only in the

An Indian family paddle their dugout canoe through part of the forest flooded by seasonal rains.

glow of the fire we lit on the riverbank. They were four women, three husbands, one older bachelor and three waist-high children, two of them boys. The older man had heavier bones, a long jaw and hair with a centre parting. The hair extended the length of his rib cage and was frizzy at the ends like wool. I thought he was a freak, but Toeleu said he was a Wayana Indian.

The Indian group weren't sure where they were going. They just wanted to get away from their village, where people with white skins had put metal sheets on top of their huts and others came to gawp at them by the plane-load. They had started in the north, by the Tumucumaque hills, and another canoe, full of their children, was two days behind them. We drank more of the cassava beer as the night wore on.

The sun was up before the Indians the next day. When I clambered out of my hammock, the forest was rattling with snores. The men, women and children were lying in untidy piles under the food store tarpaulin. The women had the first right to bathe. Then I went for my wash and Pim stole my clothes again. I was forced to wear a red Wayana loincloth. We also covered ourselves in red dye and I dipped Cashoe in a trough full of it, as the Wai-wai would have done.

Whilst most of the Indians were away all day shooting arrows at fish, Pim walked around the camp saying I was a good Indian now that I was as naked as they were. True, I was an Indian who had blue eyes, but I was still an Indian. It was the greatest compliment these people could offer me, but it made me sad. Their future was a choice between joining the parish of a Godman and being a zoo specimen in a 'guvment' reserve or, if they were determined to retain their pride, living on the run like Maipuri's Wai-wais. I was sad because being called an Indian was like being called a dodo.

Pim and the Wayana Indian called Yepe, whose name he said meant 'friend', forced me to the ground and trimmed my hair at the front into a fringe.

When Toeleu announced he wanted to leave my expedition and join these people, Pim started drinking to cheer himself up, right through the dusty afternoon heat.

Fire Dance

That night we never cooled down. As the heat of the day passed we sat in close to the fire, passing around the fish meat and *kasila* beer, a Wayana Indian recipe. The fire shot sparks at us and took so much of the air in the clearing that we were light-headed.

Every visible object was tinged red in the fireglow: the moths, the tubular roots, even our eyes. Our clothes and skin were an even deeper red from the dye. The leaves curtaining us trapped the sparks and smoke as if we were in a cave. The Indians looked into the flames with vacant expressions and seemed to relish the scorching heat, as if wanting to forget the cold world outside.

As the men wheeled around the fireside in the first major dance, the women slipped inside the men's circle and formed their own, on the very edge of the fire. They spun holding hands, so near the fire the sparks were zipping through their hair. The men stood still and watched in an outer circle. For the first time ever I was entreated to stand with the men to dance.

The women closed their eyes, upturned their heads and let their hair fall back down their shoulders. The men were beating a rhythm with their feet, but their eyes were glazed and fixed on the heart of the fire. This was a fire dance. The women were worshipping the fire with their bodies. They stopped skipping and took a stance with their feet wide apart. They let the flames lick over their skin and wriggled their hips at the fire, wailing. I thought they must be in terrible agony; they sang in high, convulsive screams, like gulls, above the furnace roar. Through the flames I saw tears running down the women's cheeks, spilling over their breasts. I winced at their pain.

Then I knew there was no pain. We men were all now pressed in there amongst them, our arms fastened in a tight circle. We began moving in a solid ring around the fire. A moment before I would never have dared approach a fire this close, but now the circle was tightening and shrinking. We were coming in closer still. I couldn't get away, and I didn't want to.

We were fused together, smelted by the fire, and this was complete unity: acceptance by the Carib Indians. I felt tears brimming in my eyes and saw them trickling down my chest. The teardrops, like everything else, were bright red.

Black vultures gather round an animal carcass, their keen sense of smell bringing them from far and wide.

A White Man's Graveyard

Yepe came away with Pim and me as Toeleu's replacement, on the second sunrise after the dance. The water was quiet and wide and had a golden-corn glow in the sun. A haze of rain came in the morning and a torrent in the afternoon, which flicked up the water and slashed the leaves in the trees, sending the monkeys clattering through the branches for cover. Afterwards, because the dust had been sponged from the air, the forest had a fresh tang and the leaves looked varnished and were swollen and soft.

We joined the Paru River, with only the Jari river system still to confront before we reached our goal. Almost immediately there were signs that we were coming out of the interior. The first was a non-Indian's hut. Pim and Yepe saw it was square, not round, and sat bolt upright in their seats. The owner was a lone trapper. His face was cross-hatched with scars and his teeth were black.

He sat in the sunlight with a crumpled shack behind. Around him was a flock of vultures. They were wrenching at carcasses lying between jaguar hides, which were staked out in the sun. The sight of us—red skins, bows and arrows—terrified him into his hut, but we got on well once we were properly introduced. The skin trade was illegal, but he, like the *seringueiros*, the rubber-latex gatherers, held the forest in esteem. The Indians could understand this and shared his disrespect for the outside world.

The trapper warned us away from the nearby village of Aldeia Bona, where, he said, the Brazilian government were busy 'integrating' Indians.

We descended the Paru, leapfrogging from hut to hut and stopping for chats with empty-headed Indians in rags. They stood by their huts with *cachaça* bottles, taking slugs of it while gutting fish. The commonest fish they called *pashina*, which had large shiny scales like shillings. When the smell of blood drew the piranhas in close and they were snapping at the gutted entrails, we bathed amongst them as if they were not there and laughed at the faces of the Brazilians who'd been taught to fear them. Yepe said piranhas were dangerous only when trapped in small pools during the dry season, and even then they had to be more than peckish before they started to shred you to pieces.

The Brazilians were a curiosity at first: real white men, goldminers in their slum shacks. We gaped at them as much as they gaped at us. We had a growing excitement, a trembling in our stomachs, as the outside world came within reach. We were paddling towards our future. The Indians didn't know what to expect of it. They just marvelled at each Coke bottle and twist of sweet wrapper that floated by as we canoed on. My excitement was the achievement of my goal, the end of my journey.

Yepe and Pim developed the habit of sifting through the junk heaps and pilfering what they could. After three or four calls—Porto Jarocomano, Tiui, Nauari—both Indians had given away their bangles, necklaces and armbands and dressed up in T-shirts and shorts. Alcohol flowed at every port of call. 'Is wonderful,' said Pim, dancing with glee, having just swopped his earrings for a deck of playing cards.

We abandoned the canoe. Pim, Cashoe, Yepe and I walked east through the forest to the River Jari. We passed through a mining camp, Santa Cruz, which had its own airstrip and a plane which had failed to clear the trees. Some pieces were still there.

Drink had been banned from the camp after two fights that had been more passionate than usual. I was shown the guns behind the bar and where the bodies fell. The sky still shone through bullet holes in the roof.

'There's gold fever here, is there?' I asked a miner.

He was a stocky, city-bred man with a nugget on a gold chain round his neck. He hated the jungle and was here only because it was a family business.

▲ **A typical trapper's riverside shack.**

'You wait till you see what they're up to where you're heading.' He told me that most of the fighting had been stamped out nowadays, because the forest had been divided up by powerful Mafia families and anyone who came scratching in the soil on those plots was in big trouble.

On the River Jari, near the mouth of the Ipitinga tributary, where we bought a new dugout, the miners were all yellow with malaria. The malaria parasite had grown accustomed to their medicines, so they drank Dr Bittencourt's Licor Amazonia—a jungle concoction of roots, nuts, leaves and fruits, 'all most rich in medical properties'. One man was green, not yellow. He was counting the days to his end. He said the malaria had developed a taste for Dr Bittencourt's medicine and thrived on it.

The sight of the decaying men changed Pim and Yepe. They became sullen. They had been led to believe that white men were strong. They stepped out of their aeroplanes, the Indian stories went, with their arms stacked with medicines. And here the men groaned all day from their hammocks and then died.

Was this the future I had brought them to, they asked. Was this it? A white man's graveyard?

'Why you bring us here?' Pim asked me.

He got so worked up Yepe had to hold him back from me.

'Do you really want to hit me? Your friend?'

He knocked Yepe to the ground, and chucked one of our brand-new paddles into the fire.

That same day they both said they were sorry, and would come with me to where the sun came out of the never-ending lake, if that was what would please me. I wasn't sure if it *would* please me any more, bringing them even closer to the edge of the forest, but whatever was just around the corner it had to be no worse than anything here.

We inched to the end of the jungle, continuing south on the Jari. For the first time a few of the men gaping at us from the trees, as they leant on their spades, wore revolvers. I remembered that I had made a promise to the Sicilian cobbler far away in El Callao. I was sad because I'd broken my word. I'd sworn never to set foot where there was gold fever.

The Lure of Gold

Alluvial gold is widespread throughout the Amazon basin, but in only a few regions has it been discovered in large enough quantities to attract hordes of prospectors. Few miners prosper, even where a rich deposit is found. Most of them experience appalling hardship, toiling endlessly in a sea of mud for little reward. And, because they lack basic medical facilities, they often suffer from diseases such as yellow fever, typhus and malaria. In the wet, unsanitary conditions in which many miners live and work, even small cuts can become dangerous through infection; foot-rot is common and is vainly treated with engine oil.

The majority endure this harrowing existence for only a few months. And when they leave, their money has in all likelihood gone to bar owners, gold dealers and other entrepreneurs who, unlike the miners, may indeed make a fortune from gold-digging.

If the miners only occasionally benefit themselves, they invariably have a detrimental effect on the land and its people. Their powerful water pumps and sieves disturb the river sediment, thus ruining natural habitats and spawning grounds. They use mercury to separate gold from sand, and often dump large quantities of this highly poisonous metal in rivers, killing fish and other wildlife. Finally, like the Conquistadors before them, the miners have brought to the forest people all the diseases of modern civilisation, from the common cold to syphilis, alcoholism and new, resistant strains of malaria.

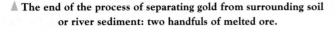

▲ **The end of the process of separating gold from surrounding soil or river sediment: two handfuls of melted ore.**

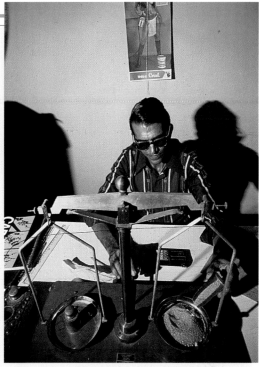

▲ A gold dealer weighing a quantity of powdered gold. Men such as this often make the greatest gain from the backbreaking labour of the miners.

◄ At Serra Pelada in Brazil, huge numbers of men toil in squalid conditions in a vast, open-cast mine. Death is commonplace here: miners are often buried in landslides after heavy rains, and as many as 40 murders are said to take place in the local town on a Saturday night.

◄ Goldminers on the Madeira River in central Brazil. The device in the foreground directs a stream of water down a series of hollow steps in which heavier gold is left behind while lighter soil is washed away. Note the high-pressure hoses and water pumps in the background, and the destruction they have caused.

▲ Panning for gold in a tributary of the Amazon. This traditional method is time-consuming and arduous, often with pitifully little reward.

◄ This *garimpeiro* or goldminer has clearly had some success, as can be seen by his gilded front teeth.

CHAPTER 8

The Eternal Prison?

I FORCED PIM AND YEPE on down the river in the canoe. They didn't know why they were coming, or where they were going to. They paddled hopelessly as if stirring soup, slowing to gawp when we passed more sickly Indians. I hoped Pim and Yepe were mourning the life that they'd left behind in the interior.

'Pim,' I said. 'Let's leave these people. Just look at them! When did you last go hunting?'

'Half moon back,' he said.

'Come on, then. Let's go.'

We tied up the canoe and I led them off into the forest. At first, they walked behind me and dragged their feet in their pinching, fake-leather shoes. Further on, brushing through the leaves, they pricked up their ears and stalked with me, as we had done together in the old days. The Indians had sold off all our weapons to the goldminers, but the spirit of the hunt was there.

We moved in and out of the spreads of palms, part of the forest again. While Pim was chasing butterflies, Yepe was talking about the jungle spirits, how he could hardly feel any here at all and how it was better in the forest we had come from.

'Yepe, I want you to take my canoe and leave me. Go up river again. Find

Swarms of brightly coloured butterflies are among the most common but wondrous sights of the jungle and its surroundings. ▶

somewhere you can live quietly with the forest.'

'Where spirits live?'

'Where spirits live, yes.'

'You not want Yepe any more?'

'I can manage. I can find someone to help. Gold men are bad people. Yepe must go a long way away and take Pim with you. Go when this sun falls low. Will you do that?'

'You good friend. I do this for you. I go long way away.'

'With Pim?'

'I take Pim. We find forest with spirits.'

We took a different route back to the river and bumped into a settlement of miners on the way.

▲ A typical *garimpeiro* mining settlement of the Brazilian Amazon.

'Let's go another way,' I said, but Pim had dashed forward and was already mingling with a bunch of silent Indians. The stench of the village, two palm huts with tumbledown roofs, made me queasy.

Pim toured the camp, running his fingers over everything he admired, which was most of the objects there. I called him back. He ran to me and grabbed my hand. 'Come, look what I find!' He pulled me over to a square, tin-roofed shack, then jerked me inside.

Our entry disturbed the flies. They pounced on us from the walls. I had to close my mouth to keep them out.

'Look what I find.'

There was a bench and on top of the bench was the thing that Pim wanted me to play with. It was made of fine metal. He flicked it with his fingernail. *Ding!* the object sang.

'Better leave this alone, Pim. This is what the gold men use for measuring gold.' He was smiling at the scales tipping up and down. 'This belongs to a gold-miner man. He's not going to be pleased to find us here.' But it was too late to escape. A big man was blocking the doorway.

'And what have we got here?'

The voice came from a frog-faced man with a pale, white skin and greased-back, black hair. He walked us out of the hut. He was smiling, but I didn't like his eyes. His leather boots squeaked. The Indians in the village kept at arm's length from him and backed off when he looked their way.

'I've already met your chum here.' He pointed a finger at Yepe, who crept up and hid behind me.

'What this man say?' said Yepe. 'He good man?'

Pim wasn't listening. He was slinking back to the hut to play with the scales. The miner went up behind him and grabbed him by the scruff of the neck. 'Oh no you don't!' he shouted and beat him over both ears.

'Does that answer your question?' I said to Yepe.

'Who are you?' the miner said.

I told him my name, the names of the others, and that we were just passing through to the mouth of the Amazon. I said the Indians were my friends and I objected to him messing them about.

The miner said his name was Mendez. 'You know where you are going on to from here?'

'Continuing south, then up the Irataparu tributary, then walking east through the forest to the road to Macapa, on the Amazon mouth.'

'I know the track through that forest. I could be your guide for a small consideration.'

'Is the river easy?'

'Easy? No.' Mendez went on to list a dozen rapids, all of which tallied with those I'd heard about. I was astounded: he really *did* know the river.

'And what is the "small consideration"?'

'That you get your two Indians to stay on and work for me. I'm on the lookout for fresh labour. These days you just can't get good workers.'

'No. Not possible. They're leaving today for the interior.'

▲ **Weighing cakes of gold dust on the scales.**

Yepe sprinted over to us. 'This man got plenty things. Here is wonderful.' It was a can-opener. 'What it do?'

'Nothing much.'

'Here, let me show you.' Mendez took a can and the opener and Yepe watched as he peeled back the bottom of the can. 'Tell him he can keep it.'

'I'm sure he doesn't want it that much.'

'Here.' He put it in Yepe's hands. 'It's all yours. What strong hands you've got.'

'It's all the swinging in the trees,' I said.

'Why don't you keep out of this?'

Pim trotted up with his hands around the neck of a *cachaça* bottle. He tossed it to Yepe, who took an over-ambitious swig and coughed and spluttered it out all over the ground.

'That drink doesn't belong to you,' I said. 'Put it back where you found it.' I apologised to the miner. 'In their society they share everything. Possessions don't mean so much.'

'Don't preach to me about Indians. There's nothing new I need to know about them. But go ahead, boy,' he said to Pim. 'That's right, tip it right back. Now your turn, Yetty.'

'Yepe,' I said. 'His name's Yepe.'

'You know what? You're beginning to get on my nerves.'

'Perhaps we'd best be off, then.'

'You American?'

'English.'

'Well, gringo, I suggest you stay out of my way.' Mendez clenched his hands around the buckle of his gunbelt. 'And keep your mouth shut when I get out the gold.'

When the Indians were reeling because of the *cachaça*, they were led off to the tin hut for a display of gold dust. I sauntered after them, but the miner barred my entrance. 'Sorry, this is private business.'

Sitting outside, I could hear Yepe's sighs and yelps of excitement from Pim. I was sad and angry, because I knew I had lost them.

'Sounds like they know a bit about gold already,' said Mendez, strolling out.

'Oh? And what are they thinking now?'

'They are thinking how rich they're going to be.'

'And *are* they going to be rich?'

'Who knows? Have you ever seen a rich Indian?'

'Only in the forest.'

'Ha! We've got ourselves a romantic.'

Pim and Yepe came away rolling drunk, hiccupping and idiotic. I pulled them back to the canoe, taking both their hands. They were very confused. It took a few hundred paces before I could shake off Mendez, but he was scared of the dark: the rustlings of mice and the snakes of the night, tree roots to trip over.

We slept in the canoe, the hull nuzzling the water reeds through the night.

It was the *creak, creak* of the leather boots which woke me. Mendez peered into the canoe from the riverbank. 'Feeling better this morning, are we?'

'What are you doing here, Mendez?'

'Haven't your Indian friends told you? I'm joining your expedition. We start off together, I show you where the track through the forest is. That gets you to the mouth of the Amazon eventually and the Indians come back and go off digging with a friend of mine called Edwardio, on the Irataparu.'

'This man good,' Yepe said. 'Tell him I think he good.'

'Yepe, I thought you were going to leave here. You *promised*. What happened?'

Pit Viper

THROUGHOUT THE AMAZON basin the most feared snakes are the pit vipers. All vipers have strong, hollow fangs for injecting venom, but pit vipers also have large sensory organs in depressions (pits) between their eyes and nostrils, which act as supersensitive heat detectors. These organs are receptive to infrared radiation and are able to identify the tiniest temperature changes (only .003°C) at a distance of at least 6 feet. They enable pit vipers to locate their prey unerringly, even if it remains invisible and completely motionless. The only possible escape from a confrontation with one of these fearsome reptiles lies in immediate, headlong flight.

The most common Amazonian pit vipers are the lanceheads, which grow to about 5 feet in length. They live on the floor of the rain forest and in cultivated areas. Others, however, are generally

▲ **The fer-de-lance, or bushmaster, is the largest of the pit vipers, sometimes attaining a length of over 10 feet. It spends much of its time comatose as it digests its prey.**

arboreal, and are often found curled round the thin branches of bushes and small trees, where they are well hidden.

Humans, fortunately, rarely die from a pit-viper bite. Nevertheless, the venom's effect is very unpleasant, resulting in vomiting, sweating, local swelling and acute headache.

'We find this man. He good. And Benedito … we going to be *rich!* We buy plenty these.' He whirled the can-opener in my face.

'Congratulations, Mendez. You seem to have won them round.'

'Move over, gringo, I'm coming aboard.'

'*Now?* What about your Indians back there?'

'Let them stew. They do nothing but drink. You can get only a couple of years' productivity out of these people as a rule and I want to move on and start afresh.'

All the way down the Jari, Mendez kept flashing his gold at Yepe and Pim, nurturing their desire for it. Over the man's gunbelt flopped two thick loops of fat. His weight slowed us down and he couldn't handle a paddle.

Just as we were reaching the first major outpost of westernisation, the Jari Project—systematic cropping of the forest for a pulp-mill floated here from Japan—we turned away into the interior again, up the Irataparu. Before we were away we heard the buzz of chainsaws and the heavy crash of a falling tree.

The river mouth was a bottleneck of rapids. There were more Indians, yellow with malaria, and rubber trees with notches where they were bleeding latex.

Well into the interior again, a week upstream of other human habitation, we glided up to Edwardio's shack.

Edwardio wasn't in. We knew this because his canoe wasn't moored. We pushed through the forest and came to a primitive hut: no smell of cooking, only a reek of urine from the clearing at the back. Edwardio came later with a rifle, after Mendez had discovered a store of tinned sardines concealed in the roof.

Edwardio was lean and had a gaunt face, a high, smooth forehead and dry skin. He looked as much like a lizard as

▲ **An armed goldminer carries home his next meal.**

Mendez did a toad. His eyes were cold and hooded. He said he wanted cash for the sardines, but was very happy that Mendez had at last got hold of two strong Indians to work for them. But what was the other stranger doing here? He said he didn't like strangers this far up the Irataparu. This was his stretch of mining country.

'I've already warned him not to come,' said Mendez.

'You did nothing of the kind.' I turned to Edwardio. 'He said he would show me the track through to the end of the forest. These are my guides. Mendez wants them to stay on and work for you, after my expedition's over.'

'That true?'

Mendez grunted. He said it was vaguely true, but it would be better for everyone if I ended my expedition here. 'I don't see the problem,' he said to Edwardio. 'This Benedito person can paddle back down the river again by himself.'

'Yepe, I must talk to you,' I said.

'Benedito, what Edwardio say?' Yepe asked. 'He good man too?'

'No. These men bad.'

The night fell. It was an inky black one and we sat in the living quarters of the hut under the soft light of the oil lamp. *Cachaça* was brought out, not a bottle but a crate.

From the goldminers' point of view, the *cachaça* worked a treat on the Indians. They had bottles to their lips for so much of the early part of the evening that I couldn't get a word in edgeways. Later, the Indians' heads crashed down on to the table. They smiled at me cross-eyed when I shook them. Yepe tried to say that he was sorry, but his lips were like rubber and no words came out.

'You'd better go to bed, Benedito. You've got a lot of canoeing to do. You should reach a settlement in a week or two if you're lucky.'

I hated Mendez. But I hated him more because of what he was doing to these Indians than because of what he was doing to me.

Running for My Life

I woke abruptly in the darkness with the feeling that something was wrong; the sensation was strong enough to make me lift my head from the cotton of the hammock to listen to the night. It was not that I knew what had disturbed me, it was just that the jungle had taught me to use my senses to the full and I trusted them. Now they had woken me out of my sleep. I would have got up to investigate even if at that moment I had not remembered the miners.

I lifted up the mosquito net, reached down for my boots, flicked them in the air to empty out scorpions and slipped them on. I heard the two Indians breathing. The miners were still up.

▲ The croaking of frogs is often a persistent background sound in the Amazon. Here, a barred leaf frog peeps over the edge of a heliconia leaf.

Still in only my loose shirt and trousers, I tiptoed through the dark to the doorway. Then I was outside standing in the dusty clearing with the scratching insects. They were quieter this night. Most were waiting for the rains. Then the frogs would come for them, the snakes would wake up to dine out on the frogs and larger snakes rouse themselves to swallow the smaller ones.

Here I was dwarfed by the trees. To see the stars I had to lift my head right back, but what I had thought were stars were in fact fireflies, skipping against the black sky.

In the clearing I heard the voices. They were speaking in Portuguese: the goldminers. They must have been in the living quarters of the hut, dragging on cigarettes. I saw the orange tips flare up, the light filter through chinks in the walls. With my nose in against a crack, I smelt the rich smoke. And I heard the goldminers say that they were going to cut my throat. All I could do was stand there in my shirt and boots and listen. Was the Englishman armed? Yes, but no problem. He only kept a dagger in his boot. Did the Englishman's Indian friends mind? No, they couldn't care less.

The words rattled about in my brain. Then I ran.

I dashed back for my hammock and mosquito net. I went right past Yepe and Pim. They were snoring like bellows. *Didn't* they care?

Then I was away, and into the black forest. At the river I heard a soft, sighing

noise in the trees and knew it was approaching rain. The river water was warm against my legs. I coiled the mooring-rope and heaved the canoe clear of the bank. Then I leapt aboard, colliding with Cashoe, and fumbled for the paddle. No one would think of going upstream to find me, I thought, and it felt good fighting against the current, so that was the direction I took.

I looked over my shoulder and saw, fading into the distance, a pale crocodile. It was Edwardio's canoe. I watched until it was lost in the darkness.

I was alone.

Rocks and branches were snared in the water, but I steered clear of them by listening to the ripples of the water flow ahead. It was a trick Yepe had taught me. The rain came, tearing at the leaves and dancing on the water. The river was swelling. Making headway was hard. I began to long for the chatter of the Indians. The canoe was so empty without them.

The sky cleared; the breeze stung my wet face. A silver crescent moon shone on the water and turned it the colour of milk.

I was on the run. I lived on fish baited with palm berries and nuts scavenged from the floor or thrown down by monkeys. At dusk I assembled a camp—just a hammock, mosquito net and canvas-sheeting roof. I tucked it in the trees a few dozen paces from the riverside. Each morning I woke in the cool mist, when it was so quiet you could hear the dew dripping, and wondered if this was a dream. But the clammy earth smell was real and so were the canopies of leaves, matted yellow orchids and moss-smothered branches. The red leaves of creepers were heaped like fishing nets over everything else.

Dog-tired, I was looking for the track from the river to the east, the one Mendez had told me led out of the forest. It was my hope; and as long as I knew I had some, that was just fine. With my stores I could make the jungle a comfortable enough home for a week or so. I kept a vision of the Amazon mouth—a sunset view of water-like, ripple-less glass—in the forefront of my mind. This image helped me to forget everything else that might go wrong.

Rapids

The third day on my own, the water ruffled and whitened. The weed didn't spiral up from the depths any more, it streamed from the lee of rocks, trailing in the current. My hands became red, flayed from hauling the canoe by rope. I missed Pim and Yepe more than ever.

'You can start bailing out the water if you want to feel useful, Cashoe!'

He was not a dog in my mind, but a member of the expedition team—the one that guarded the stores at night. So what he did now seemed like a betrayal.

Just out of the jaws of the rapids, beyond the spray but before we were safe, I jumped into the canoe and took up the paddle again. Cashoe knew how unstable the canoe was. Nevertheless he bit into a rice sack and began to tussle with it.

'Not now, Cashoe! Lie *down*!' It was already too late. The rice sack spilled, two other sacks tipped over and everything else happened so quickly the whole incident must have been over in a few seconds.

As the rice sacks shifted, giving the canoe a left-hand list, I stuck my paddle out to the right to balance it. Even then I had a feeling of inevitable disaster, like in a nightmare. There was the sight of the receding calmness of dark russet water; my panicky wild strokes with a paddle; gravel whisking up from the riverbed and clattering on the canoe underside. All the time I knew what lay behind, cataract after cataract, because I had spent the whole morning towing the canoe up through them. Back and back we jogged, Cashoe yelping. The twisting white foam streaked past as I dug and dug the water, the bucking worse and worse; the despair; and at last—a relief now—the canoe splintering against a treetrunk.

The dugout crumpled as easily as a matchbox.

Later, I caught my breath on the riverbank. I had bashed my head on a rock as I was being flushed downstream, and one of my fingernails had been split as I clawed at the shingle for a hold. The cut was painting circles of blood on my knees. I had just seen Cashoe choke to death in the surf. I was stuck in the jungle and I had lost almost everything.

I wanted to close my eyes and shrivel up in the bleaching sun.

The air was grey, dusty and hot. It buzzed gently on my face. A parrot fluttered down to the far bank and dabbled in the fingery-black tree roots. The bird was a type I had rarely seen. Its head was black, its wings chalky green and yellow and its beak like a black can-opener. Another, bigger version hurtled down from a cloud of leaves and bickered with it until the smaller bird ducked its head, shrieked and flew off.

No help was going to come my way, I had to help myself. But how?

All the excitement and drama of wild water on one of the Amazon's northern tributaries. ▼

I did what Eddie McGee would have instructed. I trampled out a clearing in the reeds and laid out everything I had salvaged. Then I began to take stock.

Survival belt kit:

1 large compass	Dried soup, 4 packets
1 spare compass	Glucose tablets, 12 packets
Waterproof (lifeboat) matches, 1 pack	A whistle
Fishing hooks, all sizes (approx. 50)	Aspirins, 20
Fishing line, 33 feet each of heavy,	Anti-malaria tablets, for 4 weeks
medium and light (breaking strain)	(All other antibiotics, etc
Explosive flares (defensive firearms), 1	too sodden to use)
Pens (2) and paper	One polythene bag containing
Water sterilising tablets	the above, as water container
(for 22 gallons)	Money belt, with passport,
Razor blades, 1 packet	airticket and dollars

With my clothes were a leg-knife, my machete and my hat (found snagged in some waterside weed). I had also rescued a cooking pan, water bottle, empty rucksack and a small strip of orange polythene. Here, too, mocking me, were Pablo's jaguar tail, the armadillo tail and the monkey's paw. It all seemed so unjust. Where were my medicine, hammock, mosquito net, shelter and food? Instead, I had two picture postcards of London and a notebook, in which I sketched a map, the one I had memorised, and filled up all the blank spaces with question marks. Then I wrote out some instructions and made myself swear never to contradict them.

According to my calculations, the edge of the forest was at worst seventy or eighty miles, as the crow flies, to the north-east. I thought I might manage two miles a day; half a dozen miles a day perhaps while I had the strength. The true distance to the road would be double my estimate, avoiding gullies and cliffs. It would be triple this if I caught a fever.

If I caught malaria, I might as well sit down and wait for a jaguar.

The evening clouds were painted red from the dying sun. I closed my eyes tight, and once again it was an English winter's day. 'Jungle Eddie' McGee was squatting at my feet.

And if you remember only one thing today, it must be this: your will to survive counts more than anything else—OK? His precise military tone was so positive and confident.

Later, I wrote in my notebook:

6.30pm. Almost dark. I have caught no fish. I made a makeshift tent of leaves. Eddie McGee would burst into fits of laughter over it. I have decided to set out tomorrow on a north-east bearing, to get as much distance behind me as possible, before I am weak with hunger and disease. The prospect of what is ahead is ghastly.

The night was hot. My scalp was prickly with sweat, and I lay wide-awake on the ground listening to the sawing and munching of insects for hours. I rolled about in my tent. If it wasn't the ants trekking across my chest, it was mosquitoes

▲ The early morning
dewy dampness of the
rain forest.

circling above my eyes, or centipedes burying into the small of my back.

The chill of dawn was already lifting when I woke. The leaves of my shelter had shrivelled and hung like walnuts. Others were stuck fast to my face like leeches. But that morning, in the dewy dampness, I was stronger. I wanted to prove to Pablo that this wasn't an eternal prison.

I disentangled the knots of fishing line, slung my rucksack over my shoulder, took hold of my machete in my right hand, placed the compass in the palm of my left and marched off in a north-easterly direction, counting every single pace. 1…2…3…4…

1st July. I have walked and walked and walked all day. Ate half a packet of dextrose tablets. This will be my ration each day (= 24 days' ration). Had a shock when I opened the packet. The tablets were all mottled: white/artificial raspberry. Make the water taste foul. Don't seem to offer much energy. The first of my four packets of soup—'Onion'—is on the boil now. I can scarcely wait. I licked the packet out for its salt.

Watching it boil, I try to think of the Indians who have always shared meals with me. But I can't picture them. I have not been able to, since the capsize. I will fight on without them.

2nd July am. Have a slight fever. Don't think it's malaria, but must wait and see if it gets worse. My rule is to move camp every day, whatever my health. I must keep going, keep putting a good distance behind me. Continuing on a north-east bearing. It is simplest. I am still convinced that my memory of the map is good. Approx. 10 miles done *total*. I count each step in a north-easterly direction, through the bars of vines, leaf plates, snaking roots. I notch every hundred paces up on a stick. The numbers tick through my mind. My head works like a clock, measuring time. I tick along. 97…98…99…100…1…2…3…

6pm. Fever worse. Chances of malaria also worse. Don't feel like eating—

lucky I haven't any food! Did approx. 1 mile today. 65 approx. to do. Slept 4–5 hours. Made myself sit in a small cool stream, forcing myself to submerge in the water every hour. My skin tingles in the water unbearably, but I'm better after.

3rd July 9.45am. Fever about the same. I have only just got up. Cold, damp ground at night must be making it worse. However deep I make my leaf bed, I can always feel the roots grinding into my back. Trying to think of ways of making a hammock. 1...2...3...4... At least the continual pace-counting blocks out thought.

4th July 9.30am. Feel better, but fever still could be malaria. Since the capsize, I have eaten only the soup, glucose tablets (six a day!), a handful of berries, the pith of a palm (you peel back the bark like a banana skin) and a few fat roots. I have some medicinal barks and andiroba nuts, which Pim taught me to find. Saving those till I'm on my last legs.

pm. Slight fever. Feel *very* weak. ½ mile done.

5th July 8am. Feel: what was all the fuss about?

5pm. Depressed. Keep making mistakes. One day I'm going to stumble into a wasps' nest, and that will be the end. The 'accident' happened on 30th June. So I have been going five days. Feels like a month. 14 miles done of approx. 75(?) total, ie only a fifth of the way. The thought is unbearable—I must do more miles, fever or not, each day.

▲ **Ants are omnipresent in the jungle. Here a group of fearsome army ants with enormous jaws overpower a grasshopper.**

The worst thing is not the gloom, the reeking moss, the ants in my eyes at night, monkeys taunting me and chucking sticks down, it is noise: the scraping of all the insects. I cannot escape from it. It's as if I've got earwigs in my ears.

Worse are the memories churning in my head. It is a battle between the weaker and stronger sides of my will. The stronger urges me on with sarcasm, 'A fool, a fool, I met a fool in the forest.' The weaker side tells me to give up this struggle: 'Out of the wood do not desire to go.'

Later. I have shaved today for the first time since the accident. It gave me a sense of triumph, that I was on top of things. I took one razor blade and strapped it with fishing line to a strong, thin twig. It also makes an effective knife, and a better one than the survival knife in my leg sheath. Who the hell designed it? It was meant for crashed aircraft pilots: a survival tool. I wonder how many poor pilots survive?

Sometimes, crouching around my camp fire, drying the slime off my skin in the sparks, I wonder if I should hang around, make a bow and arrow as Tautau taught me. Or snares, traps and spears. But I'm not trying to make this forest a home. I need to get out! (And before I catch a disease or am too weak to think clearly. But let's face it. Really, it's just a matter of time.)

The seven glucose tablets a day are almost worse than nothing. I have promised myself to stop and catch some fish at the next decent stream.

6th July 5pm. Crossed a 'decent stream'. Lost two (medium) hooks and didn't catch a thing. I imagine my stomach looks like a prune, shrunken, withered and black. I do 1,700 paces in each mile. Did five miles.

When I try to picture home, all I see are the postcards I brought with me to distribute as gifts. I still have a couple: the Houses of Parliament and Piccadilly Circus. Look at Big Ben. If only I were there!

I should be well over the Irataparu ridge by now. But it is still just exhausting up and down. The hills were only 12,000 feet. Must be over that height now.

7th July 6pm. 4½ miles done. Camped by stream with a surface like green glass. Badly stung by wasps today. Bumped into a small nest suspended from a palm, and they tipped out and poured over me like treacle. The wasps are only small yellow/orange things, but painful enough, and I walk like a hunchback—like Yakka-yakka with bee stings. Brazil-nut oil would be a balm. I have none.

8th July 6pm. Fruit, fruit, fruit! Plenty of it. Maraja berries. I'm camping by a small, icy water brook in the mosquito clouds, mashing up those juicy, purple berries, each one like a grape. For the first time my stomach is full and bloated.

I will take enough berries for many days. 4½ miles done today.

Maraja berries, looking like juicy purple grapes, hang beside the spiny trunk of their tree.

9th July. My stomach cannot take the diet. The stronger half of me shouts in my ear: 'Don't be so damn soft!' But have crippling stomach pains. These helped by chewing charcoal from my campfire, an Eddie McGee trick. 2½ miles completed today, 35 miles total. Must be almost halfway, but my pace is slower today. *Poco a poco* I will get there, Peña said. But now I know, *poco a poco* I am packing up.

10th July 5pm. Stomach pains continuing as I walk. Today I felt weak and light-headed. Is it alcohol in the maraja berries, or am I fading away through lack of sugar in my blood? Today I came across a splash of daylight on the forest floor. Yes, it's that rare. A capybara had spotted it as well and was dozing on some bark chippings. I stalked it clumsily and wanted to cry when it bolted off into the forest. The jungle is my larder. I see it as an Indian does now. Not for its majesty, or beauty, but for its food. Strange that it has taken deprivation by force to bring me close to them spiritually. And though I am not well enough to think clearly, I sense the spirits they talked of. Whatever God is, he is here.

Collected some andiroba nuts, much like brazil nuts, crunched them for my stomachache, just as Tautau showed me.

3 miles done. 38 total. No water near camp today and passed only two (pathetic) streams.

11th July noon. Not at all well. Slept in. Just cannot make myself move camp. I've therefore broken a resolution. I know I will regret the weakness. It just cannot be helped. It is stupid to try and move. Slight fever. Headache. Thoroughly tired. Just unwell. *Can you imagine what it feels like to be slowly winding down like this? To know you are petering out?* No miles done. Made tea from *quina-quina* bark to lessen the fever. Took two aspirin. Feel so weak.

12th July 6.30am. Help in the form of Cashoe! He's with me again. Is it a dream? No, he really is warm in my arms.

As I stoked the fire, I heard a whimper. An emaciated Cashoe, with his white tail high, but his ribs jutting out so far they cast shadows in the fireglow. Twelve days after the capsize he has found me. How? I don't know.

5pm. I'm up and about again, back in the race. Did three miles. Cashoe following. He is slow and easily exhausted. The stronger half of me is in the ascendant, I almost march through the greenery now, 1…2…3…4… whisking my boots through the ground creepers, kicking off those that try and hold me back, tinging my machete through the lianas, carving the jungle up. For the first time I'm convinced I'm coming out of the hill range. But today I had not a dribble of water since this morning's camp. Yet I'm sweating gallons of it. I suck pebbles to keep saliva in my mouth. I lick my arms for salt. I no longer wash my exposed skin. I have to fend off those mosquitoes somehow and sleeping in the woodsmoke is the only way.

13th July. My tongue swelled up in the night, and almost choked me. But later the rain came in torrents and I laid my head out from my shelter and let it splash in my eyes. Then I lapped it up from puddles like Cashoe.

5pm. Only about two miles done. Wallowed in the forest stream. That water

Jungle Survival

FOOD, WATER AND SHELTER are vital to the survival of any lost traveller, though none is as important as the will to survive. In the temperate rain forest, warmth is not a problem, and broad-leaved palms can easily be rigged together to keep off the rain. Water can be obtained from rivers, or from a liana sliced in two. As some of these may be toxic, however, it is probably safer to collect rainwater (of which there is no shortage) in a palm leaf folded to make a funnel.

Locating food is another matter. Most jungle animals are well camouflaged, or are small, or shy, or confined to the canopy a hundred feet up. And while young shoots and buds of palms and bamboo can be eaten raw, strangers to the forest should remember that only native forest-dwellers have the expertise to recognise other wholesome plants and fruit. The survivor's best bet is to fashion a club or spear and seek out a river: as well as providing fish, rivers attract animals, especially rodents and reptiles, which offer vital nourishment. They should not, however, be cooked over firewood containing vines since some of these emit poisonous fumes as they burn.

▲ **Benedict Allen drinks the moisture from a severed liana.**

tasted so sweet. Cashoe drank furiously. But he can't keep up. He is dying. I'm sure of that now. He came to me as a last hope. The stronger half of me whispered in my ear, 'Of course, he's a walking refrigerator.' A thought I cannot dismiss. The meat on him could make all the difference. I have had no decent protein for two weeks. I am wasting away. I cooked up my last packet soup. I did not share it. I must be firm about this. Have I the right to do this? Is it so inhumane? I'm not going to weaken my resolve. We would both die. Yet I feel like a traitor writing this. Did only two miles again. 43 miles done total.

▲ The author, like this Indian, relied on a razor-sharp machete to carve his way through the jungle.

14th July 5.30pm. Continuing without deviation on a NE bearing. I'm sure this obstinacy will pay off. My rhythm is strong. 1…2…3…4… I can last two hundred paces now, before notching them up on my stick. And the notches are not gashes any more, they are neat nicks.

Today I came across a clearing. Daylight! The sun. A burning sphere, instead of putrid stuffy air. It is so good to feel my clothes baking, the water percolating away in steam. To smell the jungle burning to a frazzle, the leaves suffering under the sun's rays.

This is a small patch of neck-high grassland only the size of a tree crown. I can't think why it's here. Not man-made. No tree stumps, burnt-out settlements, or scruffy, man-spoilt vegetation. The greatest excitement is that there are locusts here. Big, juicy, fat things. Tomorrow I may have the strength to go after them. Four miles done.

15th July 6pm. The locusts are massive and slow. Forefinger length, vivid green jobs, with red/orange-tinged bellies. They flash as bright as beetroot when they fly and edge round the other side of branches when you approach. Clobbered 15 with a stick. Netted 16 more with my shirt. I packed mud on my shoulders the way that Narru and Camahu showed me that day we spent hunting in the grey mud delta. But my back is still cracking open, red and blistered with the sun. The oil of my andiroba nuts should help soothe it. This evening I fried the last of the locusts on a stick.

I ought to have a celebration. 50 miles done! Three today. I'm in better-than-should-be-for-circumstances spirits. But why, oh why, didn't I hang around the clearing? I could have scrounged some more food. Now it's back in the darkness, with the cobwebs in my eyes and skin raw with fungi. 1…2…3…4…

16th July 5pm. I feel weak again. My lips are puffed out and chafed. They feel like tyre treads.

My cheeks have been slashed by a poisonous spiky palm. The only water nearby was black and stagnant. It smelt of tarmac. I filtered it with a trouser pocket and boiled it. I shared some boiled palm stems with the dog. We are companions again. I share my food with him nowadays.

I tapped a banana tree for water today and remembered Fritz doing the same.

17th July 5pm. Did three miles (58 total). Something sad: today I resorted to

▲ Locusts, often brightly
coloured, can be up to
3 inches long.

another non-Indian survival trick: the edibility test. I feel I am letting the Indians down.

To test if a root was poisonous, I mashed a piece up, stuck out my tongue, plonked a piece on it. Waited ten minutes. No acid taste and it wasn't dissolving away on my tongue, so I gulped a speck down. Waited half an hour, no ill effects, so took a bit more. Then more… Eventually gobbled down the whole lot. I wonder how many explorers have 'kicked the bucket' through losing patience. Later, I was trying mashed termite grubs. I've also eaten bigger white grubs which look like baby's fingers. I eat them in the Indian manner, plucking off the heads first, frying them if I can be bothered. I found 11 today peeling back bark of trees.

I'm losing interest in the struggle. The weaker side of me is taking over. I am hardly stirred by the thought: 'To die, and go we know not where.' Such words don't even scare me any more.

18th July 4.30pm. Gathered up fifty orange nuts—can't think of their name, but Pim and Yepe used to say they were good. Cast away the nuts, and kept the orange, sticky, fruit coating. Saving a quarter as a reward for when I've made my jungle tent.

Did three and a half miles. That's about what non-Indians do when they are fresh. I have done 61½ miles. Can I congratulate myself? No, because the Indians would have laughed at that. Some days the jungle is like beechwood, crinkly metallic leaves underfoot, empty spaces, like a park. Other days it is knotted and tangled like an old spider's web, gathering dust.

19th July. Violently sick. Do I eat the rest of the orange fruit or not? Stomachache and dysentery as normal. My stomach feels explosive. I'm chewing a charcoal stick as I write. The grit of the carbon on my teeth is good. My skin is red, and bleeds where the layers have been sponged away by the wetness.

20th July 6pm. 3 miles, after my greatest of struggles of will. Just wanted to carry on lying in my tent this morning. Just a bit longer than usual. Cashoe came and licked my face. I really would have just lain there, but his continual nagging forced me to my feet. As we walked, I was dizzy. My eyeballs sank to the back of the sockets—they felt right up against my brain. The trees looked black. The river's the colour of Coca-Cola. Rain came in the afternoon. I haven't even reached the Cupixi River yet and I have done 64½ miles. It makes no sense. How I long to see that river and its fish. Perhaps I am almost there.

21st July 4.30pm. Suddenly I'm struck down by bad fever. Did 3 miles. Made camp. Found two different edible fruit palms. Ate the fruit raw. I had no stream

◀ The jungle contains
an apparently limitless
variety of trees and plants.
Here a huge liana, known
as a 'tortoise ladder'
(a type of vine), snakes
its way up to the canopy,
in an area of forest that
is relatively clear
of undergrowth.

to cool in. Running water would make all the difference. Going to sleep. Don't think my stomach can take any more.

6.30pm. Slept almost two hours. Struggled awake. Fever better in cool of the evening. Boiling up the *quina-quina* bark I've been saving. If it's malaria, a sip of that tea should give it something to think about. Cashoe has eaten all my berries. I shouted at him, 'Go! Go, while you have the chance. If you want to live, leave!' He's cowering in the distance behind some palms. 'Take a chance and go. Please!'

22nd July 8am. Fever better, but it is the dewy coolness of dawn now and so would be. Going to move on to water. Chewing raw palm fruit. I have no inclination to keep writing this diary. I cannot see a use for it. I hardly have enough energy to move the pen.

5pm. Did 1 mile. With great effort. Shivering wildly. I really feel like I've had it. Please, God, let there be a road, just ahead. But why am I praying? Tautau said that God held no use for prayer. That the world is neutral and man no more important than a lizard.

Alone for three weeks, I know that this must be close to the truth. No, I won't pray. I write that; yet I know that if I don't get out of here, I will be eaten up by one of the other animals. I can hear them competing around me. An ocelot. The shriek of a rat in the talons of an owl. Today I almost trod on a snake: a brown, ropy creature. Who will God let live? Him or me? The answer is it is up to *us*. I can see why the forest people believe that now. 'The jungle is neutral.'

My feet are rotting. My toes are cold and white. They cannot feel the forest floor. I'm brewing up bark for fever, after crushing it with my knife.

Later. My *quina-quina* tea is ready. My palms are sweaty, heavily creased and bright yellow, like French Golden Delicious apples. Medicine first, then sleep. I must keep dunking myself in the stream.

23rd July 10am. The fever is bad. If only I could have ventilation. The jungle isn't like a cathedral, as some romantic said, it is like a stuffy room with everything in it—chairs, desks, etc—sodden. All windows closed.

'The jungle will be your glory, the jungle will be your grave.' The weaker side of me is winning.

Found some snails in the stream, while cooling off. Will boil them. There are 25 of them, but only an inch long.

Can hardly think. Has taken me half an hour to write today's passage. I'm not able to walk far. Just ten paces down to the stream. Shivering. Getting out of tent major effort. Taken two aspirin. I NEED VITAMINS AND PROTEIN.

4pm. Fever same or worse. It is so long since I have felt well that I find it hard to tell what condition my body is in.

Ate the snails. Also a mash of palm stems. I want only to close my eyes, but I've got to collect firewood. It is damp. I need medicine.

24th July 11-ish am. I am racked by fever. Squalid dysentery. I cannot make a fire. I hoped Tautau would come and show how you do it when the wood is wringing wet. I half-waited for him. No one came.

Keep bathing, but just feel like curling up and dropping into a long, delicious sleep. Found a large, white grub in a fallen tree. Ate it alive, still wriggling.

I just cannot make that fire I need. Perhaps later.

Tautau, Yepe, Pim, where are you?

4pm. I cannot last with much more of this. Perhaps the fever will just go away. But I know deep inside that unless someone comes for me or I move now and fight, I am *finished*. Only one thing remains for me to write today. I am resolved.

▲ Seldom observed in the forest because of their excellent camouflage, owls can more often be detected by the shrieks of their victims. This spectacled owl feeds on small mammals, reptiles and amphibians.

Fritz pulled himself out of a fever by killing a deer which 'miraculously' appeared for him. He ate the liver and kidneys. Parts 'viz all ze gootness unt vitamins'. I have been presented with an animal also. He is scratching at a burrow now. I will make a fire if I can.

25th July 8am. Yesterday I killed my companion. Sharp blow with the machete butt to the back of skull. Then slit the throat; just as I did to the Wai-wai pig.

I waited till he wasn't looking. Afterwards, all bloody. I *did* make the fire. My adrenalin carried me through. Ate both kidneys and liver. Then bound body up with fishing line and palm leaves. There is so much meat. And it will be fresh for only four days.

6pm. I stoked up the fire and smoked the legs as well as I could. Forced a broth of the meat down, though I had no hunger. I feel like a murderer. How silent it is without him.

26th July 10am. All night I tossed and turned with the sound of scavengers. Heard the patter and breathing of predators around the camp. Blasted them away once with my last distress flare. Waited all night with my machete in my hands, in case the smell drew jaguars near. The carcass was stuffed up a tree and protected from the vultures with prickly palms. That didn't stop them squabbling over it. This morning I found the skin stripped and the eyes pecked out. I'm marginally stronger than yesterday. I'm going to have another broth from the bones and take on with me flesh for fishing bait and the remaining ribs for this evening's meal.

5.45pm. 5 hellish miles. Lonely, feverish, and have all the usual stomach problems. To be expected after the dogmeat.

I plunge my hat into streams and let water dribble down from my hair when I put it on. My only luxury. Walked naked in the forest to let my skin breathe. Now my mind flits away on the slightest impulse. Today Pim stole my clothes again. He was testing me, seeing if I would last long or not. Seeing if I was as good as an Indian. And the leaves were drawing blood like razor blades today, just as they did the other time.

Now I am by my fire. The wood is wet, and smoke-blue and thick. I have to put my head in it to drive parasites from my hair. Then I will put my feet in the smoke to do the same. I am alone. Very tired. Tomorrow I must make a giant push.

27th July 5.30pm. The great breakthrough. The stronger part of me is fighting back. Did 7 miles (79½ total) and camping by a river. Can only be *the* river. The Cupixi. A silver band of water as smooth as a mirror. My liver aches, it doubles me up, but my feet are in the water, and I am in gentle evening sunlight. A milky haze kisses the trees on the far bank and I must be nearly out.

28th July 7.30am. Have caught three piranha (in only 25 minutes), with the last of Cashoe. Spent all but a minute of that time putting on new hooks. Sacrificed

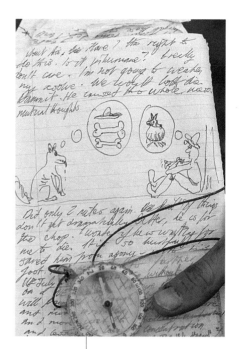

▲ **This poignant cartoon, taken from one of the author's few surviving notebooks, encapsulates his heartbreaking dilemma.**

all but a couple. They bit straight through the line, without even jerking it.

29th July 6pm. My calculations say I have done 85 miles total. What has gone wrong? Where is the road? Where is daylight? I'm still on a north-east bearing, and fought oh so hard today. Over six miles. Six miles through trees with snaky creepers up their trunks and bristly lianas.

I kept going only because the others—all my friends—were chanting for me. Calling me onward. Is it really true that they aren't here? The Italian brothers of the Orinoco, with their Warao Indians; the chief with pigtails tied with green polythene, Narru, Camahu, Zorola. The Sicilian, the *padre* of El Dorado, Peña: 'You will make it *poco a poco*.' Even Fritz barking at me to keep walking. Even Jorge the missionary, Pablo with his silver spurs clinking just a few steps behind. Maipuri, Tautau. Ak-ak skip-

▲ Another face of the rain forest: here it is almost impenetrably thick with lianas, palms, ferns and aerial roots.

ping, holding my left hand. Yimshi tugging me with the other. And Haimarha, Toeleu, Yepe, Pim and Cashoe. They were all walking with me.

But now the day is ending and here I am, still in the jungle. I have one more dried piranha for today. I am not moving.

I cannot write more. I have a bad fever.

30th July. Didn't move camp today. This is my second night here. Sometimes I just sit and swat mosquitoes for hours on end. What else is there to do? Tomorrow I must make another big push. All my strength has gone. Now I have only the strength of my friends, who keep begging me not to let them down.

31st July. I walked like clockwork, tick-tocking along in the way I had become accustomed to: 5…6…7…8…9… It was no use trying to keep my mind on the jungle any more. Being able to escape from the trees in my thoughts was what kept me alive. Tomorrow I would have been going a month. My loneliness was mixed with confusion. What had gone wrong? Why had I not reached the outside world yet? It just didn't make sense. Too weak even to cry, I walked on and let my thoughts gently lift out of the forest and drift away.

Vy are you not walking faster zan zis? It was Fritz's voice. *Get your lousy bum movings.*

Where you going, Louco Benedito? Maipuri's voice said. *Why you not walking dis way, back to decent Wai-wai forest?*

'Can you tell me the way out of here, someone?'

The jungle is an eternal prison.

'Pablo! It isn't an eternal prison, is it? I've been walking for a month, you know. But I've kept your jaguar's tail.'

Louco Benedito, said Maipuri. *If you want leave jungle, you marry Yimshi first.*

'Yimshi. Did Maipuri treat you badly after I left without accepting you that night?'

You are Mad White Giant. Mad White Giant. Mad White Giant.

'What's going on? I'm feeling weak. Why aren't any of you helping me?'

We want see if you are good Indian.

'Pim! You are here as well!'

Why you wearing clothes?

'Did you really betray me that night? Did you and Yepe really not care if Mendez and Edwardio killed me?'

I come see if jungle is your home, Mad White Benedito Giant. That was Tautau, but his image was a blur and his voice fading.

Ze jungle is your glory unt grave. Is funny, ja? Glory unt grave!

We want to see if you survive, Benedito.

Maybe you not strong enough to be good Indian, said Pim.

I was alone again and on my knees, naked. But now in the Orinoco Delta, on the mud flats. My skin was slashed by seashells. I had a pelican tied around my waist with a cord of reed. Then the dizziness was too much for me.

5pm. Collapsed today at about 11.30. Just felt faint, and blood draining from my head. Blackness. Next I knew I was face down in the leaves.

Fever is very severe, though better now. I feel weak and have more difficulty in moving my pen than ever before. Did only 1½ miles. Dizzy again. The trees are all black above my head.

Later. Barely able to make a shelter. I will sleep. Ants everywhere. Hate them. Nasty orange brutes that bite for no reason.

Later still. Putting the milky sap disinfectant of a tree, which Pablo told me about, on my cuts. Must rest. *I can hardly see.*

1st August. I've done it. Please don't take success away from me now. It would be too cruel. Dabbling in a brook this morning, my mind suddenly cleared. I saw a cut branch. Not a torn one, a ripped one, but a cut one. A beautiful, crisp, clean slice of a machete. And other cut branches are all around me. I want to remember them. Every one. And the purring of the mosquitoes, and the fragrance of the sprays of orchids which are clutching branches way up above. I want to remember the leaves shivering in the canopy breeze, and this little stream which woke me to it all.

Paths criss-cross around me. I will choose one leading north-east. I must have done it… I should hear people talking and car doors slamming. I hope I choose the right path. Success and a bed.

▲ **The fragrance of orchids pervades much of the jungle. This cattleya orchid is a typical flower of the rain forest.**

▲ Jaguars can weigh over 220 pounds. They prey on all the larger mammals in the Amazon, and will even kill and eat caymans. Fortunately, they rarely attack people.

Dangers of the Jungle

THE DANGERS OF THE RAIN FOREST are not necessarily those we expect. A sleeping explorer is more likely to be drowned by rapidly rising floodwaters than killed by a predator.

There are certainly some terrifying creatures here: venomous pit vipers; anacondas and boa constrictors that crush their prey; jaguars that can smash a man's skull with a single blow; flesh-eating piranhas; and enormous caymans. Yet, as with most animals, even these fearsome predators prefer to keep well away from humans.

They should, of course, not be underestimated. They will defend themselves if threatened or frightened; and some may look for an untypical human meal if hungry. Stingrays, for example, will retaliate if trodden on; and piranha attack in shoals when starved. On the other hand, it is estimated that only 30 per cent of victims of even the most venomous snakes actually die; indeed, many accepted antidotes are potentially more dangerous than the bite itself. Centipede, scorpion and spider bites are far more common, though fortunately very rarely fatal.

The same cannot be said of the bloodsucking insects which transmit the terrifying range of parasitic diseases endemic to this area, and which thereby pose the greatest and most insidious danger of the forest. Malaria is the most obvious of these diseases; others are much worse. Leishmaniasis, contracted from the bite of a sandfly, attacks the mucous membranes, eating away one's mouth and nose; while Chagas' disease, transmitted by the assassin bug, can induce heart failure. For this reason a mosquito net is the explorer's greatest friend, together with antibiotics to treat any infection which might otherwise turn the smallest scratch into a potential killer.

▲ A mother scorpion carries her brood of young on her back. Even these babies are fully armed with venomous stings.

▲ Red-bellied piranha. They are most dangerous when the floodwaters recede and they are trapped in a shrinking pool with no food.

▲ In the rainy season large rivers rise rapidly and overflow their banks by tens of miles. An unwary explorer camping beside a river can easily be caught at night by the floods brought about by torrential rains.

The freshwater stingray is unique to Amazonian waters. It can inflict an intensely painful wound with the poisonous, serrated barb on its tail. ▶

▲ Equally at home in the trees as on the ground, this golden eyelash viper is one of the Amazon's most poisonous creatures.

A giant anaconda crushing a cayman. It will proceed to swallow its victim whole, and then lie in a stupor for over a month digesting its meal. ▶

CHAPTER 9

Liberation

F ELLED TREETRUNKS WERE LITTERED all the way along the track, but above their stumps the remaining forest canopy was as tightly shut as ever. The trees had closed ranks. Not a single rod of light shone through. But I half-skipped along and giggled when I took a tumble over a stack of freshly cut branches.

Now the forest's stale larder reek was giving way to a dry, earthy smell: that of a newly ploughed field. I stepped in the direction of the smell, to my right, knowing I had lost the path, but not caring. I was stopped by a thicket of grey and black bamboo shoots, laced together by a strangling creeper and stretching way up above my hat. I slid my machete into my waistband, dropped to my knees and cleaved the vegetation apart with my elbows. The creeper strings were sticky with sap as they broke.

The light, I had thought, would come all of a sudden. I would peel away a sheet of the creepers and there I would be, standing in it, blinking, with my clothes already beginning to stiffen in the sun; and I would be laughing out loud.

But the light came at first in specks through the thicket, like stars in a clear night sky. The stars grew and grew, then coalesced into larger, irregular forms—triangles, diamonds and spheres—all just in front of my eyes in this dark thicket,

as I pulled more and more of it away. The quality of the light was improving, too, increasing in brilliance. When it was the most stunning of whites and the leaves and barks under my knees were crackling, not squelching, I knew the forest was behind me.

After the darkness, the light—too much of it; all this space; and everything so quiet; and dead.

I was on the verge of a cassava field. The spindly, shrubby plants looked meagre sitting there under the sun, bedded in an orange soil, which seemed to me as sterile as rock. Strangest of all, they were in orderly rows, ranks of them that continued right to the horizon, which was so low and even. On the horizon was a primitive square hut. The squareness of the hut seemed as odd as the straightness of the lines of cassava. It was all so unnatural, ridiculous after the ill-discipline of the forest.

A person came out of the square hut; a man, with a back curved from too much field work. He stared at me. I stared at him. I scuffed and tripped through the cassava crop in his direction. My feet felt less heavy than for a long time and for a second I managed a run. I slowed again; not out of tiredness, but because the man wasn't waiting with outstretched hands to welcome me back to the outside world. I'd somehow expected that he would. But no, he was just staring; more in horror than curiosity.

An arm's length away, I flipped off my hat and tried out a smile. He raised his eyebrows and his mouth fell wide open.

Along with my euphoria, my strength was going. I would fall soon. But I didn't want this man for support. He was regarding me as if I were an ogre. So instead I leant on the wooden palings of his hut wall.

I opened my mouth to speak, but the effort of explaining everything to this

◀ A cultivated field, with
the jungle encroaching to
its very edge.

With the forest looming behind them, a farmer and his wife harvest a crop of manioc tubers from their small patch of cultivated land. ▶

gaping farmer was going to be too much and I looked away, down at my boots and the mud flaking off them as it dried.

A shaft of light flashed into my eyes from the glass face of my watch. The watch was still ticking: 10.30am. My wrist was scarlet from where the watchstrap had chafed it. Sheafs of skin flapped loose like lace cuffs. I wondered what my face looked like.

The man confronting me must have been fifty years old. On his chin grew a rough grey bed of stubble and he smelt of dry clay. I saw he had his hand out. I wondered just how long it had been there. I shook it, but the grip of this weak man was so tight on my twig fingers, I grimaced.

The man was going to speak. A word of warm welcome? He said, 'The *senhor* has been out walking a long way today?'

'Yes,' I managed slowly, 'a long way.'

'Will the *senhor* stop for a second to have a coffee?'

Good grief! I thought. Can't you see I'm at death's door? 'Yes, *senhor*. I would appreciate a coffee very much,' I said.

'You wait here, *senhor*. You sit and rest awhile.'

I was unconscious when he pottered back out of the hut and the next thing I remember was lying in a hammock, gazing at the splinters of daylight that showed through the wooden tiles of the roof.

Journey's End

The man's name was José, and though I shared his rich coffee for three days and he brewed me a dozen of his family herbal remedies, he never did ask where I had come from, or how I came to stagger into his field from the jungle that morning. As for myself, I had no desire to speak at all—conversation was something I had grown to be wary of, while alone—but I owed this man much and so several times I tried to explain. José, however, was content to perch on a stool by my hammock-side, holding a warm cup of coffee ready to press to my lips. If I told him of the jungle and the Indians, he would listen out of politeness for a minute, then make an excuse and slip outside to his field with an axe or hoe. It was enough for him to know that I needed rest.

My skin was hideously yellow, but his own was stretched as tight around his stomach as anyone's I'd seen. Starvation, it seemed, was normal on the jungle frontier land dished out by the government. After another day spent scratching in the field, José confided that he was just one of hundreds of thousands who knew what the government didn't. The jungle could not sustain a decent crop for more than a year or two. He was bitter about it. The government was crazy to send people here, he said.

I was happy to be alive, as I dozed in my hammock, but the happiness was mixed with uncertainty. I felt I didn't belong to this outside world to the extent that I used to. There was a feeling of bereavement. I had entered the forest where the road had faded, and had crawled out where the same road had been abandoned five years before by construction workers beginning on it from this end. Somewhere in the 700-mile gap in the road, I had left part of myself behind.

On the third day out of the forest, I was on my feet again. A yellow government jeep came up the track to José's plantation, where the road stopped. The four surveyors pondered awhile, frowned at the forest barrier, and explained that they were wondering whether it was worth starting work on the road project again, to open the forest right up.

I said that from what I'd seen of the forest, I wouldn't bother.

'Hah!' the men laughed. 'From what the *foreigner* has seen of the forest, we shouldn't bother!' They said they appreciated the joke very much and that as I was looking pretty rough, they'd give me a lift back to wherever I'd come from. *I* laughed this time, far louder than the others had.

It took no time at all to pack. I had only to stop for my belongings: a hat, jaguar's tail, monkey's paw, armadillo's tail, machete and little else. José saluted me, smiled fractionally and, as I was hauled aboard the jeep, bent down to carry on wrenching a cassava tuber from the soil.

I took up the journey again, just like that. I was on the road to Macapa and the mouth of the Amazon. Though weak, I was strong enough to ride high on my seat, as we sped closer and closer to the river. But it wasn't the delta I was longing for any more; it was the stench of car exhaust fumes, the lick of new paint, the blare of transistors and the smooth, concrete walls. Quite suddenly, they had become beautiful, after the jungle. Though I wasn't sure why, I was yearning for these things—just as Narru and Camahu had yearned for them, bright-eyed and in their spanking new suits, only a few moons ago in the Orinoco Delta, on the day my journey first began.

Discovering the Amazon—Travel Tips

Preparing to Go

Getting there Independent travel to the Amazon is feasible but time-consuming: distances are huge and the logistics of planning an itinerary can be complex. If time is short, consider taking an organised tour from your own country.

The Brazilian national airline, Varig, and numerous international carriers fly to Rio de Janeiro and São Paulo, from where buses and domestic flights serve Belem, Manaus and other centres. Varig also flies direct to Belem and Manaus from Miami. A 21-day pass is available, giving unlimited air travel within Brazil.

Lima is the international port of arrival for Peru; domestic flights serve Iquitos, which is inaccessible by road, and other major cities.

Buses are inexpensive in both countries, but are an uncomfortable and restricted means of exploring the Amazon region, especially during the rainy season when many roads are closed. Boat travel is more convenient and far more interesting.

Visas Enquire through embassies for the latest requirements. Visas for Brazil are good for a 90-day trip, and can be extended once only for a further 90 days. For Peru, US and EC citizens receive an entry card on arrival, normally valid for up to 90 days. Other nationals may need to obtain visas in advance. Extensions can be procured at offices in Lima and Cuzco, or by leaving and re-entering the country.

Language Portuguese is the main language of Brazil; Spanish that of Peru. English and French are not widely used, but are spoken by some.

What to take Carry small-denomination $US traveller's cheques. Credit cards are useful for some hotels and for car hire, but cannot be used everywhere. Costs are often very low compared to Europe and the USA, and it is easy to find inexpensive hotels with an acceptable standard of comfort.

Take a shoulder bag or backpack rather than a suitcase: tatty-looking luggage is less likely to get stolen. Remember to pack a sweater for cool evenings, a first-aid box, a mosquito net, lightweight clothing, a practical guidebook, a phrasebook, a torch (with spare bulbs and batteries), some lightweight binoculars, a Swiss army penknife, film, suntan lotion, an alarm clock and insect repellent; additional items might include walking boots and a compass. Toiletry items are obtainable in Brazil and Peru.

When to go The months between May and September are generally driest and are thus the best. Daytime temperatures are high throughout the year. However, there is a considerable difference between the climates of the lowlands

The dark waters of the appropriately named Rio Negro flow past the stylish city of Manaus. In the bustling market (inset), the fresh catch of the day is always tempting. ▼

In Brazil, Shrove Tuesday is the occasion for exuberant carnivals.

◀ The ancient city of Cuzco nestles in a valley in the Andes at over 11,000 feet.

and the mountains, so be sure to take appropriate clothing.

Health Consult your GP on the latest health matters concerning the region you intend to visit. There are no required vaccinations, but inoculation against hepatitis, tetanus, typhoid and yellow fever is recommended. Take anti-malaria pills, sleep under a mosquito net and use insect repellent. Drink only bottled or boiled water, and avoid salads and unpeeled fruits.

In the Amazon

Boating along the Amazon Because of their excellent views of river life, boating trips are recommended, despite the risks of river sickness and poor cuisine. Beware of larger vessels and downriver trips, which keep mainly to the middle of the river from where the views are less satisfactory. ENASA, the major river transport company, have regular services connecting Belem, Santarem and Manaus, while numerous small craft depart from the port areas of all these cities. On ENASA services many travellers find second-class hammock space more comfortable than first-class cabins, which can be stuffy.

It takes four or five days to get from Belem to Manaus, and about the same again from Manaus to the border town of Tabatinga, from where it is a three-day trip to Iquitos. Downriver trips are substantially quicker.

Most upriver voyages end at Tabatinga, necessitating a change of boat before proceeding to Iquitos. Note that the accommodation is somewhat limited at Tabatinga, though it is often possible to sleep on the boats.

Belem (Brazil) This bustling city grew rich on rubber. It has a high-rise skyline as well as stylish avenues, a characterful old colonial quarter and a lively open-air market. It offers a vibrant nightlife, a range of Amazonian gastronomy and one of the best carnivals (on Shrove Tuesday) in Brazil. Upmarket hotels abound, while cheap accommodation is found near the port. Major sights include the **Basilica**, the **Forte de Castelo,** with its views over the bay, and the **Goeldi Museum**, which includes sections on Amazonian archaeology, anthropology and ecology, a fine botanical garden and a zoo of forest wildlife. Local agencies organise excursions to **Marajo Island**, a huge tract of savannah, marsh and jungle, with diverse wildlife and good beaches.

Some 500 miles upriver, the port of **Santarem** has limited tourist appeal, but is not unattractive, with its narrow streets and traditional houses. Accommodation is plentiful, and side trips can be taken up the **Rio Tapajos** or to **Alter do Chão**, a weekend resort with a beach and lagoon.

Manaus (Brazil) A port sited on the Rio Negro 7 miles north of its meeting with the Amazon and 900 miles from the sea, Manaus has tremendous atmosphere in its markets, nightlife, eating places and turn-of-the-century, European-style architecture, which includes its celebrated Opera House. There are interesting museums and numerous travel agencies that can advise on local trips, such as day excursions to the **meeting of waters** and the nearby **Parque Ecologico Janauary** for wildlife-spotting. Longer trips by boat also start here: allow several days, preferably a week, to penetrate deep into the forest, where the best wildlife sightings are likely to be.

Iquitos (Peru) Occupying a majestic site on the Amazon, this island city with stylish mansions from its rubber-boom heyday is a rewarding place to visit. Hotels are good, though not especially cheap; restaurants are acceptable. The fascinating, water-bound district of **Puerto Belen** is best explored by dugout 'taxi'. Iquitos is also an excellent base for jungle trips, and offers opportunities for river excursions, swimming, water-skiing, fishing, hunting and relaxing on beaches.

Further into Peru Although outside the Amazon region, the ancient Inca capital of **Cuzco** should not be missed. Nearby are magnificent ruins and opportunities for hiking in superb mountain scenery. It is also well-placed for jungle expeditions, notably to **Manu National Park**, one of the world's finest rainforest reserves. Trips can be organised through Manu Nature Tours, Avemida el Sol, Cuzco. Otherwise you need to apply for a permit from the Dirección General Forestal y de Fauna, Jirón Natalie Sanchez 220, Jesus María, Lima. Another excellent way to see the jungle is by scenic train journey from **Machu Picchu**, the lost city of the Incas, to **Quillabamba**, north of Cuzco.

Index

and Acknowledgments

Acknowledgments

The editors gratefully acknowledge the use of information taken from the following books during the preparation of this publication:

Aborigines of the Amazon Rain Forest: The Yanomani by Robin Hanbury-Tenison and the Editors of Time-Life Books, Time-Life 1982

Amazon Beaming by Petru Popescu, MacDonald & Co 1991

Amazon: The Flooded Forest by Michael Goulding, BBC 1989

Amazonia by Loren McIntyre, Sierra Club 1991

Amazon Wildlife Insight Guides, APA Publications 1992

'The Amazon' by Loren McIntyre, *National Geographic*, October 1972

The Amazon by Tom Sterling and the Editors of Time-Life Books, Time-Life 1973

The Amazon: Past, Present and Future, Thames and Hudson 'New Horizons' 1988

The Conquest of the Incas by John Hemming, Macmillan 1970

The Enchanted Canopy by Andrew W. Mitchell, Collins 1986

The Encyclopaedia Britannica

The Hidden Peoples of the Amazon, British Museum Publications 1985

In Trouble Again by Redmond O'Hanlon, Hamish Hamilton 1988

Jungle Nomads of Ecuador: The Waorani by John Man and the Editors of Time-Life Books, Time-Life 1982

Kingdom of the Sun God by Ian Cameron, Random Century 1990

The Land and Wildlife of South America by Marston Bates, Time Inc 1965

Narrative of Travels on the Amazon and Rio Negro by Alfred Russel Wallace, Ward Lock 1889

The Naturalist on the River Amazons by Henry Walter Bates, John Murray 1863

Out of the Amazon by Sue Cunningham and Ghillean T. Prance, HMSO 1992

Peru's Amazonian Eden: Manu National Park and Biosphere Reserve by Kim Macquarrie, Francis O. Pathey & Sons 1992

The Royal Geographical Society History of World Exploration, Hamlyn 1991

Running the Amazon by Joe Kane, Bodley Head 1989

Picture Acknowledgments

T=top; *B*=bottom; *C*=centre; *R*=right; *L*=left; *I*=insert

Cover *Spine* Colorific!/John Moss, *L(T–B)* Benedict Allen; Luiz Claudio Marigo; Sue Cunningham, SCP; Michael and Patricia Fogden; Robert Harding Picture Library/Robert Frerck; *R* Luiz Claudio Marigo, **2** Loren McIntyre, **3** Michael and Patricia Fogden, **5** Cristina Uribe Editores/Cristina Uribe Hurtado, **6** Benedict Allen, **7** André Bärtschi, **8–9** Luiz Claudio Marigo, **12** *C* NHPA/Stephen Dalton, *BL* Ardea, London/Nick Gordon, *BR* Michael and Patricia Fogden, **12–13** The Hutchison Picture Library/Jesco von Puttkamer, **13** *CL* NHPA/ Stephen Dalton, *B* Andrea Florence, **14** Gunter Ziesler, **14–15** ZEFA/H. Sunak, **15** *TR* Loren McIntyre, *BL* Günter Ziesler, *BR* ZEFA/Koblmueller, **16** *C* Robert Harding Picture Library/Derek Furlong, *BR* Mountain Camera/John Cleare, **16–17** Magnum/Stuart Franklin, **17** The Hutchison Picture Library/H.R. Dörig, **18** *TL* Luiz Claudio Marigo, *C* André Bärtschi, *BL* André Bärtschi, *BR* Luiz Claudio Marigo, *BI* Luiz Claudio Marigo, **18–19** Luiz Claudio Marigo, **20** *B* NHPA/Stephen Dalton, **20–21** Luiz Claudio Marigo, **21** *CL* Michael and Patricia Fogden, *BL* Luiz Claudio Marigo, *CR* Luiz Claudio Marigo, *BR* NHPA/Jany Sauvanet, **22** *BR* South American Pictures/Tony Morrison, **22–23** Luiz Claudio Marigo, **23** *I* Bruce Coleman/David C. Houston, *BL* Luiz Claudio Marigo, *CR* Luiz Claudio Marigo, *BR* Edward Parker Photography, **24** *C* Andrea Florence, *BL* Luiz Claudio Marigo, *BR* André Bärtschi, **24–25** Luiz Claudio Marigo, **25** *CL* Sue Cunningham, SCP, *BL* Luiz Claudio Marigo, **26** André Bärtschi, **27** *TR* Bruce Coleman/ Günter Ziesler, *CR* Luiz Claudio Marigo, *CL* Günter Ziesler GDT, *BL* Cristina Uribe Editores/Diego Miguel Garcés, *BR* Loren McIntyre, **28** *TR* Dr John Hemming, *BR* ZEFA/Jesco von Puttkamer, **29** *TC* Rex Features Ltd/Michael Friedel, *TR* The Image Bank/Marcel Isy-Schwart, *CI* Rex Features Ltd/ Michael Friedel, *CR* Camera Press/Douglas Botting, *BL* Sue Cunningham, SCP, **30–31** South American Pictures/Tony Morrison, **32** *TR* Mountain Camera/John Cleare, *BR* South American Pictures/ Robert Francis, **33** *T* South American Pictures/Tony Morrison, *L* Magnum/Stuart Franklin, *R* The Hutchison Picture Library/ H.R. Dörig, *B* Mountain Camera/John Cleare, **34** *T* South American Pictures/Tony Morrison, *CR* Bilderarchiv Preussischer Kulturbesitz, *B* Coloured lithograph, 19th century/Aldus Archive, **35** *TR* Loren McIntyre, *B* Colorific!/Maja Koene, **36** *TL* Michael and Patricia Fogden, *CR* Planet Earth Pictures/Andrew Mounter, *BL* Michael and Patricia Fogden, *BR* Ardea, London/Nick Gordon, **36–37** André Bärtschi, **37** *CL* Cristina Uribe Editores/Cristina Uribe Hurtado, *BL* Luiz Claudio Marigo, **38** *BI* Bruce Coleman/Luiz Claudio Marigo, **38–39** Still Pictures/Mark Edwards, **39** *TC* André Bärtschi, *TR* Comstock/Georg Gerster, *BR* Still Pictures/ John Maier, **40** *T* Still Pictures/Mark Edwards, *BL* Rex Features Ltd/SIPA, *BC* Greenpeace Communications Ltd/ Morgan, **41** *TL* Royal Geographical Society/Dr John Hemming, *BL* Royal Geographical Society/Luiz Claudio Marigo, **44** Engraving in André Thevet, *Cosmographie Universelle*, 1575, **45** The Bridgeman Art

Library, Diego Homen, *Atlas of South America*, 1558, British Library, London, **46** Royal Geographical Society, **47** NHPA/ George Gainsburgh, **49** Drawing in Ferdinard Denis, *Univers ou Histoire et Description de Tous les Peuples* (vol. 2), 1938, **50** *R* South American Pictures/Tony Morrison, *BL* Ancient Art & Architecture Collection, **50–51** Museo Nacional de Antropologia, Arqueologia e Historia del Peru, Daniel Gianoni, **51** *R* National Portrait Gallery, London, *BL* South American Pictures/Tony Morrison, *BR* Engraving in Theodor de Bry, *Historia Americae*, 1590, **52** Bruce Coleman/M.P.L. Fogden, **53** Rob Cousins, **55** South American Pictures/Tony Morrison, **56** Luiz Claudio Marigo, **58** Benedict Allen, **60** Benedict Allen, **62** ZEFA/Jesco von Puttkamer, **63** Bruce Coleman/Jane Burton, **64** Ron Orders, Cinecontact, **65** André Bärtschi, **66** *T* South American Pictures/ Tony Morrison, *R* Ardea London/ Adrian Warren, **66–67** Oxford Scientific Films/Aldo Brando Leon, **67** *R* South American Pictures/ Tony Morrison, *BL* Oxford Scientific Films/Jeff Foott, **69** Rob Cousins, **70** Benedict Allen, **71** Colorific!/Carlos Humberto, **73** *T* Sue Cunningham, SCP, **74** Art Directors Photo Library, **76** Benedict Allen, **77** Michael and Patricia Fogden, **78** André Bärtschi, **79** NHPA/Haroldo Palo, **80** Ron Orders, Cinecontact, **81** Günter Ziesler, **82** Reflexo/Leonide Principe, **83** Michael and Patricia Fogden, **84** Sue Cunningham, SCP, **86** André Bärtschi, **87** NHPA/Jany Sauvanet, **88** André Bärtschi, **89** Bruce Coleman/Brian Henderson, **90** *TL* Oxford Scientific Films/Kjell B. Sandved, *BL* Günter Ziesler, *BR* Oxford Scientific Films/Michael Fogden, **90–91** André Bärtschi, **91** *L* Luiz Claudio Marigo, *TR* NHPA/George Gainsburgh, *R* André Bärtschi, *BR* André Bärtschi, **93** Cristina Uribe Editores/Cristina Uribe Hurtado, **94** Nicholas Guppy, **95** Luiz Claudio Marigo, **98** Rex Features Ltd, **100** South American Pictures/Tony Morrison, **101** Magnum/Michael K. Nichols, **102** Ardea London/François Gohier, **103** Bruce Coleman/Alan Stillwell, **104** Luiz Claudio Marigo, **105** Edward Parker Photography, **106–8** Bruce Coleman/ Luiz Claudio Marigo, **107** Cristina Uribe Editores/Cristina Uribe Hurtado, **108** Nicholas Guppy, **109** The Hutchison Picture Library/Jesco von Puttkamer, **110** *TL* Benedict Allen, *TR* Michael and Patricia Fogden, *R* André Bärtschi, *BL* Michael and Patricia Fogden, *BR* André Bärtschi, **111** *TL* Oxford Scientific Films/Kjell B. Sandved, *TR* Michael and Patricia Fogden, *CR* Edward Parker Photography, *BR* NHPA/G.I. Bernard, **112** The Image Bank/Marcel Isy-Schwart, **113** The Hutchison Picture Library/Jesco von Puttkamer, **116** Cristina Uribe Editores/Diego Miguel Garcés, **117** Victor Englebert/Kaleidoscope, **118** Victor Englebert/Kaleidoscope, **119** The Hutchison Picture Library/Jesco von Puttkamer, **120** *R* Robert Harding Picture Library/Robin Hanbury-Tenison, *BL* Magnum/Cornell Capa, **120–121** Camera Press/P. Kaipiainen, **121** *T* Still Pictures/Mark Edwards, *BL* Robert Harding Picture Library/Kenneth Brecher, Royal Geographic Society, *BR* The Hutchison Picture Library/Jesco von Puttkamer, **122** Survival International/Victor Englebert, **123** Nicholas Guppy, **124** *L* Survival International/Victor Englebert, *R* Planet Earth Pictures/ Ken Lucas, **125** ZEFA/Sunak, **126** Michael and Patricia Fogden, **129** The Hutchison Picture Library/ Jesco von Puttkamer, **130** *T* Robert Harding Picture Library/ Claire Leimbach, *BL* Edward Parker Photography, **131** Robert Harding Picture Library/Robin Hanbury-Tenison, **132** *CR* Benedict Allen, *B* South American Pictures/Bill Leimbach, **134** Magnum/Miguel Rio Branco, **135** André Bärtschi, **136** *TR* The Environmental Picture Library/Irene R. Lengui, *BL* Camera Press/Harald Schultz, *BR* Colorific!/Tom Rica/Camara Tres, **137** *T* Victor Englebert/ Kaleidoscope, *BL* Rex Features Ltd/ M. Bruwier/Sipa, *BR* Survival International/Victor Englebert, **138** NHPA/James Carmichael Jr, **139** André Bärtschi, **140** Michael and Patricia Fogden, **141** Survival International/Victor Englebert, **142** Survival International/Victor Englebert, **143** The Hutchison Picture Library/Jesco von Puttkamer, **145** Benedict Allen, **146** Luiz Claudio Marigo, **147** André Bärtschi, **148** The Hutchison Picture Library/Jesco von Puttkamer, **149** Luiz Claudio Marigo, **150** Ardea London/Andrea Florence, **151** Cristina Uribe Editores/ Diego Miguel Garces, **152** Loren McIntyre, **154** Cristina Uribe Editores/Cristina Uribe Hurtado, **155** Sue Cunningham, SCP, **156** *TLI* Magnum/ Michael Nichols, *B* Still Pictures/John Maier, **156–157** Magnum/M. Rio Branco, **157** *TR* Magnum/René Burri, *BL* Magnum/René Burri, *BR* Magnum/Nick Nichols, **158** ZEFA/ Jesco von Puttkamer, **159** Still Pictures/Mark Edwards, **160** Magnum/Nick Nichols, **161** Michael and Patricia Fogden, **162** Benedict Allen, **163** André Bärtschi, **165** Loren McIntyre, **167** Robert Harding Picture Library/Brinsley Burbidge, **168** Oxford Scientific Films/Philip Sharpe, **169** Luiz Claudio Marigo, **170** Benedict Allen, **171** Magnum/Nick Nichols, **172** Cristina Uribe Editores/Cristina Uribe Hurtado, **173** South American Pictures/ Tony Morrison, **174** Ardea London/Keith and Liz Laidler, **175** Benedict Allen, **176** South American Pictures/Tony Morrison, **177** NHPA/Kevin Schafer, **178** *T* Michael and Patricia Fogden, *C* NHPA/Daniel Heuclin, *BR* Andrea Florence, **178–179** Luiz Claudio Marigo, **179** *L* Planet Earth Pictures/Ken Lucas, *R* Ardea London/P. Morris, *BR* NHPA/Martin Wendler, **180–181** Planet Earth Pictures/Richard Matthews, **182** Edward Parker Photography, **184** *LI* Luiz Claudio Marigo, *B* Luiz Claudio Marigo, **185** *TL* South American Pictures/Tony Morrison, *TR* ZEFA/L. Dantas

SEPARATIONS Litra Limited, Edenbridge, Kent
PAPER Townsend Hook Limited, Snodland, Kent
PRINTING AND BINDING Mohndruck, Gütersloh, Germany